100

Classic Hikes

of the

Northeast

100 Classic Hikes of the Northeast

Jared Gange

Huntington Graphics
Burlington, Vermont

First edition 2000, second printing 2003

Printed in Canada

Publisher: Huntington Graphics
P.O. Box 373
Burlington, VT 05402

Includes index.
ISBN 1-886064-14-8

Layout, design and maps: John Hadden, Resting Lion Studio

Editing: Laurie Caswell, Megan Manahan and Linda Young
Research assistants: Vanessa Price and Brian Schneider

Photographers as credited: Richard Bailey, Nancie Battaglia, Marty Beede, James Bond, Kate Carter, Laurie Caswell, Derek Doeffinger, Jack Freeman, Lars Gange, Carl Heilman II, Robert Kozlow, Ed Rolfe, Ned Therrien, John Winkler, and Acadia National Park.

All uncredited photos by the author.

Caution:
Hiking, like other physical endeavors, is a potentially dangerous activity. Participants in these activities assume responsibility for their own actions and safety. No guide book can replace good judgment on the part of the user. Obtain the necessary skills and inform yourself about the potential dangers before taking part in outdoor recreation activities.

Cover Photo: Nancie Battaglia
Ampersand Mountain, Adorondack High Peaks, NY
Photo previous page: Mount Washington and Tuckerman Ravine
Photo next page: Aerial view of the Great Range, Adirondacks

Adirondacks and Catskills

•

Mount Washington
White Mountains of New Hampshire

•

Massachusetts & Connecticut

•

Vermont's Green Mountains

•

Mount Katahdin
Acadia National Park
Mountains of Maine

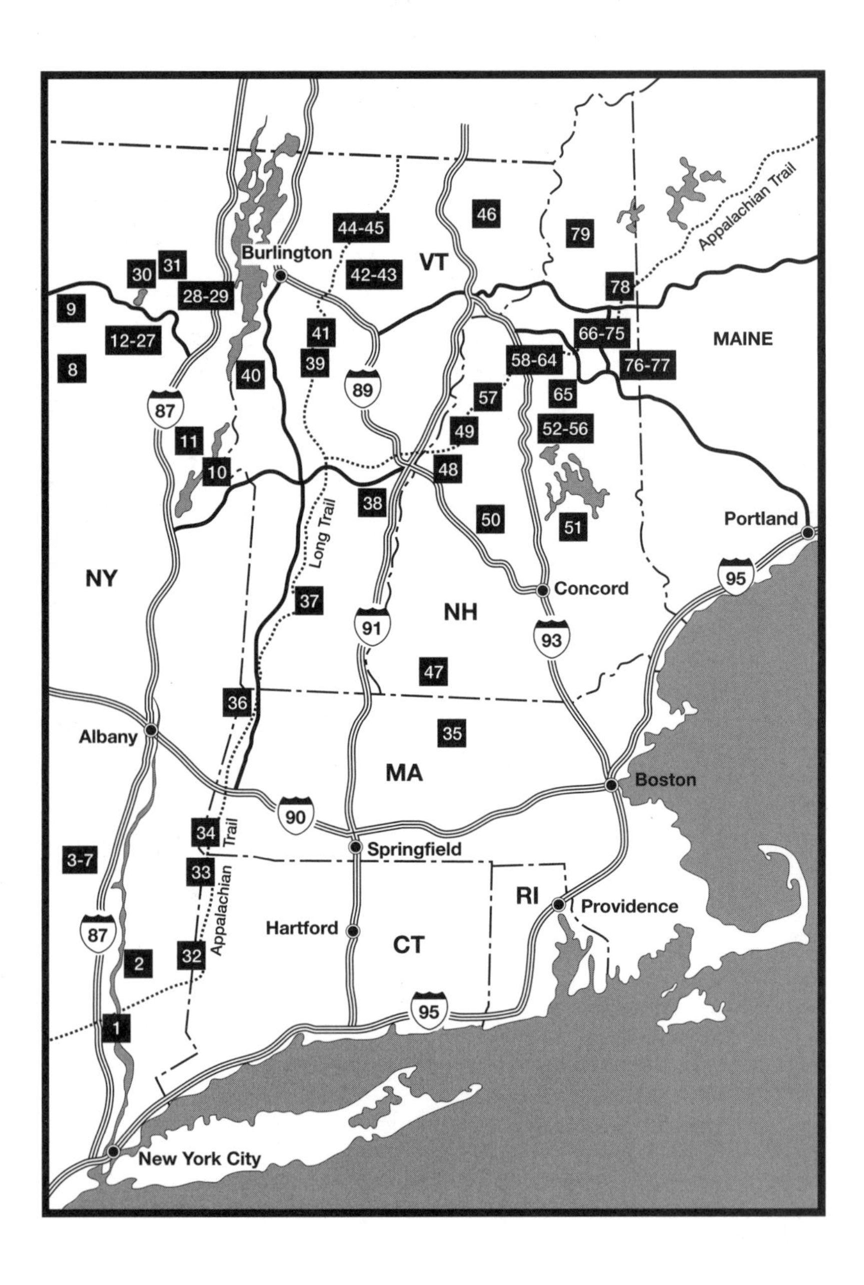

44-45
46
79
Appalachian Trail
Burlington
VT
30
31
42-43
78
28-29
9
41
66-75
MAINE
12-27
39
58-64
76-77
8
40
89
57
65
87
11
49
52-56
10
48
38
50
Long Trail
51
Portland
NY
95
37
Concord
NH
91
93
47
36
Albany
35
MA
Boston
90
34
Springfield
3-7
Trail
33
Appalachian
RI
Providence
87
Hartford
CT
2
32
95
1
New York City

Table of Contents

Introduction **12**

New York **21**

Hudson Highlands and the Catskills **22**

1 - Bear Mountain 24
2 - Breakneck Ridge 26
3 - Overlook Mountain 28
4 - North Lake and the Escarpment Trail 30
5 - Slide Mountain 34
6 - Hunter Mountain 36
7 - Black Dome Range 38

Adirondacks **40**

8 - Snowy Mountain 42
9 - Mount Blue 44
10 - Black Mountain 46
11 - Crane Mountain 48

The Adirondack High Peaks **50**

12 - Ampersand Mountain 52
13 - Mount Jo 56
14 - Algonquin Peak 58
15 - Mount Marcy 60
16 - Avalanche Lake 64
17 - Trap Dike on Mount Colden 66
18 - Cascade Mountain 68
19 - Hopkins 70
20 - Basin and Saddleback 72
21 - The Brothers and Big Slide 74
22 - Haystack Mountain 78
23 - Noonmark 80
24 - Gothics 82
25 - Giant Mountain 84
26 - Dix Mountain 86
27 - Macomb 88

North and East of the High Peaks

28 - Hurricane Mountain 90
29 - Pok-O-Moonshine 92
30 - Whiteface Mountain 94
31 - Catamount 100

Connecticut 103

32 - Mount Algo 106
33 - Bear Mountain 107

Massachusetts 108

34 - Mount Everett 108
35 - Mount Wachusett 110
36 - Mount Greylock 112

Vermont 115

37 - Stratton Pond and Stratton Mtn. 118
38 - Mount Ascutney 120
39 - Mount Abraham 122
40 - Snake Mountain 124
41 - Camel's Hump 126
42 - Mount Hunger 130
43 - Stowe Pinnacle 134
44 - Mount Mansfield via Taft Lodge 136
45 - Mount Mansfield via Sunset Ridge 138
46 - Mount Pisgah 142

New Hampshire 145

South and Central 146

47 - Mount Monadnock 148
48 - Mount Cardigan 150
49 - Smarts Mountain 152
50 - Mount Kearsarge 153
51 - Mount Major 154

White Mountains

Southern White Mountains....156

52 - Welch and Dickey....158
53 - Mount Tripyramid....160
54 - Mount Potash....162
55 - Mount Chocorua....164
56 - Whiteface....166
57 - Mount Moosilauke....170
58 - Lonesome Lake....172
59 - Franconia Ridge Traverse....174
60 - Franconia Notch to Crawford Notch....178
61 - Mount Garfield....180
62 - Traverse of the Bonds....182

Crawford Notch

63 - Middle Sugarloaf....184
64 - Mount Willard....186
65 - Mount Carrigain....188

Presidential Range....190

66 - Webster Cliff....192
67 - Mount Eisenhower....194
68 - Mount Washington, Ammonoosuc Ravine....196
69 - Traverse of the Presidentials....198
70 - Mount Jefferson, Ridge of Caps....200
71 - Mount Adams....202
72 - Mount Madison....204
73 - Mount Jefferson, Six Husbands Trail....206
74 - Mount Washington, Tuckerman Ravine....208

Other Northern Areas....212

75 - Carter Dome....214
76 - Kearsarge North....216
77 - Baldface Traverse....218
78 - Carlo-Goose Eye Loop....220
79 - Mount Percy....222

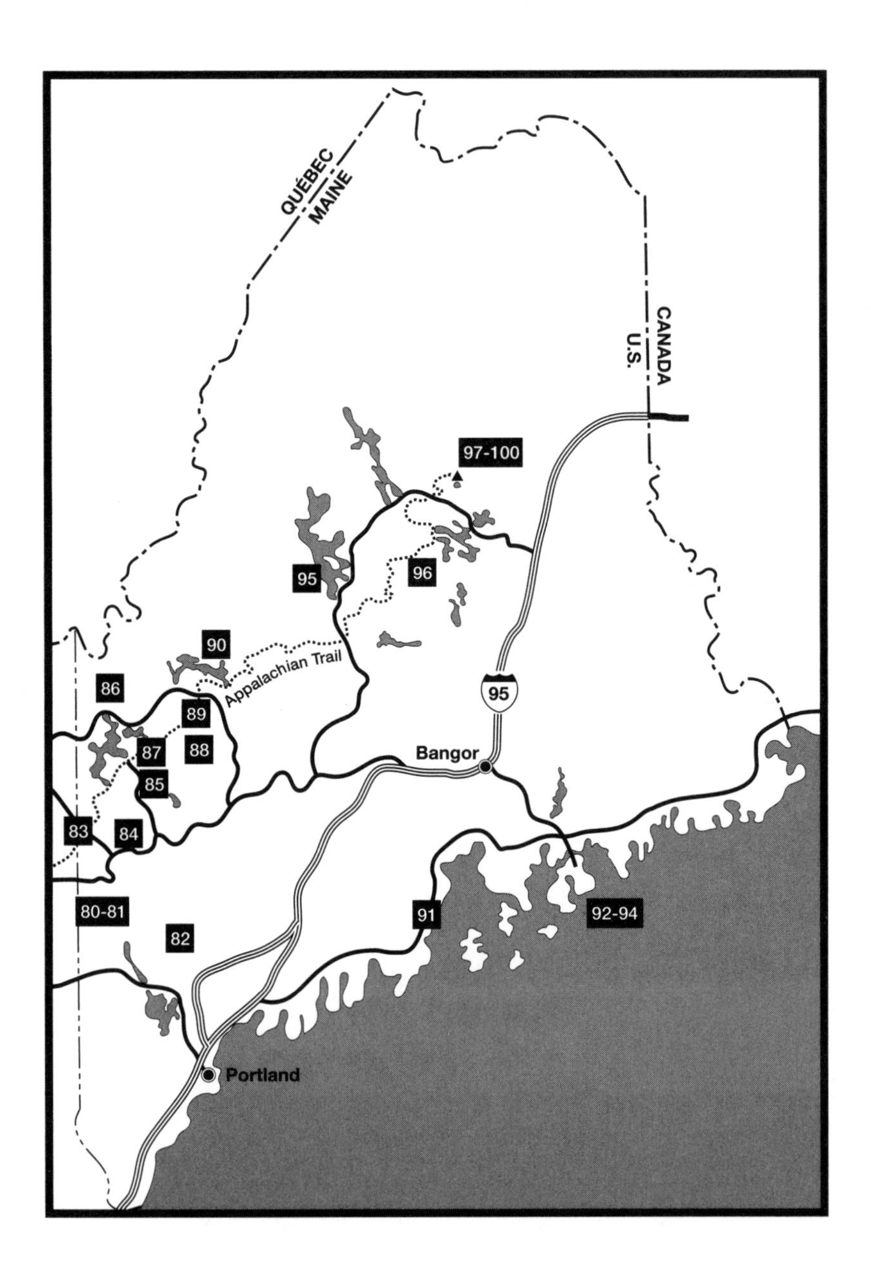
QUÉBEC
MAINE
CANADA
U.S.
97-100
95
96
90
86
Appalachian Trail
95
89
87
88
Bangor
85
83
84
80-81
82
91
92-94
Portland

Maine 225

Southwestern 226

80 - East Royce 228
81 - Caribou Mountain 230
82 - Pleasant Mountain 232
83 - Old Speck 234
84 - Rumford Whitecap 238

Western Lakes 240

85 - Tumbledown Mountain 241
86 - West Kennebago 242
87 - Saddleback Mountain 244
88 - Mount Abraham 246
89 - Sugarloaf Mountain 248
90 - Bigelow Traverse 250

Acadia National Park and Coastal Maine 252

91 - Mount Battie 253
92 - Cadillac Mountain 254
93 - Penobscot and Sargent 256
94 - The Beehive 258

Moosehead Lake and Baxter State Park 260

95 - Mount Kineo 262
96 - White Cap 264
97 - North Brother 266
98 - The Owl 268
99 - Mount Katahdin via the Knife Edge 270
100 - Katahdin via the Appalachian Trail 274

List of 4,000' Peaks 276

Glossary 280

Hiker Notes 283

Index 288

Introduction

This book has been written for visitors and residents alike. It is a presentation of the best mountain hikes — the classics — of the northeastern United States. Residents of one area should find it useful for learning about their neighboring areas, in some cases just across a river or a lake. For tourists and newcomers to the region, this guide provides a balanced and thorough introduction to the exciting mountain hiking of the Northeast.

The area covered is Maine, New Hampshire, Vermont, Massachusetts, Connecticut, and western New York state; the Hudson Highlands, the Catskills, and the Adirondacks. Although no high mountains are found here, this is a generally mountainous region with vertical differences in excess of 4,000'. New York and New Hampshire are represented with about thirty hikes each, Maine has about twenty, Vermont ten, and Massachusetts and Connecticut have five between them. The one hundred hikes described are on almost as many mountains. Four mountains—Washington, Katahdin, Mansfield and Jefferson—each have two classic routes. In addition to the one hundred featured hikes, about 35 hikes are briefly alluded to, either as a variation on a featured hike, or as a nearby hike of special interest.

Why write another hiking guide book when there are already many for New York and New England areas? The answer is that there is in fact very little in the way of a comprehensive guide to the region. We have endeavored to provide an authoritative, concise, and easy-to-use guide that is richly illustrated with photographs and well supported by maps. The Northeast, although made up of distinct regions, is a compact, accessible area; it is about the size of Iowa. Combine with this the fact that over 70 million people live within a day's drive of these mountains and the goal of providing an area-wide hiking guide seems reasonable. It should be possible to create a guide which does good service for hikers from Boston, New York City, and Montreal, as well as for residents and visitors of the mountain regions of New Hampshire, Maine, Vermont and New York. To the extent we have failed to fairly present a state or an area, we apologize in advance.

What is a classic hike? While any selection of "best" hikes will be at least somewhat subjective, we hope that our choices will be accepted by hikers familiar with these mountains. In making the selections, three kinds of classic hikes were looked at: Hikes that could be said to have a national reputation (Mount Washington, Mount Katahdin, Mount Marcy), classics within a state (Camel's Hump, Moosilauke, Giant, Bigelow, Greylock), and finally regional classics or local favorites (Percy Peak, Welch and Dickey, Mount Pisgah, Catamount, Overlook Mountain, Tumbledown Mountain, The Beehive). Coming up with exactly 100 hikes was of course arbitrary and also involved making decisions about the relative representation of the different states. Again we can only hope we got it more or less right and not stepped on too many toes in the process.

Both the Appalachian Trail and the Long Trail run through the region. The Appalachian Trail passes through the Hudson Highlands just north of New York City, enters Connecticut and continues north through the Berkshires of western Massachusetts before reaching Vermont. Here it coincides with the Long Trail for a hundred miles before heading east to New Hampshire in mid-state. The Long Trail continues north along the spine of the Green Mountains to end at the Canadian border. In New Hampshire the Appalachian Trail winds along the ridges of the White Mountains, traversing its highest summits, before entering Maine. In Maine the Trail passes through some very remote sections, including the famous 100-Mile Wilderness. The Trail ends on Baxter Peak, the highest point of Maine's incomparable Mount Katahdin. Roughly similar to the Appalachian Trail's northeasterly progression, our presentation of hikes starts in the Hudson Highlands, moves north through the Catskills to the Adirondacks, swoops back down to pick up Connecticut and Massachusetts, then takes in Vermont from south to north. We finish by travelling south to north through New Hampshire following the AT's lead into Maine and finishing on Mount Katahdin.

Mountain Weather

Mountain weather, particularly on mountains that extend above tree line, can pose a risk to the hiker. This is partly due to the fact that in terms of climate, as we climb a mountain, we are traveling north. In general, each 1,000' of elevation—about an hour of hiking—equates to moving 250 miles north. This means the upper slopes of the Presidentials have a climate similar to that of northern Labrador! The complete lack of trees or other natural protection exposes you to the full force of the wind. Thus hikers and skiers on the higher New England and Adirondack peaks, after only a few hours effort, can find themselves in arctic or sub-arctic environments, where severe storms can occur at any time.

Of course the weather can be sunny and pleasant, and a fair amount of the time it is. This what the photographs usually depict, and of course we imagine that we, too, will enjoy great weather on our excursions. But even on "good" days, lower temperatures and cooler breezes are the rule on the upper slopes. So regardless of the weather forecast and temperature when starting out, be prepared that conditions can deteriorate. This is not to say that a typhoon is always waiting at the summit. Rather, what is too often the case: hikers reach the top, tired and sweaty, with no dry or waterproof clothing to protect themselves even in moderately adverse conditions. High winds and driving rain will quickly wear down even the strongest hikers. Lastly, a bit of advice, which should be obvious, but

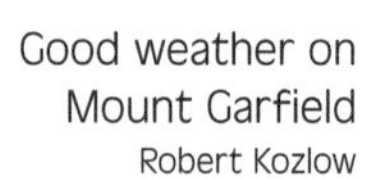

Good weather on Mount Garfield
Robert Kozlow

is often ignored: If the weather is bad, or clearly deteriorating, do not hesitate to turn back, let alone start out!

The above discussion applies with double emphasis to New Hampshire's Presidential Range. Not only is Mount Washington easily the highest mountain in the Northeast—it is about a thousand feet higher than Mount Marcy or Mount Katahdin—it has vastly more terrain above tree line. In addition, three major storm tracks converge in the area thus storms occur with greater frequency and hit with greater force. During the hurricane of 1934, the wind at the summit was measured at 231 mph, still the world record. Think of it as being inside a tornado! But more relevant for the visitor than record winds is the fact that winds reach hurricane force (75 mph) about 100 days out of the year: Your chances of experiencing strong winds are pretty good. While not everyone would agree that Mount Washington has the worst weather in the world, as is often claimed, its great accessibility and high winds give it a very strong claim to the title of "most dangerous small mountain in the world."

Lest this be only a cautionary tale, it is true that the weather in the mountains can be unbelievably fine. It's wonderful to relax on a summit without a breath of wind. The cloud formations are often fantastically beautiful and unlike anything we experience elsewhere. Alpenglow, sea of clouds, krummholz, lenticular clouds, rime-frost, sastrugi, cirques and tarns are the names of phenomena that give a hint of the wonders of the mountain world. Do go forth, just be careful!

Bad weather in the White Mountains
Robert Kozlow

Hiking times and difficulty rating

Most of the hikes in this book are accessible to the average hiker. The selection ranges from very easy excursions to the longer, more difficult climbs, including many of the most challenging hikes in the Northeast. At the top of each hike description—the summary information for every hike—an overall difficulty rating is given first, followed by an estimated round trip time. This is followed by the hike's total distance and lastly by the total amount of climbing required by you do the hike. In evaluating a hike for difficulty, we ask you to assign more importance to its estimated time than to its distance. We have attempted to give times that are correct and reasonable for an average hiker. More important is that the estimates provided are consistent from hike to hike. The importance of a consistent time rating is this: After comparing your hiking times with the times given in the book, you should be able to "tune" the book estimates to get a reliable estimate for yourself or your hiking group. Thus if you are a fast hiker, you might always use about 80 percent of the book time. The times themselves are calculated by a standard formula. If a trail is very rocky, extremely steep or in general presents difficult footing, the ascent and descent times are increased somewhat to reflect this.

The longer a hike, the more difficult it is to give a reliable fixed time, in part because fitness levels among individuals vary so greatly. For example, if you can do a 6-mile hike in three hours can you do twice the mileage in twice the time? At this point, individual variation begins to play a larger role. To address this "fitness" factor, the calculated times have been increased somewhat—or a range given—on the longer hikes.

Ultimately, rating hikes for difficulty is a subjective endeavor based in part on factual information and in part on a balanced assessment of a trail's non-objective aspects. Thus we ask you to keep in mind that the time estimates, and difficulty ratings, are only approximate and may, on occassion, not give the consistency they are intended to provide.

Maps

Maps accompany the hike descriptions throughout the book. Their purpose is to give you a general picture of where the mountains and trails are located and how to reach the trailheads. Important roads and major trails are shown. Topographic trail maps are listed at the end of each hike description under "Maps."

Until recently, the various regional hiking clubs (Appalachian Mountain Club for New Hampshire and Maine, the Green Mountain Club for Vermont, the Adirondack Mountain Club for New York) and the U. S. Geological Survey were the primary sources of topographic maps. In recent years a number of regional mapping companies have come into existence, and this has resulted in an ever-increasing selection of accurate, readable maps for hiking and biking. In the "Maps" paragraph for each hike, we list the best available topographic trail maps. Using New Hampshire's Mount Washington as an example, the three main choices are the Appalachian Mountain Club's "White Mountains, Map 1: Presidential Range" (scale 1:47 500), "White Mountains Hiking" (1:50 000) by Map Adventures, and Mount Washington "Close-up" (1:42 500) by Wilderness Map Company.

For road map information—driving approaches—we usually refer to the popular DeLorme Atlas and Gazetteer series. The appropriate page numbers from the respective state atlases are given for each hike. Thus for example, for Mount Marcy (the highest peak in New York state), page 96 of the New York State Atlas and Gazetteer shows the mountain, the surrounding region, and the roads needed to access the trailhead. The scales used are excellent for conveying detailed driving information, as well as for giving you a simple overview of your planned hike.

Hiking With Children

Most of the shorter hikes in this book, and the beginning sections of some of the longer hikes, are suitable for children. Views, especially distant views, do not always hold much fascination for kids. Their interests are usually closer at hand: stream crossings, bridges, rocky scrambles, wild animals, a lake, or a mountain hut. Try to break your hike into short, manageable sections.

Some tips: Leave your own, more ambitious hiking goals at home; there will be plenty of time for the longer hikes later. The idea is to get some walking exercise and have fun! Start out with very short trips, and if the interest is there, go with it. Hikes that last three or four hours, even with a moderate amount of climbing, are well with the reach of motivated six- or seven-year olds. Bringing a same-aged friend along can be a great motivator. Take plenty of favorite snacks and drinks. Remember to walk at a pace that suits your child, and set goals that are appropriate for their abilities. Lastly, be prepared to change your well-laid plans in mid-hike if something more interesting comes along.

Braving the wind on Owl's Head in the Adirondacks

Hiking Tips

- Allow plenty of time for your hike.
- Be realistic about your physical condition. If you are new to hiking or have not hiked for some time, you may overestimate your abilities.
- Start out with easy trips. Build confidence and experience gradually.
- Be prepared for worsening weather. Summits are usually cooler and breezier than lower elevations, and a beautiful morning can evolve into a windy, snowy afternoon.
- Consider the size of your group when planning your trip. The larger your group, the more time you will need.
- Let someone know your plans, or leave a note (but not in view) giving your route and estimated return time.
- Do not leave valuable items in your car, as break-ins do occasionally occur.
- Be careful when planning to return by a route you are unfamiliar with, especially on longer trips. Route finding problems, steep sections, stream crossings, etc. can needlessly put an already exhausted group of hikers at risk.
- Pets must be under control at all times. Some trails—those with ladders for example—are often too difficult for dogs.
- Take drinking water with you, or be prepared to treat any water you take from streams or ponds. Even the clearest mountain stream may contain the Giardia parasite.
- Pack out what you pack in.
- Be especially careful when hiking alone.
- Try to have the lowest possible impact on the backcountry.

New York

The Hudson Highlands and the Catskills

North of New York City along the Hudson River there are many popular hiking and walking areas, starting with the Palisades, the precipitous shale and sandstone cliffs on the west shore of the Hudson, just across the George Washington Bridge. Walking trails skirt the clifftop and at river level, 500' below. Heading north, the terrain on both sides of the river becomes more mountainous as we approach the Hudson River Narrows. The illustration on the next page, although somewhat exaggerated, gives a good idea of the steepness of this landscape.

Harriman State Park is the most popular trail-based recreation area near the city. Its extensive network is a great resource for longer distance walking, hiking, running, and mountain biking. The Appalachian Trail passes through the park, traversing **Bear Mountain**—the first hike in the book—before descending to the Hudson and crossing it on the Bear Mountain Bridge.

Breakneck Ridge, a dramatic headland on the east side of the river, is the second hike in this book. Together with Storm King, just across the river, these two buttress form the northern gateway to the Narrows and the Hudson Highlands.

Farther north—75 miles from New York City—is another area of cliffs and lakes, the **Shawangunk Mountains**, well-known as the site of the Mohonk Hotel. The cliffs of the Shawangunks are a Mecca for rock climbers; it is the most important climbing area in the eastern U.S. An extensive network of carriage roads provides practically unlimited walking, riding, and running opportunities. The carriage road circuit of the Trapps, the principal rock climbing area, is a fine introduction to this high-energy place.

The Catskill Mountains lie between New York City and Albany. The opening lines of Washington Irving's *Rip Van Winkle* provide a favorable introduction: "Whoever has made a voyage up the Hudson must remember the Kaatskill mountains. They are a dismembered branch of the great Appalachian family, and are seen away to the west of the river, swelling up to a noble height, and lording it over the surrounding country."

Photo previous page: Hikers on Ampersand Mountain, High Peaks Nancie Battaglia

Entrance to the Hudson Highlands, looking south from Newburgh
From an engraving by W. H. Bartlett (ca. 1850)

Lower than the Adirondack High Peaks, and farther south, the Catskills do not extend above tree line. But there are open summits and many exposed viewpoints. The highest summit is **Slide Mountain** (4,180'), and there are a total of 35 mountains over 3,500'. Geologically, the Catskills are part of the uplifted, dissected Allegheny Plateau and strictly speaking are not true mountains. Deep erosional valleys, called notches or cloves (from the Dutch "kloft"), are characteristic of the area and provide exciting visual terrain and challenging hiking.

The best known hiking is concentrated along three routes. **Devil's Path** starts on Woodstock's Overlook Mountain and runs west along a rugged ridgeline, dropping in and out of several extremely steep cloves. The **Escarpment Trail** starts south of North Lake and runs north along the abrupt edge of a 1,500'-high escarpment—the dramatic western edge of the Catskills—to the Blackhead Range before continuing to Windham High Point. The 10-mile **Burroughs Range Trail** traverses the challenging terrain of Wittenberg, Cornell, and Slide Mountains.

1 • Bear Mountain 1,306′

Rating: Moderate
Time: 3 hours
Distance: 4.5-mile loop
Total climb: 1,150′
Location: Bear Mountain State Park, at Bear Mountain Bridge
Summary: Dramatic, canyon-like setting with 100 miles of hiking trails throughout the two parks.

Dunderberg Mountain signals the gateway to the Hudson Narrows. It deflects the southward flowing Hudson over a mile to the east; to the north, on the east side of the river, a similar prow of land known as Anthony's Nose pushes the river to the west. Directly across the river from Anthony's Nose, lies Bear Mountain, the highest of the three. The Hudson River Narrows area, together with adjacent, 52,000-acre **Harriman-Bear Mountain State Parks** is a superb recreation resource: miles of hiking and biking trails in forest terrain, interspersed with lakes and picnicking areas.

From behind the Inn, pick up the red-marked **Major Welch Trail** (paved pathway) as it bears right and runs along the shore of Hessian Lake. After a third of a mile, the trail branches and leads gradually uphill as it winds north and west around to the north side of the mountain. It then turns more southerly and steepens to a moderate pitch. About one mile after starting out, the trail levels out as it crosses a ledge affording good views north and east.

The trail resumes climbing, crosses a paved road, then two gravel roads just as it reaches the summit at 2.2 miles. Continue past the summit to **Perkins Tower**; climb up and enjoy the panorama.

Now pick up the white-blazed **Appalachian Trail** and head north (left) on it to descend to Bear Mountain. The Appalachian Trail is both more gradual and more heavily trafficked than Major Welch Trail. Coming off the summit you cross the summit road once, then when you intersect the summit road again, the trail turns right (south) and follows the road for about 1/3 mile before turning to the east. The return to the base will take about 40 minutes. Before or after your hike, be sure to check out **Bear Mountain Inn**, a well-preserved example of early 20th-century lodge architecture.

Approach: From NYC, drive north to Bear Mountain Bridge. From the traffic rotary just west of the bridge, drive south 0.4 mile on Rt. 9W to the parking area (fee) for Bear Mountain State Park.

Maps: Harriman-Bear Mountain, Map #4 (NY-NJ Trail Conference) and New York State Atlas & Gazetteer, p. 32

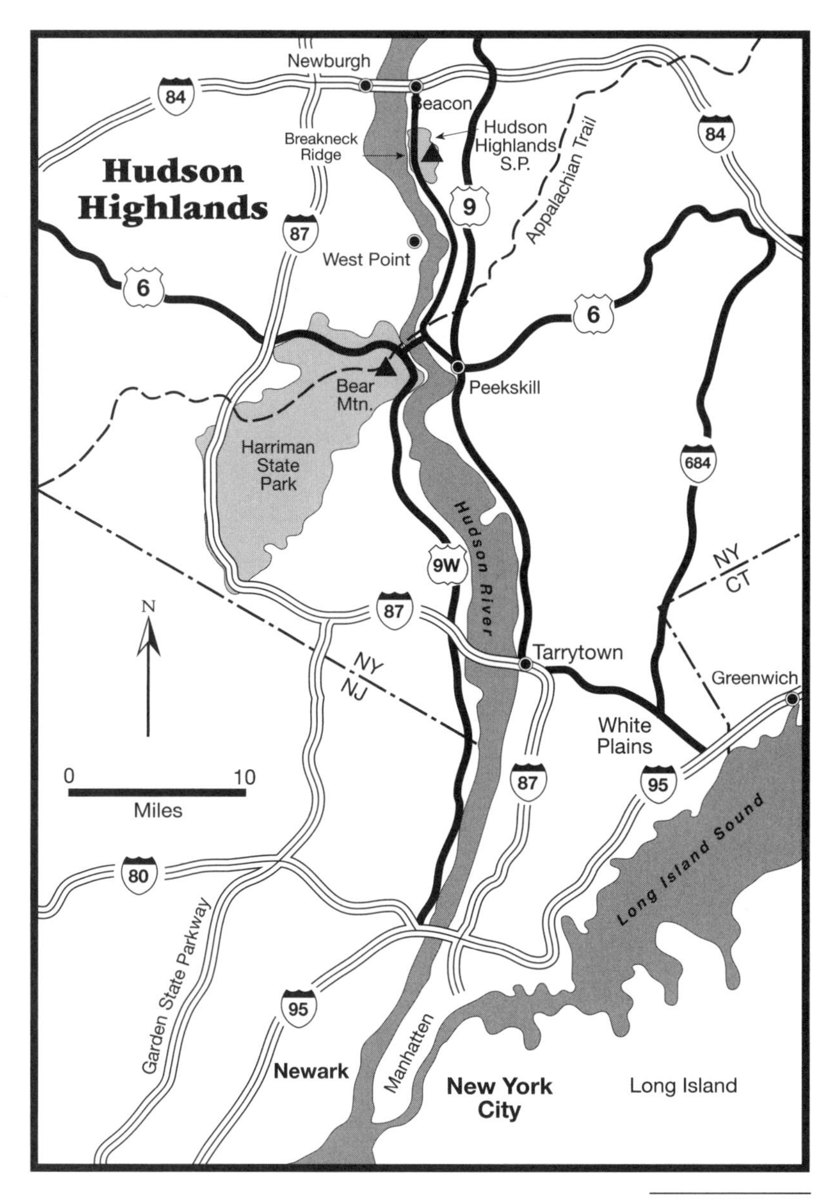
Hudson Highlands
Newburgh
84
Beacon
Hudson Highlands S.P.
Breakneck Ridge
Appalachian Trail
84
9
87
West Point
6
6
Peekskill
Bear Mtn.
Harriman State Park
684
Hudson River
9W
NY
CT
N
87
Tarrytown
NY
NJ
Greenwich
White Plains
0
10
Miles
87
95
Long Island Sound
80
Garden State Parkway
95
Manhatten
Newark
New York City
Long Island

2 • Breakneck Ridge

Rating: Difficult, with steep, exposed rock scrambling
Time: 3 hours
Distance: 2.8-mile loop
Total climb: 1,300′
Location: Hudson Highlands State Park, 50 miles from NYC
Summary: An exciting scramble on a cliff overlooking the Hudson River. Easy descent on the north side.

It may come as a surprise to some that good hiking abounds near New York City, both in terms of difficulty and elevation gain. The hike we have chosen here, perhaps the classic of the **Hudson Highlands**, certainly has both qualities. In fact, as steep climbing goes, very few hikes in the Northeast can match Breakneck Ridge. That 1,000' is climbed in the first 0.4 mile should convince skeptics! From the trailhead (unmarked), the route crosses the highway by climbing over the tunnel up a rough stone staircase. Working its way more or less straight up the bare rock, the trail, marked with white paint blazes, varies in steepness while changing back and forth from smooth slabs to jumbled rocks. In places, alternate passages (easier) are indicated. There are at least two places with significant drop-offs; exercise extreme caution. The river—it seems to be directly below—and the massive bulk of Storm King on the opposite shore, dominate the view. As you climb, you traverse a series of knolls and intervening dips, and the view gradually widens. After about an hour's climbing, you will reach a grassy area that is great for resting and taking in the sights. The Beacon-Newburgh Bridge is clearly visible to the north.

Above here, the grade eases, and the terrain is more wooded with less of a view. At 1.5 miles, after negotiating a few more dips, you come to the red-marked **Breakneck Bypass Trail** on your left. Follow this over a small rise, before beginning a relaxing, gentle descent through woods, reaching the wide, yellow-blazed **Wilkinson Trail** after about 25 minutes. Head left again, and an easy 10-minute saunter brings you back to the usually busy highway, a quarter of a mile north of your starting point.

Looking across the Hudson River from Breakneck Ridge to Storm King

Approach: From Cold Spring (8 miles north of the Bear Mountain Bridge), drive north on NY Route 9D for 2 miles where immediately after passing through a tunnel, there is parking on the west side of the road for a few cars. Two larger parking areas are a few hundred yards farther up the road.

Maps: East Hudson Trails, Map #2 (NY-NJ Trail Conference) and New York State Atlas & Gazetteer, p. 32

Although **Storm King Mountain** does not offer a climb up its river face—it is more precipitous than Breakneck Ridge—there are trails farther inland which lead to the top and have good views. This hike begins from the height of land on NY Route 9W, north of West Point, at Butter Hill.

3 • Overlook Mountain 3,140′

Rating: Moderate to easy
Time: 3 hours 15 minutes
Distance: 5 miles
Total climb: 1,300′
Location: Just outside Woodstock

Summary: A pleasant climb on a carriage road to a restored fire tower. Stupendous views of the Hudson River Valley and the Catskill Mountains.

From the parking area at the height of land—just across the road from Woodstock's impressive Tibetan temple—walk uphill to the gated carriage road that is the (red-marked) **Overlook Spur Trail**. Climbing steadily and moderately, the road winds its way up through woods with no real letup (and no views) for the first 45 minutes or so. Eventually you will start to get glimpses of distant hills, first to your left and then on the right. After about an hour, and about two miles, the ruins of a large building will appear. This 3-story, 100'-foot long structure was once intended to be a hotel but was never completed.

Immediately after passing the hotel ruins, the Overlook Trail (towards Echo Lake and Platte Clove) branches left. **Echo Lake** is a popular camping and swimming spot, but the additional four-mile round trip, involving first a descent and then a climb of 900', may be somewhat of a deterrent for those looking for that quick refreshing dip on a hot summer day. Continuing toward the summit, the gradient is now gentler, and the woods are of a younger vintage with a grassy forest floor. Glimpses through the trees make plausible the promise of good views to come. A few minutes before the summit, you pass along the base of an interesting cliff band. In fact you walk right below the tower unawares, before entering a large clearing and circling back to it.

The recently restored fire tower gets you well above the trees for a great panoramic view. (Hikers owe the "reclaiming" of this, and other historic fire towers in the Catskills and Adirondacks, to the initiative of various citizen groups.) The rugged ridge line to the northwest is home to the aptly named Devil's Path; farther beyond is the more sedate Blackhead Range. Descend by the route you came up.

Approach: Woodstock is a short distance from the New York Thruway (I-87); use exit 19 or 20. From Kingston, exit 19, follow

Fire tower on Overlook Mountain
Photo by Jack Freeman, courtesy of the Adirondack Mountain Club

signs and NY Route 28. Once in Woodstock, from the village green, turn right (north) on Meads Mountain Road and follow this 2.5 miles to the trailhead parking area on the right.

Maps: Northeastern Catskill Trails, Map #41; Catskill Forest Preserve-Official Map and Guide (free from NYSDEC); and New York State Atlas & Gazetteer, p. 52

4 • Escarpment Trail

Rating: Moderate
Time: 3 hours
Distance: 4.5-mile loop
Total climb: 900′
Location: North Lake State Campground, near Tannersville
Summary: A cliff-top walk with sweeping views of the Hudson River Valley, from Albany to New York.

Although lacking a long, difficult route to a lofty, remote summit, this area offers unusual hiking in a dramatic setting. The centerpiece is **North Lake**, perched near the edge of a precipice. It is probably the most exciting natural area in the Catskills, with a rich history, both mythical and real. The defining escarpment of the Catskills rises 1,500' from the Hudson River Valley, culminating in 100' to 200' cliffs. As you walk along the edge on a sunny morning, you see buildings in Albany catch the light; the Hudson River gleams in the distance, and below, farms and towns seem close enough to touch. Rip Van Winkle Hollow, perhaps the **Sleepy Hollow** of legend, lies practically at your feet. Nearby Kaaterskill Falls (see photo page 32) is described below.

The Escarpment Trail loops around North Lake and, true to its name, runs along the edge of the escarpment (called the Manitou Wall) before continuing north to the Blackhead Range (Hike #7). There are many famous viewpoints along the trail, including the sites of two former grand hotels. We will not attempt to describe them all in a short trail description. We present a moderate—but spectacular—hike along part of the trail.

Drive past the campground gatehouse and park at the beach parking area. From here, pick up the yellow-marked feeder trail to the Escarpment Trail. In a few minutes, you'll find yourself literally "on the edge." There are few railings, so exercise great care! Follow the blue-marked Escarpment Trail left along the cliff's edge passing in succession the fabled viewpoints of Artist's Rock, Lookout Rock, and after a little over a mile, Newman's Ledge. From here continue on the trail, leaving the escarpment's sharp edge and, after passing Badman Cave and a connector trail branching off left, reaching **Mary's Glen Trail**, which also comes in from the left. (You will use this on your return.) From this point, a 20-minute climb remains to reach the ultimate goal of this hike,

North Lake and the Catskill Escarpment as seen from North Point
From an engraving by W. H. Bartlett (1838)

North Point (3,000'). Here you will be able to appreciate more fully this unique landscape from the huge rock slabs and open grassy slopes. On your descent, head right on Mary's Glen Trail and relax on its generally moderate grade through woods—it's 1.4 miles to the campground loop road. At the road, head left for a half mile to return to your car.

Approach: From Palenville (I-87, use Exit 20), drive up Kaaterskill Clove on Route 23A to Haines Falls. Turn right on County Road #18, and follow signs to the campground. Day usage fee, map included.

Maps: North Lake Campground map; Catskill Trails - North Lake Area, Map #40; and New York State Atlas & Gazetteer, p. 52

Any discussion of hiking in the North Lake area is not complete without mention of **Kaaterskill Falls**. This slender two-tiered falls has a total drop of 260 feet—more than Niagara Falls and at one time more popular. From NY 23A (parking is 0.25 mile above the trailhead), 3.5 miles from Palenville, follow the 0.4-mile path along the stream to the base of the falls. (See photo next page.)

Kaaterskill Falls — Derek Doeffinger

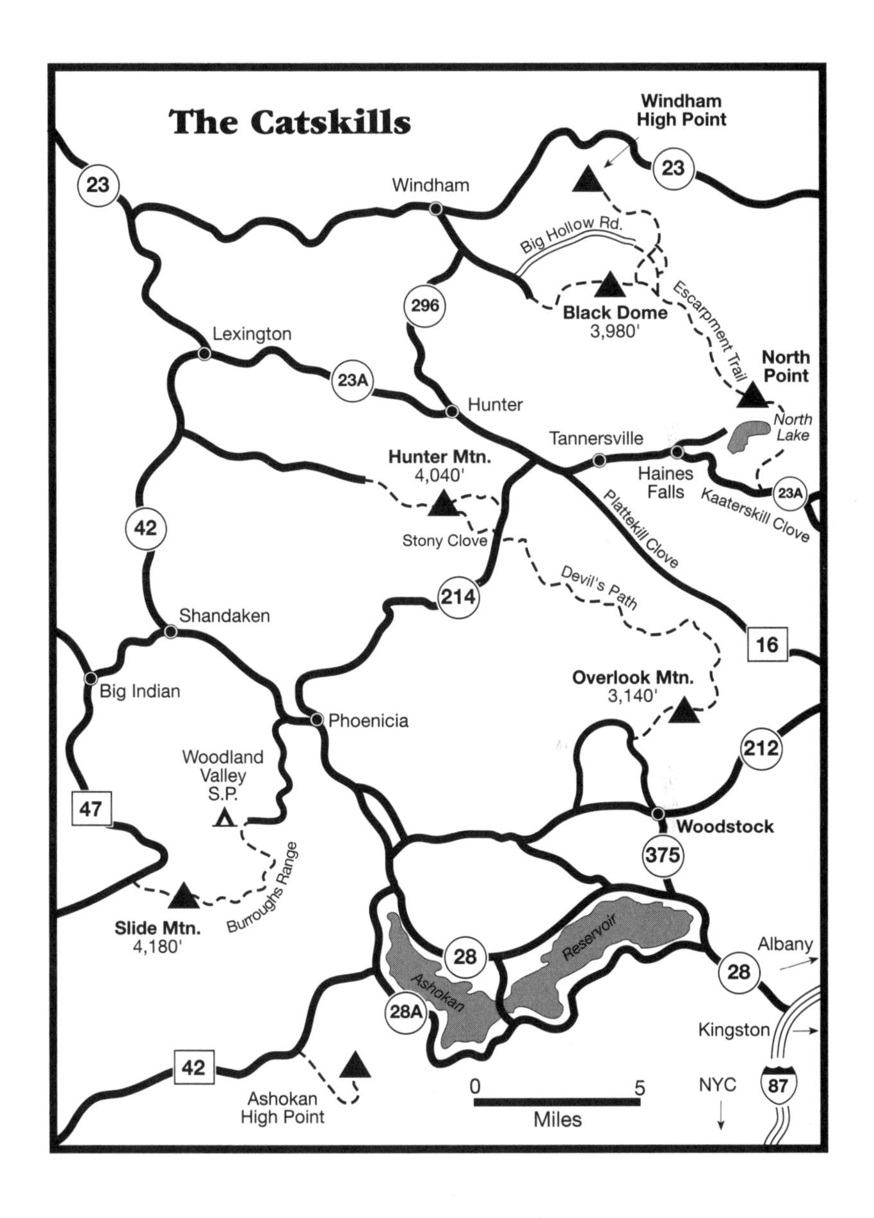
The Catskills
Windham High Point
23
Windham
Big Hollow Rd.
296
Black Dome
3,980'
Escarpment Trail
North Point
Lexington
23A
Hunter
North Lake
Tannersville
Hunter Mtn.
4,040'
Haines Falls
23A
Kaaterskill Clove
Plattekill Clove
42
Stony Clove
Devil's Path
214
Shandaken
16
Overlook Mtn.
3,140'
Big Indian
Phoenicia
212
Woodland Valley S.P.
47
Woodstock
375
Burroughs Range
Slide Mtn.
4,180'
28
Reservoir
Albany
28
Ashokan
28A
Kingston
42
0
5
Miles
NYC
87
Ashokan High Point

5 • Slide Mountain 4,180′

Rating: Moderate
Time: 4 hours
Distance: 5.5 miles
Total climb: 1,750′
Location: South of Big Indian
Summary: Highest in the Catskills, good views from the summit area.

As the highest mountain in the Catskills, Slide Mountain probably receives more than its share of visitors. The mountain is heavily forested, but there are two good viewpoints at the summit. The upper portion of the trail has gentle grades and an excellent walking surface of fine gravel.

Start out by crossing a stream and continue over easy ground in a fine hardwood forest. The **Slide Mountain Trail** (it is called the Phoenicia-East Branch Trail at this point) soon climbs increasingly steep and rocky terrain, suddenly coming out on an almost-level woods road. Follow this to the right for about five minutes, before heading left off the woods road and resuming the climb (at 0.7 mile from the car). This trail is marked in red and is referred to as the **Burroughs Range Trail** or the Wittenberg-Cornell-Slide Trail. At any rate, whatever the official name, you will soon find yourself engaged in a steady climb up a wide and very rocky trail that seems to go on forever; in fact as you look up it, you can see that it does go on forever! This is the bulk of the climb and will take a half- hour or more. At the top of this grind, you are over half way to the summit. After the grade eases, you pass the 3,500'-level (sign), and the trail traverses right and enters a zone of balsam firs. Soon the trail switches back sharply to the left, and from here to the summit the grade is generally quite moderate, pleasant in fact. After passing through an open beech woods, spruce and fir crowd the trail and narrow it to a 4- to 5-foot wide corridor. At about 2 miles, a blue-marked trail departs right, providing an alternate descent route for a loop. Note the ridge has gotten quite narrow.

The grade steepens somewhat, and about a minute before the actual summit, a dramatic ledge appears on the left. There are impressive views of nearby Cornell and Wittenberg and the Ashokan Reservoir in the distance. Continue over the summit to a large, grassy clearing just beyond. The large flat rock ledges make a good spot to rest before heading down. To find the plaque honoring **John Burroughs**, an early environmentalist and a big fan of

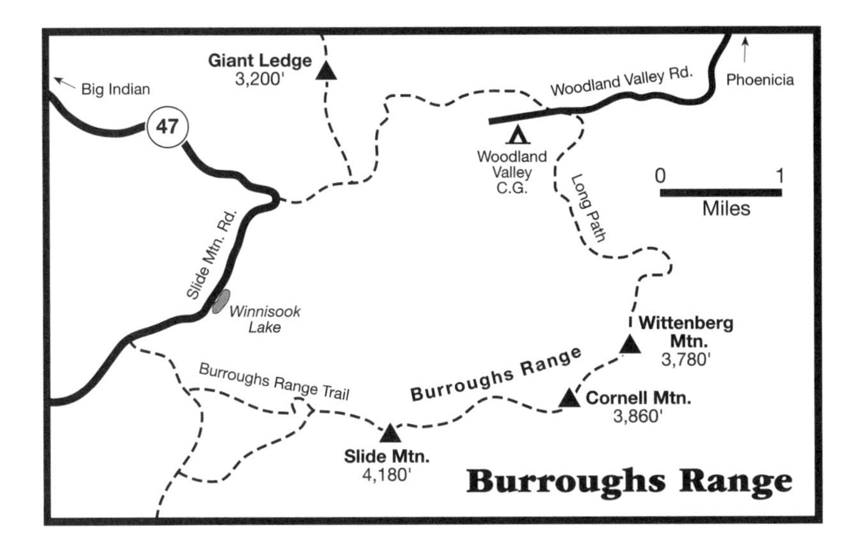

Slide Mountain, walk around to the base of the lunch ledge rock. Descend by the same route.

Approach: Exit I-87 at Kingston (when approaching from the south), and head west on NY 28. From the village of Phonecia, continue about 8 miles on NY 28 to Big Indian. Here turn south (left) on County Road #47 for 9.4 miles to the entrance (left) for Slide Mountain trailhead parking, just past Winnisook Lake.

Maps: Southern Catskill Trails, Map #43 (NY-NJ Trail Conf.) and New York State Atlas & Gazetteer, p. 51

Slide is part of the **Burroughs Range**, and the full 10-mile traverse of this ridge is a Catskill classic. (Burroughs Range or Wittenberg-Cornell-Slide Trail.) We describe it very briefly here. For a full description of this route, consult the *Guide to Catskill Trails* or *High Peaks of the Northeast.* Briefly, the traverse is as follows: From Woodland Valley State Park, a few miles south of Phoenicia, ascend **Wittenberg** (3,780', 3.9 miles), cross over to **Cornell** (at 4.7 miles, 3,860'), and, after a tough climb, reach the summit of **Slide** at 7 miles. Descend Slide as described above.

6 • Hunter Mountain 4,040′

Rating: Moderate
Time: 4 hours
Distance: 4.4 miles (or 6-mile loop)
Location: Off Stony Clove highway, south of Tannersville
Total climb: 2,200′
Summary: A prolonged, steep climb to a restored fire tower. A longer variation descends into spectacular Stony Clove.

This popular hiking peak, also home to the Catskill's best known ski area, is second highest in the Catskills. Unlike many ski mountains, the actual summit is some distance from the ski area. There are four main routes up Hunter; from Stony Clove via Devil's Path (3.8 miles), from the west via Spruceton Trail (3.6 miles), from the Colonel's Chair (2.1 miles from the restaurant at the top of the chairlift), and the **Becker Hollow Trail**, described below.

From the small parking area just off the highway, walk through the stone portal, into the hardwood forest and along a stream. At about a half mile, after a stream crossing, the wide, well-maintained trail begins its steady climb, always in woods, reaching a sign noting the 3,500' level at 1.8 miles. Continue climbing very steeply to where the **Becker Hollow Connector Trail** (yellow markers) branches right. Just beyond the junction, you can cool off with water from a piped spring. From here it is a relatively easy 0.35 miles up to the summit clearing. Climb the 70' fire tower to enjoy the sweeping views. Hunter Mountain's tower was restored in time for the summer 2000 season—part of an ongoing effort to bring back some of the old fire towers which have suffered neglect over the years. The majority of hikers climbing Hunter from Becker Hollow return directly to Becker Hollow.

A worthwhile **variation** is to follow **Devil's Path** as it descends very steeply into the dramatic notch of **Stony Clove**. It is then only 1.6 miles along Route 214 back to your starting point—an easy shuttle or downhill walk. For those feeling a little ambitious, the Devil's Path variation (3.8 miles) is as follows. From the summit, take the blue-marked **Spruceton Trail** 0.2 mile south to Hunter Mountain Trail. The **Hunter Mountain Trail** descends gently, reaching Devil's Path 1.4 miles from the summit. Now head left (east), continuing a moderate descent for another 20 minutes. From here on down, Devil's Path lives up to its name, dropping 1,500' to the road. After a mile and a half of varying degrees of

Hunter Mountain from the east

steepness, you will descend a more or less vertical section (50') known as the Devil's Portal. Below this, walk across some nicely placed stones and past large boulders before finally descending into Stony Clove, reaching the highway.

Approach: Head west on NY 23A from Tannersville. Just before Hunter village, head south on NY 214 towards Stony Clove, and park on the right at 1.3 miles.

Maps: Northeastern Catskill Trails, Map #41 (NY-NJ Trail Conf.); New York State Atlas & Gazetteer, p. 51

Devil's Path: Devil's Path is touched upon briefly in the foregoing description. The full 25-mile trail is one of the most challenging hiking trips in the Catskills. It starts just south of Route 16 in Plattekill Clove, and after gaining the ridge at Indian Head Mountain (3,573'), leads you on a wild up-and-down ride over high summits and into deep cloves. After traversing Hunter Mountain, Devil's Path ends a little west of Spruceton.

7 • Black Dome 3,980'

Rating: Moderately strenuous
Time: 5 hours 30 minutes
Distance: 7 miles, one-way traverse
Total climb: about 2,900'
Location: Northern Catskills, about 5 miles northeast of Hunter village
Summary: A classic ridge walk across a succession of summits, offering a number of great views.

The traverse of the Blackhead Range is one of the finest ridge walk in these mountains. Although not especially long or strenuous, this hike offers great views as it runs across three of the highest Catskill summits: **Thomas Cole Mountain** (3,940'), **Black Dome**, and **Blackhead Mountain** (3,940'). There are a number of shorter variations, including a 4-mile round trip of popular Black Dome, third highest mountain in the Catskills.

From the Barnum Road trailhead, the **Blackhead Range Trail** (also called Black Dome Range Trail) ascends moderately, reaching the top of Caudal after 1.2 miles. At 1.8 miles, you cross the summit of Camel's Hump, and at 2.5 miles reach the top of Thomas Cole Mountain. After enjoying the excellent southerly views, descend into a saddle and make the 250'-climb to the top of Black Dome. Here the views are the finest of the entire trip, with Hunter Mountain and Devil's Path clearly visible about 9 miles to the south. From the top of Black Dome, it is 3.25 miles back to Barnum Road. For the shortest conclusion to the traverse, continue on the Range Trail (red markers), bypass Blackhead Mountain and reach Big Hollow Road in 2 miles. To do the complete traverse, head down the Range Trail towards Big Hollow Road, but after 0.6 mile, in the saddle between Black Dome and Blackhead, pick up yellow-marked **Blackhead Mountain Trail** and make the 500-foot climb to the summit of Blackhead Mountain. There are great views a little before halfway but nothing much at the top. Now head down the north ridge of Blackhead Mountain on the **Escarpment Trail/Long Path** (blue markers) for 1 mile, before turning left onto the **Batavia Kill Trail** (also 1 mile), which brings you back to the Blackhead Range Trail 0.5 mile from Big Hollow Road, for a grand total of 7 miles.

Baby porcupine on summit of Black Dome

Approach: From Hunter, drive north on NY 296 to Hensonville and head right on County Route 40 to Maplecrest. Turn south (still on C.R. 40), then left on Barnum Road to the end. This hike is given as a point-to-point traverse. The Black Dome trailhead is at the end of Big Hollow Road (C.R. 56), a few miles from Maplecrest.

Maps: Northeastern Catskill Trails, Map # 41 (NY-NJ Trail Conference) and New York State Atlas & Gazetteer, pages 51-52.

Black Dome only: As noted above, it is 2 miles (and 1,800' of climbing) to the top of Black Dome from Big Hollow Road—a very popular hike to the "gem" of the Blackhead Range. Plan on 3-4 hours for this 4-mile round trip. From the parking area at the end of Big Hollow Road, take the red-marked Black Dome Range Trail to the top. Return by the same route.

The Adirondacks

New York's 6 million acre **Adirondack Park** is about the size of the state of New Hampshire and is larger than Yosemite, Yellowstone, and Grand Canyon National Parks combined. Home to hundreds of lakes and mountains, the park contains the greatest wilderness acreage in the United States east of the Mississippi River. The Adirondack Park is not a national park, nor even a state park in the usual sense. It is a complex patchwork of private and public lands, towns, and wilderness. Almost half the park—referred to as the Forest Preserve—is protected from development of any kind by New York's constitution. In the words of environmentalist author Bill McKibben: "It remains the site of a great experiment about whether humans and nature can make their living in the same place."

Although heavily logged in the mid 1800's, the Adirondacks were largely unknown to the American public until after the Civil War. Soon, these mountains and lakes were discovered by vacationers. Summer homes were built, some on an almost inconceivably grand scale; vast tracts of land came under private control; a tradition of mountain guides was born, and the Adirondacks became a testing ground for nascent conservation ideals.

From a hiking perspective the relatively compact **High Peaks Region**, with more than 40 summits over 4,000', contains most of the exciting hiking. Although not as high as New Hampshire's White Mountains, the High Peaks' concentration of high summits is unequalled in the eastern U.S. A well-developed system of trails and lean-tos invite exploration of this fascinating mountain world.

West of the High Peaks, the Park's seemingly countless rivers and lakes are fantastic for canoeing and fishing. Many of the lakes, for example Saint Regis, Saranac, Placid, Indian, Blue Mountain, and Tupper, have rich histories of their own. See the sidebar on Adirondack Traditions, pages 76-77.

North of the core High Peaks, Whiteface and Catamount are two outstanding hikes; to the south, in the Lake George area, Black Mountain and Crane Mountain are excellent moderate excursions; and towards the southwest, Blue Mountain and Snowy Mountain are two classics.

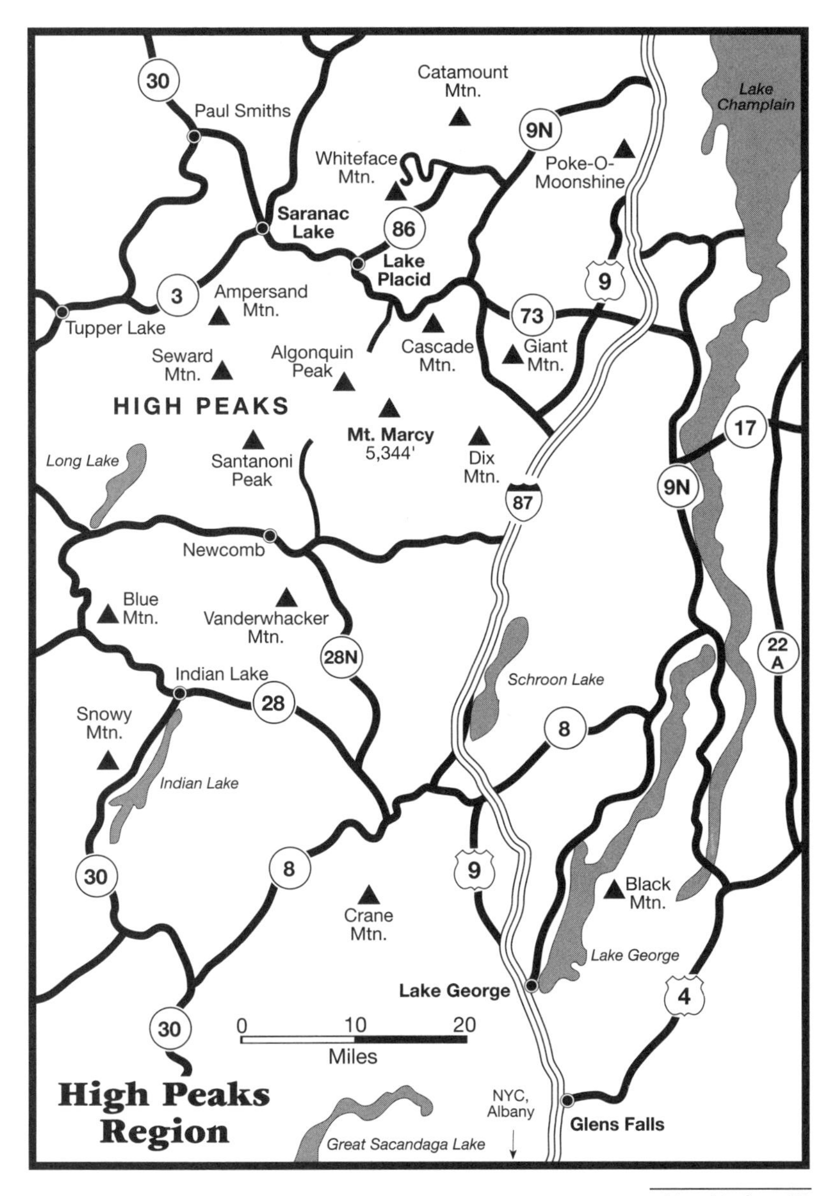

Catamount Mtn.
Lake Champlain
30
Paul Smiths
9N
Whiteface Mtn.
Poke-O-Moonshine
Saranac Lake
86
Lake Placid
9
3
Ampersand Mtn.
73
Tupper Lake
Cascade Mtn.
Giant Mtn.
Seward Mtn.
Algonquin Peak
HIGH PEAKS
17
Mt. Marcy
5,344'
Long Lake
Santanoni Peak
Dix Mtn.
9N
87
Newcomb
Blue Mtn.
Vanderwhacker Mtn.
28N
22 A
Indian Lake
28
Schroon Lake
Snowy Mtn.
8
Indian Lake
30
8
9
Black Mtn.
Crane Mtn.
Lake George
Lake George
4
30
0
10
20
Miles
NYC, Albany
Glens Falls
Great Sacandaga Lake
High Peaks Region

8 • Snowy Mountain 3,899'

Rating: Moderately strenuous
Time: 5 hours
Distance: 7.4 miles
Total climb: about 2,300'
Location: West side of Indian Lake

Summary: A Doctor Jekyl and Mr. Hyde hike: very easy in the beginning but with a long, extremely steep finish. Great views from a ledge near the summit.

Sometimes referred to as the Mount Marcy of the southern Adirondacks, Snowy Mountain is a major landmark. As described by O'Kane in his 1928 *Trails and Summits of the Adirondacks:* "The summit of Snowy, as one looks at it from the region on the east or northeast, gives an impression of a darkly wooded mass, like a battered and dented block, set upon the top of a broad, high foundation. The sides of that elevated block drop off almost sheer." Sweeping upward 2,250 feet from Indian Lake, it is an intriguing mountain and something that calls out to be climbed! With its height (50th highest in NY) and solid vertical gain, Snowy Mountain is a kind of honorary 46-er. It is a very popular hike for summer vacationers in the Indian Lake-Blue Mountain area.

The one and only trail up the mountain, **Snowy Mountain Trail**, is well-worn and heavily used. Initially, the terrain is easy; in fact the first 2.5 miles gains only 800 feet. After a first mile of pleasant woods, the trail reaches a stream, crossing it and various side brooks a number of times in the next mile or so. Eventually, the real climb begins. Moderate at first, it soon becomes hideously steep; the worst sections are direct assaults up steep, bare rock. Exercise caution here because loose gravel, sand, and mud make the rock surfaces slippery. This last section climbs 1,300' in 1.2 miles: it's among the steeper trails in this book.

A little below the summit, you abruptly come out on a broad, grassy shelf with fine, sweeping views to the east. Take a well-earned break here. Mount Marcy lies 40 miles to the northeast. Given a clear day and binoculars, Marcy and many of the High Peaks can be identified—32 in fact. The actual top (viewless) is about five minutes farther via a somewhat confusing trail (and its variations) that snakes through the dense woods of the summit block. Unfortunately the summit fire tower is unsafe to climb. Exploring around on the summit area will yield a few other lookouts with interesting views. Return by the same route.

Snowy Mountain John Winkler

Approach: From the village of Indian Lake, the trailhead is 6.5 miles south on NY 30. Approaching from the south, Indian Lake is 60 miles north of Amsterdam (exit 27) on I-90.

Maps: Trails of the Adirondack Central Region (ADK) and New York State Atlas & Gazetteer, p. 87

Two and a half miles west of Newcomb, and 11.5 miles east of Long Lake on Route 28, is the trailhead for **Goodnow Mountain** (2,690'). The one and a half mile (1,200' of climbing), well-maintained route to the summit makes an excellent short hike. Figure on 2 to 3 hours for the round trip. From the parking lot, the trail climbs gradually, then runs gently up and down over easy terrain. After crossing a bridge (0.5 mile), begin a steady climb, gaining the main ridge after swinging around to the south (0.9 mile). After passing an old barn at 1.5 miles you soon reach the summit. From the fire tower you can pick out 23 (half) of the High Peaks. The Seward and Santanoni Ranges are nearby, while Marcy and its companion peaks are visible about 25 miles to the northeast.

9 • Blue Mountain 3,759'

Rating: Moderate
Distance: 4 miles
Time: 3 hours 30 minutes
Total climb: 1,600'
Location: Between Blue Mountain village and Long Lake
Summary: Panoramic view from the summit tower. Upper trail is primarily on bare slabs.

High and standing alone, Blue Mountain is the landmark for the Blue Mountain Lake region. While the lower section of the trail is a typical, heavily used, rocky, and often rough path, the upper third of the trail ascends along bare rock. At times disconcertingly smooth, at times heaved and buckled, and at times fissured by cracks carrying runoff, this portion of the route is a joy in dry conditions. The trail maintains a fairly steep gradient and will require care on the descent, especially when wet. The summit fire tower has been restored (Spring 2000) and is a great finish to this interesting hike.

From the highway (there is a sign), the trail starts out as a woods road, soon narrowing to a rocky trail. This is an interpretive trail; there are numbered markers along the route which are keyed to informative blurbs on the natural environment found in the handout (stocked in the box located at the beginning of the trail). The trail climbs generally moderately with occasional level sections. The flatter areas tend to be wet. Frequent use of puncheons, however, help to keep your feet dry. At about the halfway point, the trail climbs across roots and rocks before commencing the interesting slab section. You will be climbing on this exposed bedrock for the next 20 to 30 minutes. About 10 minutes before reaching the summit, the grade eases abruptly, although you are still walking on bare rock. The dense woods persist until the last minute or so, when you finally emerge onto a small, rocky knoll, ringed by forest. Views from the fire tower include Raquette Lake, Ampersand, Algonquin, Colden, and Marcy.

Descend the same route. Because of the extensive slab section, individual descent rates will vary, depending on hiking experience and footgear. This is especially true in wet or snowy conditions.

Approach: The trailhead parking lot is on NY 28, 1.3 miles north of the village of Blue Mountain. Approaching from the north, drive south on NY 28 from Long Lake for 9.3 miles.

Blue Mountain from Blue Mountain Lake

Maps: Trails of the Adirondack Central Region (ADK) and New York State Atlas & Gazetteer, p. 87

On a non-hiking note, a visit to the **Adirondack Museum** in Blue Mountain Lake is highly recommended. Twenty-three exhibit areas explore the Adirondack themes: wooden boats, including the Adirondack Guide boat; rustic furniture; Adirondack painters; early road and rail transportation; the history of mining and logging; ice harvesting; the history of tourism in the Adirondacks (its hotels, camps, and clubs); plants and animals of the Adirondacks; and outdoor recreation and environmental issues. The Museum is located on Route 30, just up the hill from the hamlet of **Blue Mountain Lake**, and a little over an hour's drive from Lake George or Lake Placid. It is open from late May to mid-October. Admission is charged. Call 518-352-7311 for information.

10 • Black Mountain 2,646′

Rating: Moderate
Time: 3 hours 30 minutes
Distance: 5.6 miles (loop optional)
Total climb: 1,050′
Location: Lake George, east side

Summary: Sweeping vista of the Champlain Basin, as far north as Mount Mansfield. Dramatic views down to Lake George from ledges near the summit.

Starting out as an old road, the trail (marked with red disks) climbs briefly then runs over easy terrain before passing to the right of a run-down farm. Bear right at a junction (about 1 mile) where a sign indicates it is 1.6 miles to the summit. At about the halfway point, you cross a small brook, and a snowmobile trail joins the hiking trail, coinciding with it almost to the summit. The trail ascends more directly now—in places it is very steep but for a few short sections almost level—as it ascends to the main ridge. Reaching the narrow ridge (about three-quarters of the total effort to the top), you are rewarded with dramatic views of Lake George, far below. Take a minute to climb out on the rocks just off the trail to get a better vantage point. The trail now veers sharply left and works its way up very steep slopes for a short distance before making a gentle traverse across the face of the mountain. Where the snowmobile trail continues straight ahead, the hiking route swings back to the right, making the final climb to the summit.

The top is adorned with an old ranger cabin, various sheds and a fenced-off area containing communications equipment. From the immediate summit area, the view is to the north, sweeping around to the east and south. The northern part of Lake George, Lake Champlain, and a big slice of Vermont are visible: a great arc of lakes and distant mountains. However, a little extra effort yields the best view. Take the trail that continues down the back side (west) of the summit. An enjoyable five-minute descent brings you to a grassy, ledgy area. From here the view down to Lake George, 2,300' below, with the little island group off Montcalm Point is quite remarkable. The Tongue Mountain Range is directly across the lake. Retrace your steps to return to your car.

Note that it is possible to continue below the ledges mentioned above, past Black Mountain Pond and Lapland Pond, making a loop slightly longer than the up-and-back route.

Lake George from Black Mountain

Approach: From Ticonderoga (north end of Lake George), drive south on NY 22 for 17 miles to County Road #6. (Coming from the south, County Rd. #6 is 7.3 miles north of Whitehall.) Turn west (towards Huletts Landing on County Road #6), continuing 2.5 miles to Pine Brook Road. Head left for 0.8 mile to the trailhead and parking.

Maps: Adirondack Eastern Region (ADK); The Adirondacks, Lake George Region (Adirondack Maps); New York Atlas and Gazetteer, p. 89

The **Tongue Mountain Range** occupies the peninsula on the west side of Lake George. It is bounded on the west by NY Route 9N. A network of trails makes possible several options, including a complete traverse of the main ridgeline. Fivemile Mountain, at 2,256', is the range's highest point.

11 • Crane Mountain 3,264'

Rating: Short, but steep
Time: 3 hours
Distance: 3.8-mile loop
Location: Near Warrensburg and west of Lake George
Total climb: 1,150'
Summary: A fun, very steep trail leads to great views from ledges. Swim in a beautiful mountain pond on the way back.

Finding this mountain is an achievement in itself! Those still wishing to climb it after the somewhat tedious driving approach will be rewarded with an exciting climb. As an isolated, relatively massive, steep-sided mountain, Crane makes a distinct impression as you drive towards it. From the trailhead parking, take the trail branch (straight), which heads for the summit. After an easy stroll for a few minutes, the trail makes an abrupt change. For the next half-mile it powers 700' up the steep south face of Crane—this is one of the steepest trails in this book. The clambering ascent up through the smooth, gray boulders—call them elephantine—is so steep that it's amusing. After a section that runs near the edge of a cliff—it is easy to jog left to the ledges for a view—the trail comes to a junction. The left branch leads directly to **Crane Mountain Pond** (0.4 mile), but our route (right) takes us over the summit first. Heading onward, the trail steepens, with the final pitch straight up a rock face; a 24-rung ladder makes this easy.

After enjoying the summit ledges (views are blocked to the north), make the pleasant descent to the pond. Just a few minutes off the summit, a short side trail (left) leads to a great overlook of Crane Mountain Pond, directly below. When you reach the pond, contour left along the shore; you soon reach a fork. Heading left takes you back to the trail you came up, at the junction mentioned above, and this is the shorter way back. The somewhat longer and more interesting variation is to continue along the edge of the pond, and just after crossing the pond outlet, swing sharply left and begin your descent. Right before the outlet are a couple of great spots to relax by the pond, including a wonderful slab that any self-respecting swimmer will find impossible to resist. Below the pond outlet, the trail runs out onto a sloping slab. Descend along the right edge of the slab to the woods, where the trail is once again obvious. Like the ascent route, the trail here is not shy about taking a steep line. After about 30 minutes, you will come to

Crane Mountain Pond

a woods road (Putnam Farm Road). Head left here over easy ground for a little less than a mile to return to your car.

Approach: In Warrensburg (6 miles from Lake George), drive west (left) on US 418 and cross the Schroon River. About a mile after crossing the Hudson River, and 3.7 miles from Warrensburg, turn right on Athol Road. Continue through the settlement of Athol; at 5.5 miles, make a sharp right onto Glen-Athol Road. Stay on this road to Garnet Lake Road South—you are now 11.7 miles from Warrensburg. Turn left, and continue for 1.3 miles to Sky High Road. Turn right and continue 2 more miles to the trailhead.

Maps: The Adirondacks, Lake George Region (ADK) and New York State Atlas & Gazetteer, pages 80 and 88

The High Peaks

Just south of the resort town of Lake Placid, lies an area of rugged, roadless mountains, the High Peaks of the Adirondacks. With a vast network of hiking trails, dozens of lean-tos and camping sites, spectacular alpine scenery and a rich and storied tradition, the High Peaks are unique in this country. The region is a paradise for hikers, skiers, and climbers. The High Peaks include all but two (Hunter and Slide are in the Catskills) of New York State's 46 summits over 4,000'. And while the high mountain terrain in New Hampshire's White Mountains tends to be along ridges, the concentration of complex mountain terrain in the High Peaks is probably unequalled in the Northeastern U.S.. In places the forested mountainsides have been stripped by landslides, leaving the long, fan-shaped scars which are a characteristic of these mountains. The highest summits are above tree line; breathtaking views of wild mountain landscapes and sparkling lakes are found everywhere. On steeper terrain, and on the ridges, much of the walking is on rock slabs and exposed ledge.

The highest summit is **Mount Marcy** (5,344'), followed by **Algonquin Peak** (5,114'). The 4,000'-ers are regularly climbed, despite the fact that about half of them have no officially maintained trail. Generally hikers show little enthusiasm for crashing through dense stands of spruce, clambering over blowdowns and wading across mucky swamps, but here in the High Peaks "herd paths" and rock slides are an essential part of the experience.

In the High Peaks not all trails have formal names, and there is no dominant trail like the Appalachian Trail or the Long Trail, something which is very much the theme in Vermont, Maine, and New Hampshire. To help differentiate among the trails, a system of colored metal disks is used. **The Adirondack Mountain Club** (**ADK**), the NY State **Department of Environmental Conservation** (NYSDEC), and the **Adirondack Trail Improvement Society** (ATIS) are the primary trail maintenance organizations. The most important trailhead is at **Heart Lake** (eight miles south of Lake Placid), where the **High Peaks Information Center** is open year round. The authoritative guide is the ADK's *Guide to Adirondack Trails: High Peaks Region.*

From Haystack, looking across Panther Gorge to Mount Marcy

12 • Ampersand Mountain 3,352′

Rating: Moderate with a steep climb
Time: 4 hours
Distance: 5.4 miles
Location: Southwest of Saranac Lake
Total climb: 1,900′
Summary: A lower, isolated peak with exceptional views of lakes and mountains in all directions from its open summit.

Cross to the south side of the road, and pick up the red-marked trail. It starts out as an enjoyable stroll through a hemlock forest, coming to a boggy area in a little less than a mile. After a section of puncheons and several small bridges, the trail begins to climb and reaches a small clearing (a former cabin site) at 1.7 miles. Soon after this point, the ascent begins in earnest with approximately a half mile of sustained, quite steep climbing, eventually bringing you up onto the final ridge. (The last mile climbs almost 1,500—this is steep stuff.) At this point, a short but intricate bit of trail remains before you can stand on the summit. After walking beneath the cliffs on your left, you climb steeply (left) past huge rocks up to a little saddle. The actual summit is on your right. The trail now takes an indirect approach, as it drops down a short distance before turning sharply right to take on the short and steep finale. Then it's across easy rock slabs to the wide-open summit. This last section is marked with yellow paint blazes—you will find them to be essential on your way down if the visibility is poor.

Although a relatively low mountain, Ampersand does offer an unobstructed view in all directions. Dozens of lakes lie scattered to the west and north. Only 5 miles to the south, the Seward Range, with 4,361-foot Mount Seward, dominates the view. Algonquin, Marcy, and many of the other High Peaks loom on the eastern horizon. The sharp profile of Whiteface is hard to miss. Descend by the route you came, carefully following the paint blazes. It is possible to wander off in the wrong direction.

Approach: From Saranac Lake drive west 8.6 miles on NY 3 (from its junction with NY 86) towards Tupper Lake. Park on the north (right) side of the highway.

Maps: Trails of the Adirondack High Peaks Region (ADK); The Adirondacks, High Peaks Region and New York State Atlas & Gazetteer, p. 95

Whiteface Mountain from the summit of Ampersand

Adirondack Mountain Club

The Adirondack Mountain Club (ADK) is the primary hiking club in the Adirondacks. Based in Lake George, the club has 26 chapters and over 30,000 members. Its mission statement reads in part: "The Club, founded in 1922, is a member-directed organization committed to public service and stewardship. The ADK employs a balanced approach to outdoor recreation, advocacy, environmental education and natural resource conservation." The ADK publishes various guide books, including the definitive 8-volume series on the Adirondacks and the Catskills.

At Heart Lake, the northern entrance to the High Peaks, the ADK's High Peaks Information Center provides information on trail conditions and hiker supplies. Nearby Adirondak Loj is one of two lodges maintained by the ADK for its members and the public. The full-service lodge is open year-round and offers rustic, comfortable accommodations and is an ideal starting point for hiking and skiing excursions. Johns Brook Lodge (JBL) is located at the foot of the Great Range, a 3-mile walk in from the Garden, the main trailhead in Keene Valley.

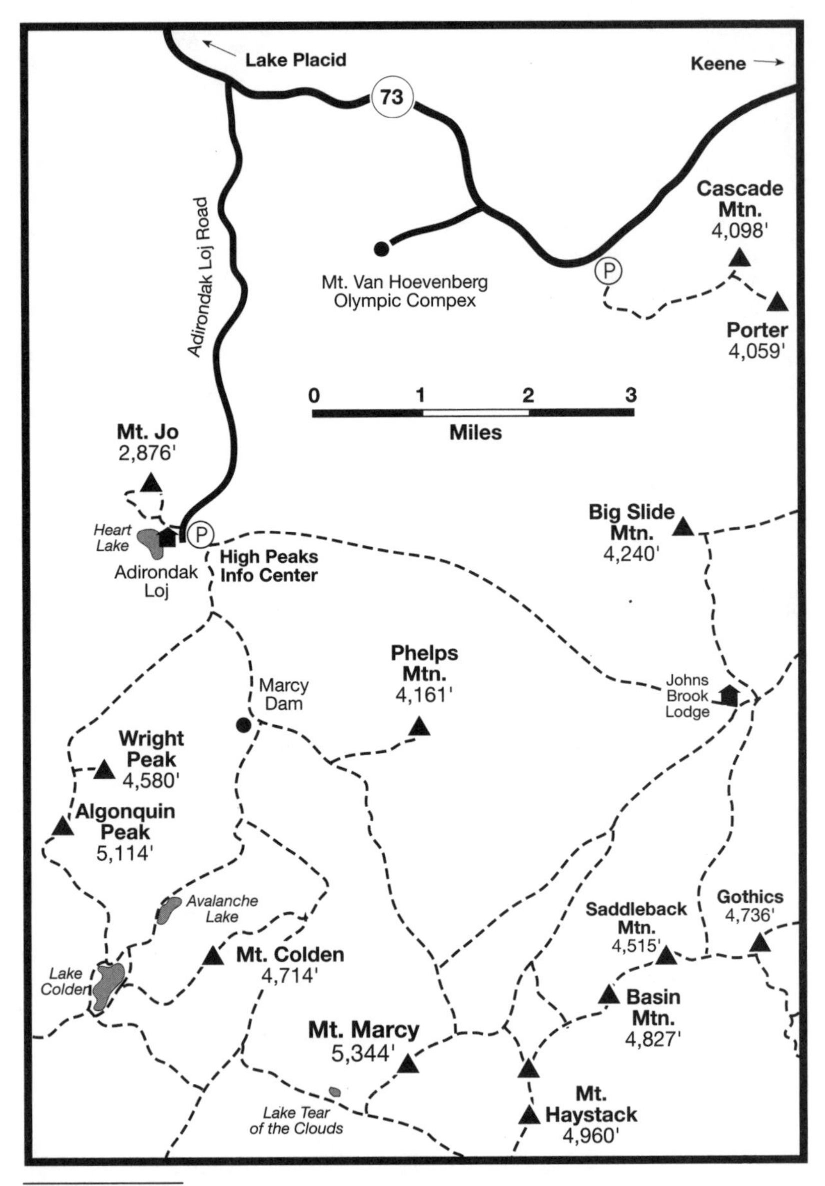
Lake Placid
Keene
73
Adirondak Loj Road
Mt. Van Hoevenberg
Olympic Compex
Cascade
Mtn.
4,098'
Porter
4,059'
0
1
2
3
Miles
Mt. Jo
2,876'
Heart
Lake
Adirondak
Loj
High Peaks
Info Center
Big Slide
Mtn.
4,240'
Phelps
Mtn.
4,161'
Marcy
Dam
Johns
Brook
Lodge
Wright
Peak
4,580'
Algonquin
Peak
5,114'
Avalanche
Lake
Mt. Colden
4,714'
Lake
Colden
Saddleback
Mtn.
4,515'
Gothics
4,736'
Basin
Mtn.
4,827'
Mt. Marcy
5,344'
Lake Tear
of the Clouds
Mt.
Haystack
4,960'

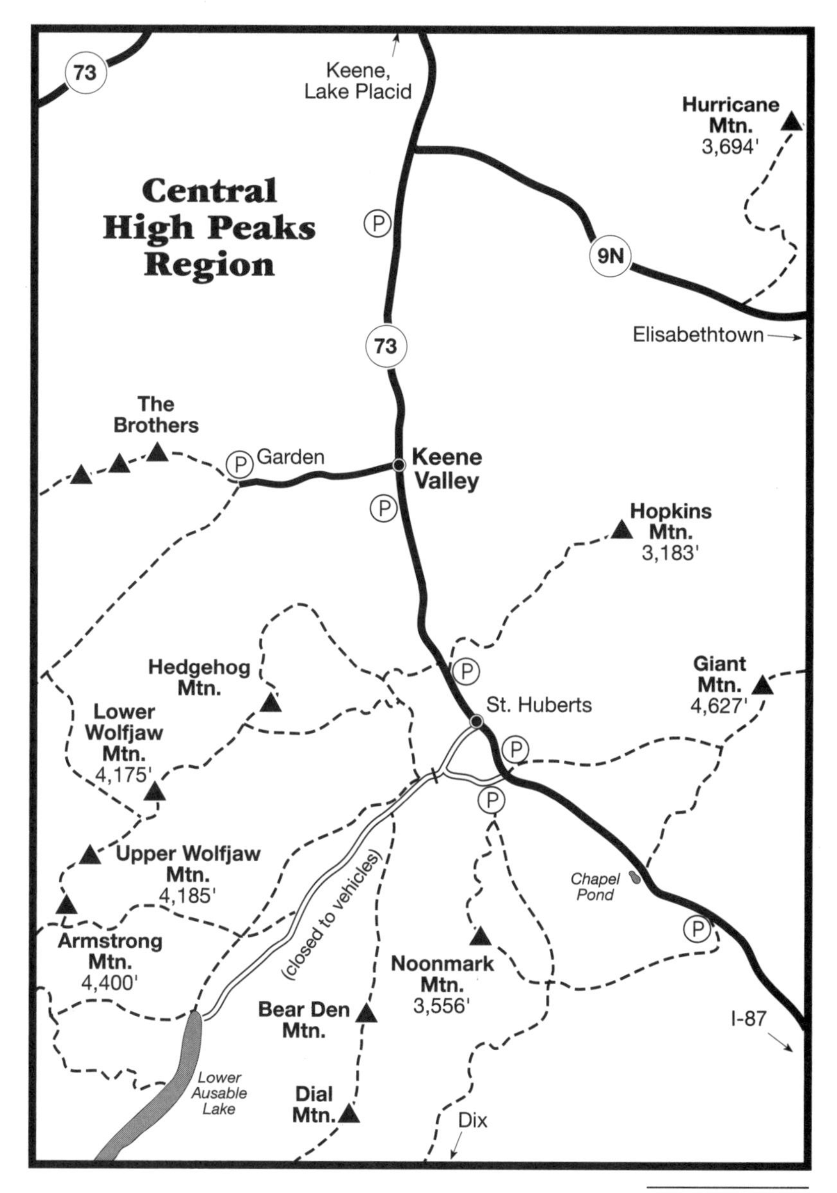

Central High Peaks Region
73
Keene, Lake Placid
Hurricane Mtn. 3,694'
9N
Elisabethtown
73
The Brothers
Garden
Keene Valley
Hopkins Mtn. 3,183'
Hedgehog Mtn.
Giant Mtn. 4,627'
St. Huberts
Lower Wolfjaw Mtn. 4,175'
Upper Wolfjaw Mtn. 4,185'
(closed to vehicles)
Chapel Pond
Armstrong Mtn. 4,400'
Noonmark Mtn. 3,556'
Bear Den Mtn.
I-87
Lower Ausable Lake
Dial Mtn.
Dix

13 • Mount Jo 2,876′

Rating: An easy hike
Distance: 2-mile loop
Time: 1½ to 2 hours
Location: Heart Lake, about 8 miles from Lake Placid
Total Climb: 700′
Summary: Classic short hike right above Heart Lake. Stunning, close-up views of Algonquin and the core of the High Peaks.

Mount Jo is probably the best-known small mountain of the High Peaks region, and it is the classic kids' hike in the Adirondacks. Climb it to have a good look at Colden, Algonquin, Wallface, and many of the High Peaks.

The trail up Mount Jo has two variations, which are called the **Short Trail** and the **Long Trail**. Various combinations are possible, and the route described here uses both trails, making a loop trip. From the parking area, return to the road, head right, and in about 100 yards you will come to signs for Indian Pass. Follow this trail a short distance to **Heart Lake**, turn right, and immediately come to the sign for Mt. Jo. Begin climbing, reaching an intersection at 0.3 mile. Keep right for the Short Trail, which climbs an impressive, steep gully—you weave your way up through boulders—to the summit ridge at 0.7 mile. Here, you'll meet the Long Trail coming in from the left. Bear right over generally easy terrain to the summit, about a mile from your starting point. There is one short but very steep rock pitch just below the summit ledges. From the top, the views of Heart Lake directly below and the High Peaks in all their glory immediately to the south are well worth the effort. On your return, at the last intersection you encountered on the way up, continue straight to take the Long Trail down (for variety, and it is easier on the knees), or, bear left to drop down steeply the way you came up. Up and down the Short Trail gives a total of 1.8 miles.

Approach: From NY 73, about 4 miles east of Lake Placid, turn south on Adirondak Loj Road. At 4.3 miles, you come to the information booth where a small day usage fee is charged. The parking area is just beyond on the left.

Maps: Trails of the Adirondack High Peaks Region (ADK); The Adirondacks, High Peaks Region; and New York State Atlas & Gazetteer, p. 96

Heart Lake and Algonquin from Mount Jo

On your right, after you enter the parking lot, is the all-important **High Peaks Information Center** which is run by the Adirondack Mountain Club. Club personnel can provide up-to-date trail and weather information, and last-minute supplies can be bought. There is a campground, and at nearby Heart Lake, the ADK's **Adirondak Loj** offers bunkroom style lodging with meals.

14 • Algonquin Peak 5,114'

Rating: Strenuous
Time: 6-7 hours
Distance: 8 miles
Location: Heart Lake, a few miles south of Lake Placid
Total climb: 2,940'
Summary: Spectacular, panoramic views. One of the great classics of the Adirondacks and one of the best day hikes in the East.

Algonquin Peak, together with Mount Marcy and Mount Colden, form part of the central core of the High Peaks. It is these three summits that catch the eye when viewed from the north and the Lake Placid area. Algonquin is also the centerpiece of the group of summits known as the MacIntyre Range, the other peaks in this compact range being Wright, Iroquois, and Boundary. The 4-mile trail to the summit—short by Adirondack standards—makes Algonquin Peak a logical choice for one's first major hike. The view from the high, open summit is one of the best in the Adirondacks. This is a popular mountain, summer and winter!

From the trailhead, follow the **Van Hoevenberg Trail** (the same as for Mt. Marcy) over easy ground toward Marcy Dam. After 1 mile, continue straight at the trail junction (the left fork continues to Marcy Dam and Mt. Marcy). From here, the trail continues over more easy terrain with some steep sections, reaching another intersection at 1.4 miles (keep right). Now climbing more steadily and crossing several streams, the trail passes a small waterfall at 2.4 miles. The view opens up as the trail alternates between steeper and easier sections, and the 0.4-mile spur trail to **Wright Peak** (4,580') branches inconspicuously to the left at 3.1 miles.

The next half mile has some very steep sections; in fact there is a crux: a narrow, nearly straight-up slab of exposed bedrock, about 100' high. At 3.6 miles, you pass through the last of the trees and begin the final enjoyable climb along moderately pitched ledges, with cairns and yellow-paint blazes leading the way across the open rock. The alpine character of the view is one of the most dramatic in this book: mountains and lakes are everywhere. Across an abyss, the slides of Mount Colden command your attention, Marcy reigns supreme just beyond, and to the south, the waters of the curiously named Flowed Lands sparkle in the sunlight. Most of the High Peaks—46 mountains are on the official 4,000-footer list—to the east and south are in plain view. Return by the route you came

Marcy and Colden from the summit of Algonquin

up, carefully following the cairns and paint blazes off the top. Note that the trail continues down the south side of the mountain to Iroquois Peak (4,830') and to Lake Colden.

Approach: The trailhead is located at the end of Adirondak Loj Road, at the High Peaks Information Center. A small parking fee is charged. Adirondak Loj Road branches south from NY 73, 4 miles east of Lake Placid.

Maps: Trails of the Adirondack High Peaks Region (ADK); The Adirondacks, High Peaks Region (Adirondack Maps); and New York State Atlas & Gazetteer, p. 96

15 • Mount Marcy 5,344′

Rating: Strenuous day hike or as an overnight trip
Time: 9-12 hours
Distance: 14.8 miles
Total climb: 3,200′
Location: Center of the High Peaks, south of Heart Lake
Summary: Highest in New York state and a Mecca for hikers. Wonderful open summit.

Mount Marcy is New York's highest peak, and the Van Hoevenberg Trail is far and away the most popular way to make the ascent. It is an immensely popular hike. Although the route is over 7 miles each way, every year thousands of relatively inexperienced hikers tackle it as a day hike. As it is one of the toughest of the popular day hikes in this country, this would seem to be a proof of the mind over matter doctrine.

The starting point—the **Heart Lake** area—is the most important trailhead in the Adirondacks, comparable to New Hampshire's Pinkham Notch. Here, the Adirondack Mountain Club's **High Peaks Information Center** is staffed year-round, providing information and supplies. There is also a large campground and two large parking areas. These are usually overflowing on busy days. Adirondak Loj and Heart Lake are a just a short walk from the hiker parking area—well worth a visit. After any last minute purchases, filling of water bottles, offerings to the gods, etc., sign out, and follow the wide and pleasant hiker highway—the **Van Hoevenberg Trail**, marked with blue disks—over very easy ground for 2.3 miles to the small lake known as **Marcy Dam**.

Marcy Dam is an excellent short hike in its own right and is a logical goal for members of your party who may not feel compelled to go all the way up Marcy. It is also a popular camping site, serving as a base for forays into the High Peaks. There are six lean-tos and a number of campsites available on a first-come first-serve basis. Just after crossing the dam, the trail to Avalanche Lake branches off to the right. (Avalanche Lake is covered in hike #16.) At 3.2 miles, you pass the side trail (left) to Phelps Mountain (1.2 miles, 1,200 feet of steep climbing). If today doesn't turn out to be your day to do Marcy, Phelps (4,161') is a good consolation prize, as it has first rate views. After more steady climbing, some of it steep, you reach the ledges of **Indian Falls** at 4.4 miles. Here you can sit and relax on the smooth slabs and cool your feet in the little

Approaching the summit of Mount Marcy

ADK Summit Stewards on Mount Marcy

stream. (Walk down the slabs a short distance to get the best views.) Leaving the warm, sunny rocks behind, make the generally steady ascent—there are a couple of sections with easier grades—reaching the yellow-marked Hopkins Trail (it enters left from Johns Brook Valley) at 6.2 miles. You are now about 900' below the summit of Marcy. After negotiating some ups and downs—Marcy's summit is now in full view—the trail passes the Phelps Trail (red markers), the main route from Keene Valley. Bear right, pass through a small wet area, and then comes the finale, a clamber up open ledges to the summit! If the weather is with you, relax and contemplate the incredible panorama: the Great Range, Giant, Dix, Johns Brook Valley, and Whiteface are especially compelling.

Most hikers return by the same route, but there are a couple of loop alternatives as well. The longer and more interesting **variation** is as follows: Descend from the summit into the col between Mount Skylight and Marcy, head right (continuing on the Calamity

Brook Trail) past **Lake Tear of the Clouds** (highest pond source of the Hudson River) to Lake Colden, 4.8 miles from Marcy's summit. Now head north to Avalanche Lake, over Avalanche Pass and down to Marcy Dam, closing the loop. (Consult one of the standard trail maps to better understand this.) This variation adds 3.5 miles to the basic out-and-back version, for a total of 18.3 miles.

Approach: From Lake Placid, drive 4 miles east on NY 73, and turn right on Adirondak Loj Road. Follow this 4.8 miles to the High Peaks Information Center and parking area.

Maps: Trails of the Adirondack High Peaks Region (ADK); The Adirondacks, High Peaks Region (Adirondack Maps, Inc.); and New York State Atlas & Gazetteer, p. 96

Fragile vegetation

It is commonly known that the higher one goes on a mountain, the harsher the climate becomes. In fact as we gain altitude, the changes in weather, and in plant and animal life are identical to those encountered when traveling north. This is dramatically illustrated in the Adirondacks and on the higher summits of New England when mountains reach a height of four to five thousand feet—trees are no longer able to survive, and sub-arctic conditions prevail. Interestingly, the transition to this so-called arctic-alpine zone is quite abrupt, giving rise to a distinct "tree line." One minute you are in a dense woods; the next minute you are completely out in the open.

While wind and the relatively featureless terrain present special dangers to hikers, these areas also need protection from humankind. The arctic-alpine zone is far from lifeless; grasses, mosses, lichens and a profusion of delicate alpine flowers thrive. The long, brutal winters and short, cool summers are the facts of life here. Human foot traffic is much more destructive than the harsh weather. Once a delicate plant is damaged, recovery is extremely difficult. Thus the plea to visitors: When above tree line, do not step on plants, and walk only on rocks! Keep dogs leashed. Camping above tree line is not allowed, except in winter with adequate snow cover.

16 • Avalanche Lake

Rating: Moderate
Time: 5 hours
Distance: 10 miles
Total climbing: 1,100'
Location: Between Algonquin Peak and Mount Colden

Summary: A gentle stroll leads to a narrow pass in a dramatic setting. South of the pass lies Avalanche Lake, one of the gems of the Adirondacks.

From the **High Peaks Information Center** (HPIC) at the end of the Adirondak Loj Road, sign out at the kiosk and follow the blue-marked **Van Hoevenberg Trail**. This wide, heavily used path is the primary access to the High Peaks from the north. Starting out in a pine forest, the trail dips across several wet spots and small streams; it takes you over easy terrain to a fork at one mile. Now bear left for 1.3 miles to **Marcy Dam**; the right fork is the route up Algonquin Peak. The trail continues over very easy ground but changes character somewhat; the footing is slightly rougher and it pitches a few moderate hills at you. At 2.3 miles you emerge from the woods and cross Marcy Dam. This peaceful lake—both the lake and the dam are referred to as Marcy Dam—nestled right at the base of the High Peaks, is a good spot to take a break. Marcy Dam is also an important "base camp" for excursions into the High Peaks; there are six lean-tos and a ranger outpost.

Cross the dam, and paying close attention to signs, leave the Van Hoevenberg Trail about two hundred yards past the dam, heading right on the yellow-marked **Avalanche Pass Trail**. A mile past Marcy Dam, cross the stream (good swimming here), and at the fork, continue straight. (The left fork leads to Lake Arnold and Mount Colden.) Soon the trail climbs more steeply, with occasional steps and short ladders. The ski trail variation criss-crosses the hiking trail in this section. The trail over **Avalanche Pass** itself was impacted seriously by a major slide in the fall of 1999. The demolished forest—trees were shattered and flung every which way—the immense piles of debris and a new clearing are testimony to the forces unleashed by this earth and rock avalanche off Mount Colden. Continue through the pass area, walk along a cliff band, and make the easy descent to Avalanche Lake. Here precipitous mountain flanks plunge into the lake on both sides: Mount Colden on your left and Algonquin on your right. Implausible as it may

Avalanche Lake

seem, the trail continues along the right edge of the lake by using a system of ladders and walkways bolted to the cliffs and boulders. This famous section is known as **Hitch-up Matilda**, named in honor of the young woman whose skirts dragged in the water as her guide carried her across the shallow water at the base of the cliffs. The current trail does not feature wading. Either end of the lake serves as a good turnaround point. The near end, where there is a small beach, is about 4.5 miles from your starting point, and the far end is about five miles. Return by the same route.

Approach: From NY 73, 4 miles east of Lake Placid, drive south on Adirondak Loj Road 4.8 miles to the High Peaks Information Center's trailhead parking at Heart Lake.

Maps: Trails of the Adirondack High Peaks Region (ADK) and The Adirondacks, High Peaks Region (Adirondack Maps, Inc.)

17 • Trap Dike and Mount Colden

Rating: Very difficult, a rock climb
Time: 6 to 8 hours
Distance: 11 miles
Total climb: 3,000′ (rock climb portion is about 2,000′)
Location: West face of Mount Colden, above Avalanche Lake
Summary: The original rock climb and now a classic. Although an easy climb, it is not a hike.

There are dozens of prominent "slides" in the Adirondacks—gashes on the mountain sides—caused when steep mountain slopes slough off their thin layer of soil and trees, exposing the smooth bedrock underneath. The Trap Dike climb starts out in a recessed dike, eventually transitioning to an adjacent slide, which leads to the top of Mount Colden (4,714').

The climbing route proper starts from **Avalanche Lake**. The normal hike in to the lake is from the High Peaks Information Center at Heart Lake. Follow the **Van Hoevenberg Trail** to Marcy Dam; head right on the trail to Lake Colden, crossing **Avalanche Pass** at 4 miles and reaching the far (south) end of Avalanche Lake at 5 miles from the car. (Hike #16 describes this approach in detail.) As you traverse along the edge of the lake, you have ample opportunity to study Trap Dike across the lake. At the far end, leave the trail and bushwhack along the opposite shore of the lake until you come to the deep recess of Trap Dike. Climb up the dike—it is like a giant, super-steep staircase—until the side wall is low enough to allow an easy exit. Parties that exit the dike too early often experience difficulties on the very steep lower slabs. Thus be sure to continue in the dike until you reach the cairn. This is the signal that it's time to move to the right and out onto the slide.

Once you are on the slide, it is exhilarating, with exposed scrambling leading to the broad summit ledges. Avalanche Lake lies directly below. How difficult is this climb? Under good (dry) conditions, experienced climbers will not need a rope, as this is a class 3 climb. Novice climbers must carry a rope and be led by an experienced guide. After enjoying the views and paying your respects to the summit, descend on the red-marked trail (1.6 miles) very steeply to Lake Colden, 2,000' below, or alternatively, head left to Lake Arnold on yellow blazes. Back at **Lake Colden**, bear right and continue to Avalanche Lake. Now use the approach route to return to Marcy Dam and your starting point.

Trap Dike from Avalanche Lake

Approach: From the High Peaks Information Center at Heart Lake, eight miles south of Lake Placid.

Maps: Trails of the Adirondack High Peaks Region (ADK).

18 • Cascade Mountain 4,098'

Rating: Moderate
Distance: 4.8 miles
Time: 3 hours and 45 minutes
Total climb: 1,940'
Location: A few miles north of Marcy, on the south side of NY 73
Summary: An easy and accessible mountain, with terrific, close-up views of the High Peaks.

For an Adirondack 4,000-footer, the effort needed to climb Cascade seems almost negligible compared to the typical 12- to 15-mile trips. You have the added bonus that the views from the summit ledges are superb. Algonquin, Colden, and Marcy are a few miles away to the south, and to the left of Marcy, the magnificent Great Range stretches away to the east.

The roadside parking is fairly limited and can pose a problem for this very popular hike. Note that the trail for Pitchoff Mountain (3,477') starts just across busy Route 73.

From the road, the trail drops down a small bank, then begins its pleasant climb. A bit awkward at the outset—ankle-banging rocks—it soon climbs without any particularly steep sections and without much of a view until you reach a small clearing at 1.8 miles, i.e. after about an hour and a half of climbing. After another 0.3 mile, bear left at the trail junction, move out across the huge ledges, and climb the gentle hunk of granite that is the actual summit. At the highest point you are on the edge of a cliff looking almost straight down onto the highway far below. Whiteface Mountain and its ski runs looms 10 miles to the north. Far away to the east, the mountains of Vermont barely ruffle the horizon. But the real action is south: the wild mountain mass of the High Peaks. If the weather is good, these ledges are a great place to hang out for hours and contemplate life. When you are ready to descend, head down the route you came up.

Approach: The trailhead is on NY 73, 6.8 miles west of Keene and 4.5 miles east of Adirondak Loj Road (8.5 miles east of Lake Placid).

Maps: Trails of the Adirondack High Peaks Region (ADK); The Adirondacks, High Peaks Region (Adirondack Maps, Inc.); and New York State Atlas & Gazetteer, p. 96

Colden and Algonquin from Cascade John Winkler

Aspiring forty-sixers and those with extra energy might want to extend their hike of Cascade and climb another of the High Peaks in the same day. The summit of **Porter Mountain** (4,059') is only 0.7 mile, albeit a very rough 0.7 mile, from the trail intersection you passed on the way up (just below the summit of Cascade). As you head left (west) from this junction, the trial drops into a dip before climbing to the summit. A short distance from the summit, you will have to negotiate a huge boulder that is placed squarely in the trail. From the top of Porter, you have a great view in all directions. The detour over to Porter will add about an hour to your total hiking time.

19 • Hopkins Mountain 3,183′

Rating: Moderate
Distance: 6.4 miles
Time: 4 hours 30 minutes
Total climb: 2,200′
Location: Keene Valley
Summary: Great summit ledges with an unusual eastern perspective on the High Peaks.

From the road, the **Mossy Cascade Trail** initially runs next to the river, soon reaching a house at 0.4 mile. After bearing right, then left, the trail veers sharply right and ascends beside Mossy Cascade. (At 0.7 mile, there is a short spur trail left to the base of the cascade.) After passing through a rough clearing, you settle into a fairly steep climb, coming to a viewpoint at about 1.5 miles. This is about the halfway point. Continuing, pass through a little dip and climb a steep ridge, pass a trail junction (stay right) before finally gaining the ridge and another trail junction, at 3 miles. While the right fork heads toward Giant, we go left up the final climb to the summit ledges. The view is practically panoramic, sweeping from Dix in the south, past the Great Range to Whiteface in the north. (It is blocked to the northeast by Tripod Mountain.)

Approaching the summit of Hopkins

The Ausable Club and the lands of the Adirondack Mountain Reserve are directly visible to the southwest, and finally, the summit slabs of Giant gleam to the south. Twenty-two of the High Peak summits can be picked out. The summit's huge granite slabs, interspersed with mossy patches, and in season, blueberries, make this a summit worth lingering on. Descend the same route.

Approach: Park on NY 73, 2 miles south of Keene Valley, just south of the Ausable River bridge. The trailhead is on the left (east) side of the road.

Maps: Trails of the Adirondack High Peaks Region (ADK); The Adirondacks, High Peaks Region (Adirondack Maps, Inc.); and New York State Atlas & Gazetteer, p. 96

The Forty-sixers

For many hikers, climbing all the Adirondack summits over 4,000 feet is an important goal. In fact for some it is the Hiker's Holy Grail! Without a tempting long-distance trail like the Appalachian Trail, "peakbagging" has perhaps assumed greater significance here than in other areas. The fact that about half of the summits have no maintained trail makes this quest especially challenging. Over time, as more and more people have hiked "trailless" peaks, rough paths have established themselves. Most of these "herd paths" are easy to follow, but in a good number of cases (for example, Allen, Couchsachraga, the Sewards) solid map and compass skills are essential. Some of the routes ascend slides for hundreds of feet (Macomb), and this greatly reduces bushwhacking time.

Enthusiasm for the 46er quest is not shared by all hikers, and quite a few of the lower summits—Noonmark, Catamount, Mount Jo, Hopkins, Pyramid—to name a few, are intrinsically more interesting than many on the 4,000'-er list. However, let there be no mistake, becoming a 46er is an outstanding achievement! Modern surveys have shown four of the original forty-six mountains to be less than 4,000 feet, but for continuity and the sake of tradition, the original list is still the official list. Those wishing to embark on this project can contact the 46er Committee at the Adirondack Mountain Club.

20 • Basin and Saddleback

Rating: Strenuous and very difficult
Distance: 16.3-mile loop
Time: 10-12 hours or overnight
Total climb: about 4,000'
Location: Great Range

Summary: Spectacular traverse between two high summits. Probably the most exposed and difficult hike regularly done in the Adirondacks.

When viewed from a distance, Saddleback (4,515') and Basin (4,827') make a rather mild impression, at least when compared with Gothics, Dix, Giant, or even Noonmark. However the slabs on the west face of Saddleback present the most difficult bit of scrambling in the entire High Peaks. The views, of Haystack, Marcy, and especially Gothics, are outstanding. Starting from the **Garden**, take the enjoyable walk on the **Phelps Trail** (yellow markers) into DEC's **Interior Outpost** at 3.1 miles. (This area, and higher up at **Johns Brook Lodge**, are the main camping spots.)

At the ranger cabin (outpost), pick up the **Orebed Trail** (blue markers) and cross Johns Brook on the little suspension bridge. Paying heed to the blue markers, stay on Orebed Trail through two intersections, and make the long, and at times very steep, 2,400-foot climb to **Gothics Col**, 6.2 miles from the Garden. You are now on the ridgeline of the Great Range, with Gothics' summit 0.6 mile (a 700'-climb) to the left. Head right on the **Range Trail**, also marked in blue, and reach the summit of Saddleback after 0.5 mile and 500' of climbing. As you ascend from the col, the view across to Gothics is so stunning that it may cause you to abandon the Saddleback-Basin traverse and climb Gothics instead!

At any rate, from the summit of Saddleback, let the yellow blazes lure you over the precipice. Be careful and take your time on these steep slabs: this is the most difficult part of the route. Now continue down into the main col separating Basin and Saddleback. Then ascend through sparse woods, climb a bump on the ridge, and drop into a shallow col. The final climb is very steep with some scrambing and a classy little traverse just below Basin's summit. The view is panoramic, with Marcy and Haystack dominating to the west. Dix, Big Slide, Saddleback, and Lower Ausable Lake are all in view. From the summit, make the descent on ledges of varying steepness, to the junction with **Shorey Short Cut**, about 0.7 mile below the top. Take this trail. It climbs for a few minutes, passing a good

Gothics from Saddleback

view of Haystack, before descending steeply to the **Phelps Trail**. Follow this to **Slant Rock Lean-to**. From here it is simply a matter of following the Phelps Trail (yellow markers) all the way back to the Garden, a distance of 6.8 miles; **Bushnell Falls Lean-to** and the crossing of Johns Brook is 1.8 miles, Johns Brook Lodge 3.3.

Approach: From the Garden, 1.6 miles from Keene Valley. Keene Valley is on NY 73, 3 miles south of Route 9N.

Maps: Trails of the Adirondack High Peaks Region (ADK)

21 • The Brothers and Big Slide

Rating: Moderately strenuous
Time: 6-7 hours
Distance: 9.5-mile loop
Total climb: 2,800'
Location: West of Keene Valley

Summary: A rolling ridge climb culminating on a 4,000'-summit. Stunning views of Giant and the Great Range.

This hiking route climbs a ridge and then passes across a succession of minor, open summits before climbing steeply to the ridge's high point, **Big Slide Mountain** at 4,240'. It then makes a direct descent into the valley and provides you with a well-earned and gradual saunter back down to your starting point.

From the **Garden**, pick up the trail for Big Slide by immediately heading right and following signs for the Brothers. Our trail runs up along the edge of the parking lot. The main trail leads straight ahead from the trailhead kiosk and up the valley to Johns Brook Lodge. (You will return on this.) At first, the trail climbs generally moderately, reaching a rather steep, rocky section at 0.7 mile, and shortly afterwards you come to the first of many open ledges. After some enjoyable, mixed climbing, you come out on the open summit of **First Brother** at 1.5 miles. Here the views of Giant and the Great Range, directly across the valley, are guaranteed to stop you in your tracks, at least for a few minutes.

After descending a bit, you climb up and over **Second Brother**, and from here the trail descends gradually before climbing again, reaching the summit of **Third Brother**, at 2.6 miles and an elevation of 3,681'. There are excellent views of Giant, the Great Range, and Big Slide. Now descend gently, cross a couple of streams, and make the climb up to the junction with **Slide Mountain Brook Trail**. Bear right here (use the left fork on your descent) and make the final very steep clamber to the top, passing a couple of side trails which offer views out over the slide. From the top, the view stretches from Giant in the east, along the Great Range, and all the way over to Algonquin Peak in the east.

To begin the homeward journey, and to continue on the loop, return to the junction, but stay on the Slide Mountain Brook Trail (head right) as it descends first steeply, then more moderately. The trail crosses and recrosses Slide Brook (a beautiful stream, great for cooling off and relaxing), eventually bringing you down into

Giant from First Brother Nancie Battaglia

Johns Brook Valley and the **Phelps Trail**, 2.4 miles from the top of Slide Mountain. From here, head left on Phelps Trail and make the easy, generally downhill walk (3.2 miles) back to the Garden. Those wishing to visit **Johns Brook Lodge** head right on the Phelps Trail—up the valley—0.3 mile. The trail is almost flat; it's worth the extra effort. The ADK-run "JBL" has drinking water, snack food, and accommodations with meals. After checking it out, return on Phelps Trail, following it back to your car. Note that the total walking distance, inlcuding the detour to JBL, is about 10.1 miles.

Approach: From the Garden, a small parking lot 1.6 miles west of the village of Keene Valley. This is the primary hiking access to the Johns Brook Valley, and the parking lot is generally full on weekends and other busy times. A shuttle service to the overflow parking in Keene Valley was initiated in 1999.

Maps: Trails of the Adirondack High Peaks Region (ADK); The Adirondacks, High Peaks Region (Adirondack Maps, Inc.); and New York State Atlas & Gazetteer, p. 96

Adirondack Traditions

Up until the early 1800s, the area we know as the Adirondacks was largely ignored, by Native Americans and European settlers alike. However by 1830, iron mining was underway, and about the same time logging began in earnest; by 1850 New York was the biggest producer of timber in the United States. The area remained largely unknown to the general public. However with the post-Civil War prosperity, and ensuing leisure time, things began to change.

Tourists began to come to the Adirondacks in large numbers; hotels and private "camps" were built, and the Adirondack guiding tradition was born. Local men were hired by city dwellers to show them the way of the woods: to hunt, to fish or simply to "tramp." Key to navigating the many lakes were the Adirondack guide boats (photo at right). These marvels of boat building are light and fast, yet can easily carry two men and their equipment, even a bagged deer. As wilderness conservation principles received broad acceptance, the forested wilderness was no

Slant Rock Lean-to on the way to Mount Marcy and Haystack

Adirondack Guide Boat on Upper Ausable Lake

longer seen as a dangerous, threatening place, but rather as a cherished resource, itself threatened by man.

As a more positive attitude to the woods experience evolved, vacationers wanted to embrace nature in its least altered state, while maintaining a comfortable, even luxurious, standard. **Adirondack style** is a rustic furniture and building style that distinguishes itself by using wood—logs and branches—as unaltered as possible. Bark is left on logs and the natural crookedness of branches is prized for its decorative qualities.

As more people spent more leisure time in these mountains, climbing the High Peaks gradually became popular, and in 1922 the **Adirondack Mountain Club** was formed. Trails to the major summits were cut, and more and more lean-tos were built. By 1924 the Marshall brothers had completed their ascents of all the High Peaks—the 46 Adirondack summits over 4,000'—and another Adirondack tradition was born. Today those who manage to climb all of the original 46 peaks are called 46ers. Completion of this goal is generally a multi-year project. Some hard-core hikers set themselves the decidedly more difficult goal of climbing all 46 summits in the winter.

22 • Mount Haystack 4,960′

Rating: Very long and strenuous
Distance: 17.8 miles
Time: 10-12 hours or two days
Total climb: about 4,000′
Location: 1 mile southeast of Marcy

Summary: The connoisseur's favorite: Its view is more dynamic than Marcy's and it is more remote and much less crowded than the popular High Peak summits.

Sometimes a lower summit has the best view. Such is Haystack: Marcy looms high overhead, while Panther Gorge, invisible from Marcy's heights, plunges into the void.

From the **Garden**, follow the yellow-marked **Phelps Trail** over very easy terrain, passing the **DEC Interior Outpost** at 3.1 miles and soon afterwards, at 3.5 miles, **Johns Brook Lodge**, an Adirondack Mountain Club facility offering lodging during hiking season. From here, it is 5.4 miles and over 3,100' of climbing to the summit of Haystack. JBL (or nearby lean-tos and campsites), the Bushnell Falls Lean-tos at 5.1 miles (elev. 2,800'), or Slant Rock Lean-to at 6.8 miles (elev. 3,500') are the camping choices. Continuing, the Phelps Trail runs along Johns Brook at first, then after a short, steep section returns to a moderate grade, reaching the junction with the Hopkins Trail 1.6 miles from JBL. Bear left on the Phelps Trail and cross Johns Brook—there is a high-water crossing just upstream—to reach **Bushnell Falls Lean-to** and its excellent camping sites. Proceeding to **Slant Rock Lean-to** (at 6.8 miles), the pace is slower, the trail somewhat steeper, with more roots and rocks to contend with. Continue up terrain that alternates between steep to quite moderate, reaching the junction with the **State Range Trail** another mile farther on, at 7.8 miles. Here, just below the col between Haystack and Marcy, the Phelps Trail continues toward Marcy (1.2 miles). Head left on the blue-marked Range Trail, and after a mix of terrain—there is one extremely steep section—you come out onto an open ledge, where you first get the dynamite views of Marcy, Skylight, and Haystack. Drop steeply into a saddle (here the Range Trail heads left towards Saddleback and Gothics) and continue on the yellow-marked **Haystack Spur Trail** up the bare rock of **Little Haystack** to incredible views. Following cairns and paint blazes, descend the precipitous (but not difficult) south face of Little Haystack, using a convenient system of ramps, which zigzags down the steep rock.

Haystack and Little Haystack

Finally, with more pleasant scrambling on bare rock, you reach the summit of Haystack. The view is unique; steep mountain slopes are everywhere, above, across and below. Big mountains like Basin, Gothics, Skylight are right up close. At your feet the mountain slides out of sight into the abyss of Panther Gorge. Mount Marcy soars skyward on the other side, its summit towering over you. (See the High Peaks Introduction photo on page 51.) Return by the same route.

Approach: Haystack is located in the middle of the High Peaks, and there is no way to drive close to it. Our approach is from the east, from the small parking area known as the Garden, 1.6 miles above Keene Valley. Overflow parking is available in Keene Valley.

Maps: Trails of the Adirondack High Peaks Region (ADK); The Adirondacks, High Peaks Region; and New York State Atlas & Gazetteer, p. 96

23 • Noonmark 3,556′

Rating: Difficult, but short
Distance: 5 miles
Time: 4 hours
Total climb: 2,300′
Location: Keene Valley
Summary: Superb panorama from the summit. Views of Dix and Giant. A relatively short hike, but the upper section is extremely steep.

Noonmark is the landmark of Keene Valley. It is the steep-sided, truncated cone due south of the village. Of the two main routes up Noonmark, the hike described here, the **Stimson Trail**, ascends the mountain from the north. The trailhead is quite near the Ausable Club, just opposite the southern end of the golf course, but the hiker's parking area is located about 0.25 mile farther south, down the hill almost back on NY 73. When driving south from Keene Valley, the turn off to the Ausable Club is at 2.5 miles, and the turn off to the hiker parking area is another 0.5 mile farther.

Walk up the gravel road to the trailhead on the left, where there is a trail sign. The trail proper starts up a small driveway, passes several structures, then switches to a path. At 0.3 mile, after passing through a gate, the gradient steepens, and at 0.5 mile reaches the intersection for the trail (left) to Round Mountain. Stay right. From this point on, the trail gets down to business, climbing quite steeply in places. There are numerous short scrambles up bare rock which are very enjoyable if you like this sort of thing. And finally, for the last 20-30 minutes, you are increasingly out in the open, and the views just keep getting better.

The compact, wide-open summit of this sharp little peak offers an unrestricted panorama. Just across the highway to the northeast, massive, complex Giant Mountain dominates the view. To the south, only 3 miles away, the great rock scars on Dix command one's attention. To the northwest, the Great Range is laid out clearly, as it sweeps upward from Keene Valley to Rooster Comb, over the Wolfjaws, across Gothics, Saddleback, and Basin to Haystack.

Descend by the same route. Because of the many "cliffy" sections, individual descent times will vary quite a bit.

Noonmark from the north — John Winkler

Approach: From Keene Valley, drive 3 miles south on NY 73 to a side road right where the hiker parking areas are located. Park here and walk up the road (towards the Ausable Club) 0.25 miles to the actual trailhead and sign on your left.

Maps: Trails of the Adirondack High Peaks Region (ADK); The Adirondacks, High Peaks Region (Adirondack Maps, Inc.); and New York State Atlas & Gazetteer, p. 96

24 • Gothics 4,736'

Rating: Strenuous
Distance: 11.5-mile loop
Time: 8 hours
Total climb: 3,650'
Location: Great Range, 5 miles southwest of Keene Valley
Summary: The classic route on one of the most imposing mountains in the East. Dramatic alpine views.

From the parking area, walk up the side road to the Ausable Club, and enter the private holdings known as the **Adirondack Mountain Reserve** (AMR) after signing in at the gatehouse. Note that dogs are not allowed in the reserve. Walk up **Lake Road** 3.1 miles, almost to the end. The **Weld Trail** branches right and crosses the bridge just below the dam at **Lower Ausable Lake**. It coincides briefly with the **Sawteeth Trail** and the Rainbow Falls Trail. Now, climbing up moderate terrain, pass the spur trail right to a viewpoint for **Rainbow Falls** at 0.3 mile. At 0.9 mile, you cross an old slide (overgrown), and after about another mile of rough and steep trail, you reach the saddle between Sawteeth and Pyramid, 1.7 miles from Lake Road and 4.8 miles from the Ausable Club. From here to the summit of **Pyramid** the climb is very steep, without letup, but the top makes it all worthwhile. Although 4,595' high, Pyramid is not an official 4,000'-er because it is not high enough above the col separating it from Gothics. However, the views from Pyramid are quite possibly the best in these mountains: Gothics looms overhead; you are standing on the edge of a cliff, and the sheer cliffs of Saddleback and Gothics confront you. From here, the summit of Gothics is only about 500 yards away. Drop into the col and make the steep climb up the final wall of Gothics. At the junction with the **ADK Range Trail** 0.3 mile past Pyramid, bear right over easy ground to the summit of Gothics, a short way beyond. You are now 5.8 miles from the Ausable Club gatehouse. The view is spectacular and panoramic; 30 High Peak summits can be picked out, clouds permitting.

When you are ready to head down, continue on the ADK Range Trail; it descends steeply, reaching **Gothics Trail** after 0.4 mile. Head right on it. After negotiating three short ladders and traversing across the shoulder of Armstrong (good views back toward Gothics) the trail drops steeply, passing a balanced rock on the left, about a mile from the summit, before continuing its steep descent.

Gothics, Pyramid and Giant from Haystack

After crossing several streams, the grade becomes very moderate, although there is a ladder just before you reach Beaver Meadow Falls and the intersection with **West River Trail**. Cross this trail, and the river, and bear left on **East River Trail** a short ways before bearing right again. It's now 0.5 mile to **Lake Road** and from there, 1.8 miles on the road back to the gate at the Ausable Club.

It is possible to avoid walking on Lake Road—partly or totally—if one chooses. The scenic East River and West River Trails run from the Ausable Club area to Ausable Lake, closely paralleling the river which drains the lake. See either topo map noted below. Either of these trails will bring you back to the Ausable Club.

Approach: Drive three miles south from Keene Valley on NY 73; the hiker parking areas are on the right. Walk up the hill on the Ausable Club road. At the Club, turn left to reach the entrance to the Lake Road which is 0.4 mile from your car.

Maps: Trails of the Adirondack High Peaks Region (ADK) and The Adirondacks, High Peaks Region (Adirondack Maps, Inc.)

25 • Giant Mountain 4,627′

Rating: Moderately strenuous
Distance: 6 miles
Time: 5-6 hours
Location: Keene Valley, just east of the core of the High Peaks
Total climb: 3,050′
Summary: This massive, isolated mountain offers a tough climb to an awe-inspiring summit. One of the great Adirondack landmarks.

From the highway, the **Ridge Trail** climbs, eases, then climbs more steadily and at 0.7 mile, reaches a good viewpoint down to Chapel Pond. Dropping down slightly to the small mountain pond known as **Giant's Washbowl** (and a trail heading left), the trail skirts the pond, climbs up past another trail on the left (0.9 mile), before reaching yet another intersection (at 1.0 mile). This third trail leads left for 0.5 mile over **Giant's Nubble** with its interesting views of the Giant. Over the next 1.2 miles (and 1,400' of climbing), the route works its way up a succession of ledge areas (including one that is quite large), followed by easier ground, eventually reaching the Roaring Brook Trail at 2.2 miles from the highway. Now follow the **Roaring Brook Trail** on to the summit over generally moderate terrain. Note the impressive slides on Giant's west face a short way past the trail junction. Two tenths of mile before the top, the **Rocky Peak Ridge Trail** comes in from the right. See the trail description at right.

All but seven of the High Peaks can be seen from the summit of Giant! In any event, the view, from distant Lake Champlain and Vermont to nearby Ausable Club at the base of the precipitous west face, is spectacular, as one would expect from a large mountain which stands alone. Giant's rounded shape, and in winter, its snow-covered slides, make it perhaps the most recognizable of the High Peaks from across Lake Champlain in Vermont.

Descend by the same route, taking care to make the correct choices at the trail junctions on your way down. On a warm day, a swim in **Chapel Pond** makes for a fine conclusion to this hike.

Approach: From Keene Valley, drive south on NY 73 for 5 miles to Chapel Pond. The well-marked trailhead with its somewhat limited roadside parking is along the left (east) side of the road.

Maps: Trails of the Adirondack High Peaks Region (ADK); The Adirondacks, High Peaks Region (Adirondack Maps, Inc.) and New York State Atlas & Gazetteer, p. 96

Giant from the Ausable Club John E. Winkler

Rocky Peak Ridge variation: During fall foliage, the long and complex ridge running east off Giant Mountain offers what some consider to be the most exciting hike in the Adirondacks. Open for about half its length—a forest fire raged here in 1913—the 8-mile **East Trail** traverses the lower summits of Blueberry Cobbles (blueberries in season) and **Bald Peak** (3,060', at 3.9 miles) before reaching the spectacular, open summit of **Rocky Peak Ridge** (4,420') at 6.7 miles. A close-up view of the massive rockslides on Giant's east face greets you. Now descend over 600' into a saddle before making the final 900'-climb to the top of Giant. On your descent, use the route to Chapel Pond described above. In summary, this is a long, exposed route with over 5,000' of climbing. It will generate a lot of thirst, especially on a warm summer day; take plenty of water. Start from the parking area on Rt. 9, 5 miles north of the intersection of Rts. 9 and 73, and arrange to be picked up at one of the trailheads on the Keene Valley side of Giant.

26 • Dix Mountain 4,857'

Rating: Strenuous
Distance: 13.6 miles
Time: 9-10 hours or overnight
Total climb: 4,000'
Location: South of Keene Valley
Summary: A mellow approach culminates in a very steep and sustained climb to a spectacular summit.

Dix is one of the great Adirondack summits and is counted among the outstanding climbs in the East. Lying to the south of Giant, its scarred east face makes it easy to pick out from the Vermont side of Lake Champlain. The route given here is the normal approach, although the Elk Lake routes (southerly) are important as well.

Marked with blue disks, the trail ascends moderately from the road before dropping down to **Round Pond** (0.5 mile). After a gentle climb, pass over generally very easy terrain with occasional wet areas, reaching a four-way trail intersection at 2.3 miles. The right fork leads in 2.3 miles to the Ausable Club, and straight ahead, the trail leads to the summit of Noonmark in one mile. We continue left over easy ground — there are some beautiful stretches along the river — with gentle ups and downs for the next two miles, reaching the **Boquet Lean-to** (elevation about 2,400') at 4.2 miles. If you are doing Dix as an overnight, this is the logical spot to camp. After crossing the river, the trail climbs more steadily, closely paralleling a tributary for a time.

Finally at 5.8 miles, you suddenly come out of dense forest onto scoured rock and avalanche debris, with stunning views of the rock slides trailing off the summit ridge of Dix, high overhead. The trail, marked here with yellow paint and rock cairns, angles up and across the slide before re-entering the woods and commencing a murderously steep and direct ascent (1,600') to the top. The angle does ease about 10 minutes before the **Hunter's Pass Trail** junction. At the junction, the trail to Elk Lake departs right. We head left (yellow markers) up the increasingly open ridge which is again extremely steep for a short section before finally cresting on the narrow and relatively level summit ridge. The views of the Great Range, Marcy, Giant, Lake Champlain, and the distant Vermont hills, as well as island-dotted Elk Lake are worth studying at length from the special vantage point that Dix provides. Return by

Dix from the summit of Noonmark Lars Gange

the same route, via Bouquet Lean-to and Round Pond.

Approach: From the village of Keene Valley, drive south 5.3 miles on NY 73. Parking is on the right, 0.1 mile north of (before) the trailhead. Approaching from the south, you drive 3.2 miles north on NY 73 from NY 9.

Maps: Trails of the Adirondack High Peaks Region (ADK); The Adirondacks, High Peaks Region; and New York State Atlas & Gazetteer, p. 96

Dix Mountain, described above, is the tallest member of the Dix family. It is also the only one with a regular trail. The rest of this high, trailless group lies off to the south and southeast from the summit of Dix. These mountains are generally approached from **Elk Lake**. The other summits in the family are East Dix, South Dix, Hough, and Macomb. The next hike description (Hike #27) treats Macomb.

27 • Macomb 4,405′

Rating: Fairly strenuous
Time: 6-8 hours
Distance: About 7.5 miles
Location: Northeast of Elk Lake, in the southern High Peaks
Total climb: 2,500′
Summary: Introduction to slide climbing on a trailless peak. Offers an opportunity to do three other trailless 46-ers.

Of the 46ers—the Adirondack summits over 4,000'—about half are "trailless peaks." Macomb is one of them. Traditionally, reaching the top of a trailless peak meant complete reliance on one's ability to follow compass bearings and accurately read topographic maps in order to plot a course through steep, rough, and completely trackless terrain. Over the years, however, the passage of many hikers, all more or less following the same route has created primitive trails on these mountains. These are known as "herd paths." In fact, all the formerly trailless peaks now have herd paths leading to their summits. These routes are not maintained however, and in many cases confusing variations exist. Some of the paths are quite long and will involve hours of careful route finding, so hikers on these routes need a high degree of self-sufficiency. In particular, strong compass and map reading skills are mandatory for a safe hiking experience. A comprehensive understanding of the topography of the general area, before setting out, is essential.

With the foregoing in mind, the standard, relatively straightforward, "trailless" route up Macomb is as follows. From **Elk Lake**, follow the **Elk Lake-Dix Trail** 2.3 miles to Slide Brook. (Slide Brook Lean-to is just beyond.) At Slide Brook, leave the trail and head (right) up the mountain, following the stream's north bank. After about a mile, you come to the base of the slide, on your right. Ascend the slide, and at its top, keep climbing another 15-20 minutes to reach the ridge. Then head right (south) along the ridge for about five minutes to reach the summit. Return by the same route.

Approach: From I-87 at North Hudson (exit 29), head west on NY 2 four miles to Elk Lake Road, on the right. Drive 5.1 miles up this road to the trailhead parking area on your right.

Maps: Trails of the Adirondack High Peaks Region (ADK); The Adirondacks: High Peak Region (Adirondack Maps, Inc.); and New York State Atlas & Gazetteer, p. 88 and 96.

Slides on Macomb — John E. Winkler

Extended trailless variation: Once you are on the top of Macomb, you can do **South Dix** (4,060'), **East Dix** (4,012') and **Hough** (4,400') on the same day, making for an all-out day of summiting frenzy! The main summit, Dix Mountain (4,857', Hike #26), is about a mile northwest of Hough. Lying a few miles south of the main grouping of the High Peaks and somewhat detached from it, this high, isolated group of summits—known simply as the Dixes—offers sweeping views of Mount Marcy, the Great Range and many, many other Adirondack summits. Two of Vermont's major peaks, Mount Mansfield and Camel's Hump, stick up on the eastern horizon. From the summit of Macomb, South Dix is the closest, one mile away via a good herd path. The route dips about 600' into the intervening col (at 3,790') before ascending South Dix via its north ridge. As you ascend the open rocks below South Dix's summit, fantastic views of the Great Range and the High Peaks unfold. The trip to South Dix and back to Macomb adds about 1,700' of climbing and two miles to the trip total. Consult the ADK's *High Peaks Guide* for route information on the other summits.

28 • Hurricane Mountain 3,694′

Rating: Moderate
Distance: 5.2 miles
Time: 4 hours
Location: Between Elizabethtown and Keene Valley
Total climb: 2,000′
Summary: A fun hike with a brisk climb to views that sweep from the High Peaks across Lake Champlain to Vermont.

Hurricane is the first high mountain you encounter as you approach the Adirondacks from the east, and its summit views are among the best. Lake Champlain stretches out to the east while the High Peaks beckon from the west. Like its near neighbor, Giant, Hurricane enjoys a perspective on the High Peaks that a few miles of separation can provide. It is easy to pick out from the vicinity of Elizabethtown because of its height and summit fire tower.

From the highway, the trail climbs steeply up a bank and continues very steeply for a short distance before leveling off and crossing an open, boggy area on a succession of planks, called puncheons. (The trail is marked with red DEC disks.) From this point—you've now done about 40 percent of the hike—it's a steady climb (with some quite steep sections) to the ledges below the summit. As you come out into the open, the summit tower serves to guide you to the top, assuming you are not in the clouds! It is advisable to note the final, open portion of the route for your return, as the paint blazes and cairns are a little infrequent. At any rate, the final easy clamber to this outstanding summit is spectacular. The fire tower is in a state of disrepair and climbing it is not recommended.

Although Hurricane is not a 4,000-footer, the relatively modest effort required to reach the top and the first-rate views of the High Peaks, Lake Champlain, and Vermont make this hike an absolute must! Return the way you came up.

Approach: The trailhead is on the north side of NY 9N, 6.8 miles west of Elizabethtown and 3.6 miles east of the junction of routes NY 9N and NY 73 in Keene Valley.

Maps: Trails of the Adirondack High Peaks Region (ADK); The Adirondacks, High Peaks Region (Adirondack Maps, Inc.); and New York State Atlas & Gazetteer, p. 96

Fire tower on the summit of Hurricane John E. Winkler

29 • Poke-O-Moonshine Mtn. 2,180'

Rating: Easy
Time: 2 hours
Distance: 2.4 miles
Location: Just off I-87, about 23 miles south of Plattsburgh
Total climb: 1,280'
Summary: A favorite with rock climbers. Great views of Lake Champlain make Poke-O-Moonshine popular with hikers, too.

As seen from I-87, Poke-O-Moonshine's various cliff bands—some over 300' high—suggest this might be a good area for rock climbing. It is. The rock is firm and the routes accessible, making this a popular venue for climbing, summer and winter. The hiking route is very popular as well. It begins from the southern end of **Poke-O-Moonshine State Campground**. The heavily used trail, sparsely marked with red disks, gets quite steep a short way from the campground. Soon encountering one of Poke-O-Moonshine's typical cliff bands, the trail ascends left along the base of vertical rock before swinging around to the right, reaching the top of the cliff but without any rock climbing skills needed. The grade then slackens a bit, and you come to the saddle between Poke-O-Moonshine and the mountain to the south. A stone chimney is all that remains of a cabin. Now head right, at times climbing steeply, working your way around to the back of the mountain. The trail finishes on easy terrain, reaching the old fire tower on open ledges. The tower is open to the public but is in neglected condition. The long views of the Lake Champlain Basin — Lake Champlain is over 100 miles long — provide great reward for this short hike. To the southwest some of the High Peaks, for example Giant and Whiteface, can be seen. Return by the same route.

Approach: The trailhead is in the Poke-O-Moonshine State Campground on NY Route 9, 3 miles south of I-87 exit 33 (northern approach). When approaching from the south, take exit 32, and drive north on NY 9 for 9 miles.

Maps: The Adirondacks, High Peaks Region (ADK) and New York State Atlas & Gazetteer, p. 97

Whiteface from Poke-O-Moonshine Mountain

30 • Whiteface Mountain 4,867′

Rating: Strenuous
Time: 8-9 hours
Distance: 10.4 miles
Total climb: 3,620′
Location: Wilmington

Summary: An impressive, isolated peak. The top is rather civilized—there is a snack bar and even an elevator—but Whiteface offers a very solid hike.

One of the most alpine mountains in the East—the summit ridge would be at home in the Swiss Alps—Whiteface stands alone, about 10 miles north of the main concentration of the High Peaks. Although isolated from its 4,000' brethren, this is no lonely outpost. It sports a major ski area; Whiteface was the alpine skiing venue for the 1980 Olympics. A paved highway allows summer visitors to drive to the top, and a paved path, complete with railings, leads up the final, quite spectacular ridge.

There are several excellent hiking routes up the mountain, and the summit highway is used in winter by skiers and snowmobilers. The trail we have selected, the **Wilmington Trail**, is probably the most popular, in part because it provides easy access to **Esther**

Lake Placid from the summit of Whiteface

The summit of Whiteface

Mountain (4,240'), a trailless High Peak on the 46-ers' to-do list. From the trailhead parking, immediately cross a brook and soon thereafter an old road (0.3 mile), and continue over easy terrain on a very pleasant trail. After a mile, the trail begins a steady, moderate climb, and at 2.2 miles from the car, you find yourself on the top of Marble Mountain, once the site of a ski area. The next mile is a mix of gentle and steep sections; at 3.3 miles, the trail descends a bit, and the unmarked trail to Esther Mountain (1.3 miles to the summit) branches right. Continue descending for a half mile or so, cross a wet area, and resume climbing.

At 4.8 miles, you arrive at the base of one of the highway's massive stone embankments. This spot is called the **Wilmington Turn**. Stay to the left, and scrambling up and over rough boulders, climb up to the pavement. From the highway, clamber up a bank, and after a brief section of dense forest, you finally emerge at the base of an exposed rock ridge, the beautiful finale to this hike. The summit with its weather observatory is just ahead. As you make the final climb, ponder the glaciers which long ago sculpted this mountain, carving out ravines and shaping the rock ridges. Upon reaching the summit ridge, walk left to reach the actual top. The views are panoramic, and the perspective on Lake Placid far below, is unique. The High Peaks lie to the south. Return by the same route, or vary it as follows. Descend the paved "tourist walkway," railings and all, to the upper terminus of the highway. Then walk down the highway a few minutes to the Wilmington Turn (described above) where you again pick up the trail. Follow it back down to your starting point.

Approach: From the eastern edge of Lake Placid, drive north on NY 86 to the ski village of Wilmington. At the traffic light, head left for 0.6 mile up the Whiteface Mtn. Memorial Highway to a road on the left. Park 0.2 mile up this road at the trailhead parking area.

Maps: Trails of the Adirondack High Peaks Region (ADK); The Adirondacks, High Peaks Region (Adirondack Maps, Inc.); and New York State Atlas & Gazetteer, p. 96

Slide Route: Whiteface, like Giant and Dix, seems to have more than its share of slides. In winter the snow-covered scars on the mountain's east side make it easy to identify from across the lake in Vermont. However, the slide on the southwest side—facing Lake Placid—offers perhaps the best "scrambling" route. Unfortunately, it is a little hard to get to. You need to get to the north end of Lake Placid. One approach is via the **Connery Pond Trail** which starts 0.5 mile in from Route 86, a distance of 2.5 miles. (Drive 3 miles from Lake Placid and turn left.) The other approach is by lake. From the village of Lake Placid, take a boat (canoe, kayak, or motorboat) the length of Lake Placid to the trailhead at Whiteface Landing.

From **Whiteface Landing**, continue up Connery Pond Trail about 1.8 miles to where it veers right, away from the brook. Continue straight on here, leaving the trail, and soon you will encounter an old phone line. Now bushwhack (short distance) left to the brook and above it, the slide. Ascend the slide to the summit ridge, enjoying the views of Lake Placid as you climb. The final cliff can be avoided on the right. The summit, in plain view, is just a short walk to the right. To descend, head south off the summit ledges, following signs and blazes for the Connery Pond Trail.

Winter in the High Peaks

The High Peaks see plenty of activity in the winter. Snowshoers tackle most of the trails, while skiers are active on the relatively few routes that lend themselves to skiing. As in the summer, the **Heart Lake** area is the most popular starting point. The trails to Marcy, Avalanche Pass, and Algonquin Peak have ski trail variations in their steeper sections. Lack of adequate snow cover can sometimes be a problem, especially early

Winter climb of Gothics Carl Heilman

in the winter or in lean periods. As a rule, snow at the trailhead means adequate snow farther in on the trail. Once past Marcy Dam, the trails are rougher, but the deeper snow of higher elevations compensates.

Perhaps the classic ski tour in the High Peaks is the 10-mile intermediate round trip from Heart Lake via Marcy Dam, over **Avalanche Pass** to **Avalanche Lake**. If Avalanche Lake is the classic tour, then the climb of **Mount Marcy** (15 miles round trip, elevation gain 3,300') is the Big One. Only skiers in excellent shape and who are at least advanced intermediates should attempt this. If the snow conditions are less than ideal, you

Skiing on Avalanche Lake

should be an advanced or expert level skier. Note: The slightly longer approach from South Meadow—the turnoff is a mile north of Heart Lake—offers a better-quality skiing route to Marcy Dam than the Van Hoevenberg Trail from Heart Lake.

Moving to east side of the High Peaks, from the trailhead (the Garden) 1.5 miles from **Keene Valley**, the heavily used trail to **Johns Brook Lodge** (3.5 miles) is quite skiable with a (packed) foot of snow cover. This is a classic trip with skis or with snowshoes. However, less than a mile beyond JBL, steeper terrain elevates the skiing to a completely different level of difficulty.

The other access from the east is the very gradual **Lake Road** from the Ausable Club (in St. Huberts, just south of Keene Valley) to **Lower Ausable Lake**. After skiing the 3.5 miles to the lake, ski down along the lake (2.5 miles) and marvel at the cliffs and plunging mountain slopes. Lower Ausable Lake is one of the great showplaces of the Adirondacks. Howeve, the Lake, together with adjoining lands, is privately owned and summer access is quite restricted.

A little to the north of the core High Peaks, **Whiteface Mountain** provides a moderate, if rather long and monotonous ski route. From Wilmington, drive to the base of the (gated) **Whiteface Mountain Memorial Highway**. This 5.5-mile, paved road up Whiteface Mountain is popular early in the season, when there is little snow. Its steady uphill angle makes it a bit of a grind, but the ski run down is fun and easy.

Those wanting skiing that is less challenging than a backcountry tour should check out the **Jackrabbit Trail**. Named in honor of the famous Norwegian ski pioneer, Herman "Jack Rabbit" Johannsen, the trail runs from Saranac Lake to Lake Placid and continues to Keene, linking up inns and ski centers along the way. Its total distance is 24 miles. Consult the ADK's *Classic Adirondack Ski Tours* for descriptions of 50 ski tours.

A note on etiquette: If there is sufficient snow cover to ski, then all trail users *must* use snowshoes or skis. This is because the boot holes made when hikers walk in soft snow—this is known as post holing—pose a danger for skiers.

31 • Catamount Mountain 3,168′

Rating: Moderate effort, with rock scrambling
Time: 3-4 hours
Distance: 3.6 miles
Total climb: 1,600′
Location: Six miles north of Whiteface Mountain
Summary: A fun climb, about half of it is on bare rock. There are panoramic views from the summit.

Although Catamount Mountain rises impressively above Plank Road, the unsigned trailhead is much less obvious. But for the locals, and others who treasure this gem, a little red paint and surveyor's tape are sufficient to locate the starting point. The trail starts off as a pleasant meander through evergreens. After about 15 minutes the climbing begins, and the spruces and pines immediately give way to a mix of hardwoods, with birch dominating for a time. The trail steepens as you get your first introduction to the rocks and slabs that this mountain is known for. Using cairns, follow the route across a brief semi-open ledgy area, and a little less than an hour into the hike, you find yourself at the base of a short "chimney." In climbing terminology, a chimney refers to a more or less vertical section of rock that is enclosed on three sides. After you surmount this little obstacle, you are on the upper mountain. From here to the first summit, the trail is out in the open a great deal, with plenty of sloping bare rock. From this first summit (called a "false" summit), the actual summit beckons, another 20-30 minutes away. The route negotiates some awkward terrain (with rock "steps" or short cliffs) and passes through dense woods before tackling the final climb. Once again the climbing is primarily on bare ledge, a refreshing change from trail walking.

From the top, the views of nearby Whiteface Mountain and the more distant High Peaks are fine indeed. Linger for a while before carefully working your way down this rather rigorous little mountain. Oh, but there were more of them!

Catamount and similar "ledgy" hikes are excellent training for those who plan to hike and climb in more alpine terrain, for example the Rockies or the Alps. With this in mind, getting used to walking on uneven rock surfaces for extended periods is essential. In fact, for all hikers, improving one's ability to move easily up and down friction surfaces (slabs) uses less energy and reduces the chance of injury.

Catamount Mountain from the west

Approach: From Wilmington (12 miles northeast of Lake Placid), take the Whiteface Mountain Memorial Highway. At the actual toll gate entrance (2.9 miles from Wilmington), stay right, and continue to a junction at 6.1 miles. Turn right here, and at the T-intersection for Plank Road (Forestdale Rd.) at 7.0 miles, turn right again, and drive another 2.1 miles to the trailhead (roadside) parking. The minimally marked trail is on your left.

Maps: Trails of the Adirondack High Peaks Region (ADK); The Adirondacks, High Peaks Region; and New York State Atlas & Gazetteer, p. 96

Connecticut
&
Massachusetts

Connecticut and Massachusetts

Although it is the least mountainous of the states covered in this book, **Connecticut** has good hill hiking, especially in the beautiful and pastoral northwest region of Litchfield County. Without a list of high summits to conquer, Connecticut offers hikers an impressive system of lower elevation "through trails" totaling over 450 miles.

The Appalachian Trail enters from New York state about midstate a little south of Kent and runs north over sharply hilly terrain before crossing the state's highest summit, **Bear Mountain** (Hike #33), and passing onto higher ground in Massachusetts. Popular Macedonia State Park, a little north of Kent, has a 13-mile trail network. Farther south, near Milford, hikers can enjoy some steep scrambling on Candlewood Mountain to reach views of the Housatonic Valley hundreds of feet below.

The Appalachian Trail runs through the western part—Berkshire County—of **Massachusetts,** and it is here that the state's highest mountains are concentrated. The Berkshire Hills, as they are usually called, reach their greatest height in the north, with **Mount Greylock**, 3,491'. There is intense hiking activity here in the Williamstown area with a good network of trails and a strong hiking and skiing tradition associated with Williams College. Farther south, near Great Barrington, Monument Mountain offers a fun, short hike to a curious boulder pile of a summit. In the extreme south of Berkshire County, just south of South Egremont, the area around Mount Washington State Park is a major recreation area. The well-known summits of Mount Alander and **Mount Everett** (second highest in Massachusetts) offer solid hikes. The Appalachian Trail traverses Everett from north to south, and the mountain can be climbed by a fine, steep trail from the east, Race Brook Trail (Hike #34). On the north slope of Alander, and just a short walk from the road, is famous Bash Bish Falls, worth a visit when in the area.

In the central part of the state, Mount Wachusett (Hike #35) is one of the most visited mountains in the United States. Despite an elevation of just over 2,000 feet, its rocky trails and thousand-foot vertical gain provide a good workout.

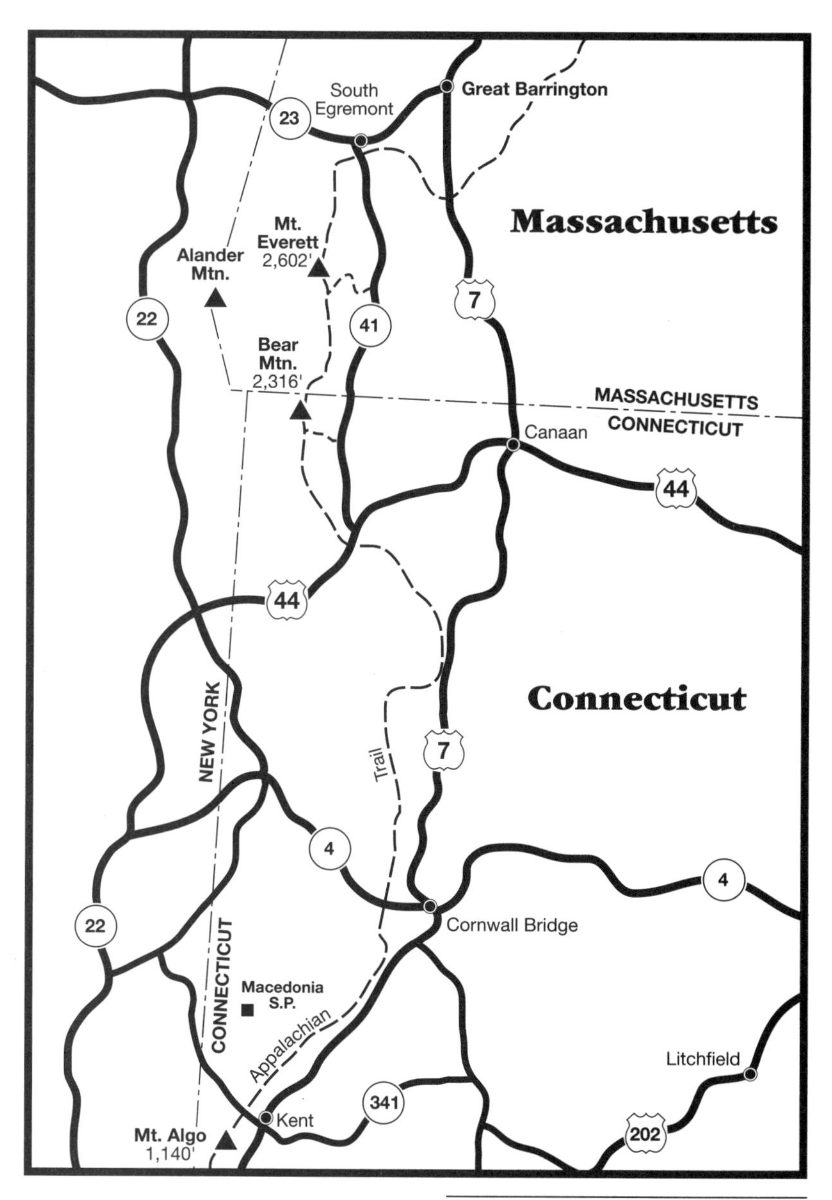
South Egremont
Great Barrington
23
Massachusetts
Mt. Everett 2,602'
Alander Mtn.
22
41
7
Bear Mtn. 2,316'
MASSACHUSETTS
CONNECTICUT
Canaan
44
44
NEW YORK
Connecticut
7
Trail
4
4
22
Cornwall Bridge
CONNECTICUT
Macedonia S.P.
Appalachian
Litchfield
341
Kent
Mt. Algo 1,140'
202

32 • Mount Algo 1,200'

Rating: Moderate
Time: 5 hours (or 3 hours)
Distance: 7.6 miles (or 4.6 miles)
Total climb: 2,200'
Location: Near Kent, western edge of Connecticut
Summary: Out-and-back jaunt on the AT. Good views from ledges.

From the highway, follow the white-blazed **Appalachian Trail** south as it climbs first steeply, then more moderately in a mixed forest. After about thirty minutes of walking you come to the spur trail (right) for Mount Algo Lean-to. Just off the main trail, the shelter is pleasantly located in open woods, on a gentle slope, and with a good stream nearby. Now the climbing is steady but rather moderate, gradually slackening as you reach the wooded top.

From Algo's mellow, indistinct summit area, descend into a ravine (Thayer Brook) formed by Mount Algo and the ridge of neighboring Schaghticoke Mountain. Cross the brook and ascend the ridge, and after traversing just below the summit for a while—you hike along below the ridge top, never actually climbing to the top—the trail begins to drop down, and you soon come to a rock ledge with views south. This spot (2.3 miles) is the turnaround point for the short version of the hike. For the full hike, read on.

Continue on moderate terrain, and after an easy descent you come to a brook and the blue-blazed side trail to Schaghticoke Mtn. Campsite. Continuing, make the steep descent into boulder-strewn **Dry Gulch** at 3.5 miles, before taking on the very steep climb to the hike's endpoint at **Indian Rocks**. Here you can relax and enjoy the views of the Housatonic River Valley, about 800 feet below. When you are ready to return, head back the way you came.

Indian Rocks is equidistant between Bull's Bridge and the hike's starting point on CT Route 341. As this entire 7.8-mile section of the AT offers great hiking, if you can arrange to be picked up at the other end, consider doing it as a one-way traverse. It is worth noting that in late June and early July the mountain laurel is in full bloom, making for a spectacular display of snow-white blossoms.

Approach: From Kent, on US Route 7 about 30 miles north of Danbury, drive west on CT 341 0.9 mile to where the Appalachian Trail crosses the highway.

Maps: ATC Massachusetts and Connecticut, Map #5 (Appalachian Trail Conference)

33 • Bear Mountain 2,316'

Rating: Moderate
Time: 4 hours
Distance: 5.4 miles
Total climb: 1,600'
Location: Salisbury, in northwestern Connecticut
Summary: A mellow, pleasant route to Connecticut's highest summit.

Bear Mountain is one of the most visited mountain tops in Connecticut, partly because it is the highest summit (although not quite the highest point) and also because it lies on the Appalachian Trail. From the parking lot just off CT Route 41, follow the blue-blazed **Undermountain Trail** over very easy ground. The trail soon settles into a steady but generally quite moderate climb through a pleasant deciduous forest reaching the **Appalachian Trail** (AT) after 1.9 miles. About two-thirds of the way to the AT, the Paradise Lane Trail (see variation below) branches off to the north. Once you reach the AT, bear right and continue climbing; it is about 0.8 mile to the summit. The trail blazes are now white, the standard for the Appalachian Trail and other major "through" trails. Views start to open up as you ascend the increasingly bare south ridge of Bear Mountain. To the west, various Connecticut and New York summits can be picked out; on a really clear day New York's Catskills can be seen. The trail leads in and out of pockets of scrub oak.

At the summit a reduced version of a once grand stone monument greets you. Scrambling up on this will help get you above the low forest cover. By walking a bit to the north, it is possible to get a good view north to Mount Everett, at 2,602 feet, Massachusett's second highest mountain. Like Bear Mountain, Everett is traversed by the Appalachian Trail. Descend the way you came.

Approach: From Salisbury, drive north 3.2 miles on CT 41 to the trailhead parking lot on the left side of the road. Salisbury is only a few miles south of the Connecticut-Massachusetts border.

Maps: USGS Bashbish Falls

Loop variation: A loop hike over Bear Mountain is possible by following Paradise Lane north to the AT, then heading left and climbing to the summit (on the AT, heading south). Now return by the route described above to close the loop. The total distance for this variation is about 6.5 miles.

34 • Mount Everett 2,602′

Rating: Moderate
Time: 4 hours
Distance: 5.4 miles
Total climb: 1,900′
Location: Extreme southwest corner of Massachusetts
Summary: Varied, at times steep, trail leads up past waterfalls and cascades to summit views.

After Mount Greylock—the state's highest mountain—Mount Everett is the outstanding peak in Berkshire County. Berkshire County forms the western part of Massachusetts and is home to the Berkshire Hills, the name given to the Appalachian Mountains in Massachusetts. Mount Everett and Mount Alander (2,006'), form opposite sides of the enclosure which defines a high basin, home of popular Mount Washington State Park. Massachusett's best known waterfall, **Bash Bish Falls**, is part of the drainage off the north slopes of Mount Alander.

Starting out from Route 41 in Salisbury, the **Race Brook Falls Trail** dips to cross a stream bed and runs briefly over easy terrain. At the trail junction for the spur trail to the Lower Falls, the Race Brook Trail bears left and commences a steady, moderate climb. The relatively mature hardwood forest gives a nice open feeling, while the omnipresent mountain laurel lays claims to the understory. There are two sections to this hike. In the first, the trail ascends the ravine or "draw" between two mountains, Mount Race and Mount Everett, crossing and recrossing Race Brook. The second section is the ascent of the south ridge of Mount Everett along the Appalachian Trail. After you are about a half hour into the hike, you reach a beautiful cascading waterfall deep in the recesses of this hemlock-forested ravine. It is worth noting that for those wanting a shorter hike, this 70'-high waterfall is a good destination in its own right. After leaving the waterfall, the trail is rather steep for about 15 minutes before traversing sharply to the left across ledges—there are views to the east—and returning once again to the brook. From here to the ridge, the trail stays close to the stream as it climbs more moderately.

Two miles from the highway, the Race Brook Trail terminates at the **Appalachian Trail**; it is 0.7 mile right (north) to the summit. From here, the trail is gradually more out in the open and is mostly on bare ledge. There are mountain views to the south through

On the Race Brook Trail in January

the trees, and when the leaves are off the trees there is fine, open feeling. Along the way you pass scrubby oaks and curiously stunted pines. The last five minutes or so are more or less level. Unfortunately the abandoned fire tower is unsafe to climb and has been fenced off. However there are viewpoints near the summit which offer unobstructed views in various directions. The return route is the same as your ascent route. Although there is a sign at the junction, take care not to walk past the Race Brook Trail as you head back down the AT.

Approach: From Great Barrington, drive southwest to South Egremont (on Routes 23 and 41), then turn south on Rt. 41 for 5.2 miles to a parking pullout on the right.

Maps: Southwestern Massachusetts (AMC); Ashley Falls (USGS)

35 • Wachusett Mountain 2,006'

Rating: Easy
Time: 1 hour 30 minutes
Distance: 2 miles
Location: In Princeton, north of Worcester and west of Leominster
Total climb: 600'
Summary: A short, fun hike on a steep and rocky trail to panoramic views. A favorite hike for young children and families.

Not many mountains feature a goldfish pond on the summit, but this one does. As the biggest mountain for miles around, Wachusett is an extremely popular family outing. It is only an hour from Boston, and with its excellent trail network, a ski area, and a paved road to the summit, this is one well-used rock pile! Over 250,000 people reach the summit each year, admittedly most of them by car, but many thousands make the enjoyable hike from the base. In fact, Wachusett may rival New Hampshire's Mount Monadnock as the most climbed mountain in the U.S.. The Visitor Center is open and staffed year round. Stop in and pick up the free trail map.

Of the dozens of possible routes on this mountain—there are 18 named trail segments—the combination of the Bicentennial and Pine Hill Trails offers a fun, direct route to the top and is one of the most popular. From the parking lot at the visitor center, pick up the **Bicentennial Trail** as it slabs left across the very steep mountainside, climbing gently along a wide, but unimproved, rocky trail. After about ten minutes, bear sharply right onto the **Pine Hill Trail** which ascends in a direct fashion to the summit. It maintains a steep pitch—at times you clamber up bare bedrock—until a few minutes below the top. A little over half way through the climb you cross the **Summit Road**; painted footprints on the pavement make it difficult to miss trail's continuation on the other side. Both trails on this route are marked with blue paint triangles. The summit itself is a large, flat, gravel expanse, with an old fire tower (closed) on one side. The ski area's quad chairlift ends just below the summit. Mountains in western Massachusetts (Greylock) and southern Vermont (Stratton) and New Hampshire (Monadnock) can be seen, although they appear as blips on the horizon. Surrounding towns and nearby lakes and hills can be picked out as well; use the State Reservation map for its careful labeling of the view. The goldfish? Just below the summit, in the picnic area, is a

Family hiking on Wachusett Mountain

small pond where the little critters hang out—even throughout the long winter. Head down the way you came up, or use the map to take a longer route, for example the somewhat gentler Loop Trail.

Hikers wanting more of workout can start at the ski area base on Balance Rock Trail. This gives a thousand feet of vertical instead of the six hundred afforded by the route described above. Note that hiking on the ski trails is not allowed.

Approach: From Route 2 (exit 25), drive south on MA 140 2.2 miles to the access road for the Wachusett Mountain ski area on the right. Drive up this road, past the ski area entrance, to the Wachusett Mountain Reservation Visitor Center, at 1.8 miles.

Map: Wachusett Mountain State Reservation Trail Map (free)

36 • Mount Greylock 3,491'

Rating: Moderately strenuous
Time: 5 hours
Distance: 7 miles (or 9-mile loop)
Location: Williamstown, in northwestern Massachusetts
Total climb: 2,400'
Summary: Classic route up Massachusett's highest mountain. Ascends the edge of the huge ravine known as the Hopper.

Of the many hiking trails on Mount Greylock—there are two roads to the summit as well—the historic Hopper Trail is the best known. Ancient by American standards, it was worked on by students from Williams College as early as 1830. The **Hopper** itself is the gigantic ravine on the mountain's west side, and is the dominant physical feature of the mountain. Its funnel-like appearance—it resembles a grain hopper—explains the name.

From the parking area, walk through the farm area on the old farm road which leads towards the mountain. After passing through a meadow for a few minutes, the route forks, with the blue-blazed **Hopper Trail** branching sharply to the right. Continuing straight is the Money Brook Trail, which is used on the descent if the loop variation is chosen. Initially negotiating some wet areas, the trail climbs steadily without much letup, passing the Money Brook Cutoff after about 35 minutes and reaching a campground and road (Sperry Road) after about an hour. From here to the top—it is steep in places—will take about a half hour. Follow the blazes carefully here: stick with the blue blazing for about another 15 minutes until the white-blazed **Appalachian Trail** appears, then follow it to the top and **Bascom Lodge**. The amenities of the AMC-run Bascom Lodge—a rustic but comfortable mountain lodge—are warmly appreciated by tired hikers, AT thru-hikers in particular. Nearby, the War Memorial Tower, a 100'-high stone tower, is an interesting curiosity. Views from the summit area encompass a wide area and include chunks of five states. For your return, either head back down the way you came up, or, for a longer **variation**, follow the AT north off the summit before taking the Money Brook Cut-off (and a short section on the road) to Money Brook Trail. Here head left and descend into the confines of the Hopper, eventually rejoining the Hopper Trail at the intersection mentioned above.

Bascom Lodge on the summit of Mount Greylock Richard Bailey

Approach: From US Route 2 in Williamstown, drive south on Water Street (it turns into Green River St.) two miles to Hopper Road at Mount Hope Park. Turn left and continue on Hopper Road 2.7 miles to the farm and trailhead at the end of the road.

Maps: Mount Greylock Reservation State Park map and Trail Guide and Map (Williams Outing Club)

Pine Cobble (1,894'), is probably the most popular short hike for Williamstown folks, and especially for students from Williams College. There is a panoramic view from the top. The Williams Outing Club maintains the 1.6-mile Pine Cobble Trail, which is the most direct route. To pick up the trail (blue blazes) from the campus, cross the river on Cole Street, head right, then immediately left up the hill. It takes a little over an hour to make the climb.

Note: The locator map for Mt. Greylock is on page 119.

Vermont

Vermont's Green Mountains

Southern Vermont has relatively few high summits, although it has two distinct mountain ranges: The Green Mountain Range and the Taconic Range. Manchester sees the majority of hiking activity with Stratton and Bromley the best known summits, but it is Mount Equinox (3,825') that makes an impression as it looms over Manchester with its great bulk. Most visitors reach the top by car, but there is a good hiking route on the west side, starting in Manchester village. Lye Brook Falls and Prospect Rock are popular, shorter hikes in the area.

Killington Peak (4,241') is the dominant peak of **Central Vermont**. It in turn is pretty much dominated by the Killington Ski Resort. Hiking routes unaffected by the ski resort are the Bucklin Trail, on the west side, and the Long Trail from the south. The satelite peaks of Pico Peak and Shrewsbury Mountain both have trails. Nearby Deer Leap Rock offers a good view for little effort. Snake Mountain, Middlebury's local favorite, has stunning views of Lake Champlain and the Adirondacks. East of Killington, Woodstock's Mount Tom and Ludlow's Okemo are local favorites. Farther east, near the Connecticut River, Mount Ascutney has a very well-developed network of trails on its steep slopes.

It is **Northern Vermont**, from Lincoln Gap north, that seems to have snagged most of the interesting mountains of Vermont, Mount Abraham, Mount Ellen, Burnt Rock, Camel's Hump, Mount Mansfield (Vermont's highest at 4,393'), Mount Hunger, and Jay Peak are the best known. Mount Mansfield is several miles long, and its one and a half mile long, above-tree line summit ridge provides one of the best mountain walks in Vermont—in the Northeast for that matter. The pointed, barren summit of Camel's Hump (4,083'), completely unspoiled by roads, towers or ski lifts, is another cherished gem. Stowe Pinnacle and Sterling Pond (Smugglers Notch) are great as short excursions for younger hikers. Lesser known Belvidere Mountain, north of Johnson, and in the Northeast Kingdom, Burke Mountain, Mount Wheeler, Mount Hor, and Mount Pisgah, round out the main selection.

Photo previous page: Camel's Hump from Huntington

Photo at right: Mount Mansfield summit ridge, seen from the Forehead

37 • Stratton Mountain 3,936'

Rating: Moderately strenuous
Time: 6 hours
Distance: 12-mile loop (includes one mile along the road)
Total climb: 1,900'
Location: East of Manchester and west of the ski area
Summary: Views of five states from the fire tower on top of Stratton. Visit to Stratton Pond.

Follow the white-blazed **Long Trail** (the Appalachian Trail coincides with the Long Trail in southern Vermont) from Kelley Stand Road north over easy terrain as the route mixes with old logging roads and crosses wet areas. About a half mile past a beaver dam, at 1.2 miles from the road, you come to an old farm site (stone wall, apple trees). Soon thereafter, you cross a Forest Service road (FR 341) and begin climbing in earnest, crossing more logging roads. The Stratton Mountain Trail comes in from the right at 2.5 miles. About ten minutes farther on, there is a view of Somerset Reservoir and Mount Snow, and another half mile of walking in balsam forest brings you to the summit fire tower, 3.8 miles from Kelley Stand Road. In addition to nearby Mount Snow and Somerset Reservoir, Mount Ascutney, Mount Equinox, and even New Hampshire's Mount Monadnock can be seen. A ranger-naturalist is present during the summer. The north summit of Stratton (3,875') is 0.7 mile north on a spur trail. This is the top of Stratton Mountain Ski Area.

To do the loop including **Stratton Pond**, continue north on the Long Trail. For a much shorter trip, return the way you came up. Continuing on the loop, pass a lookout after 0.1 mile (view of Stratton Pond), and a half-mile past the top, start descending steeply as the trail gets rougher, soon meeting the Forest Service road crossed earlier. Continue on the LT/AT another mile, and after a total distance of seven miles from Kelley Stand Road, you reach Stratton Pond. The trail around the lake provides access to the shelters and campsites. A Green Mountain Club caretaker is in residence here during the summer. This beautiful spot is in danger of being loved to death, so please treat it with special care.

From Stratton Pond, pick up the **Stratton Mountain Trail** and follow it 3.7 miles south over very easy terrain back to Kelley Stand Road. From here it is 0.9 mile back along the road (east) to your starting point, the Long Trail parking lot.

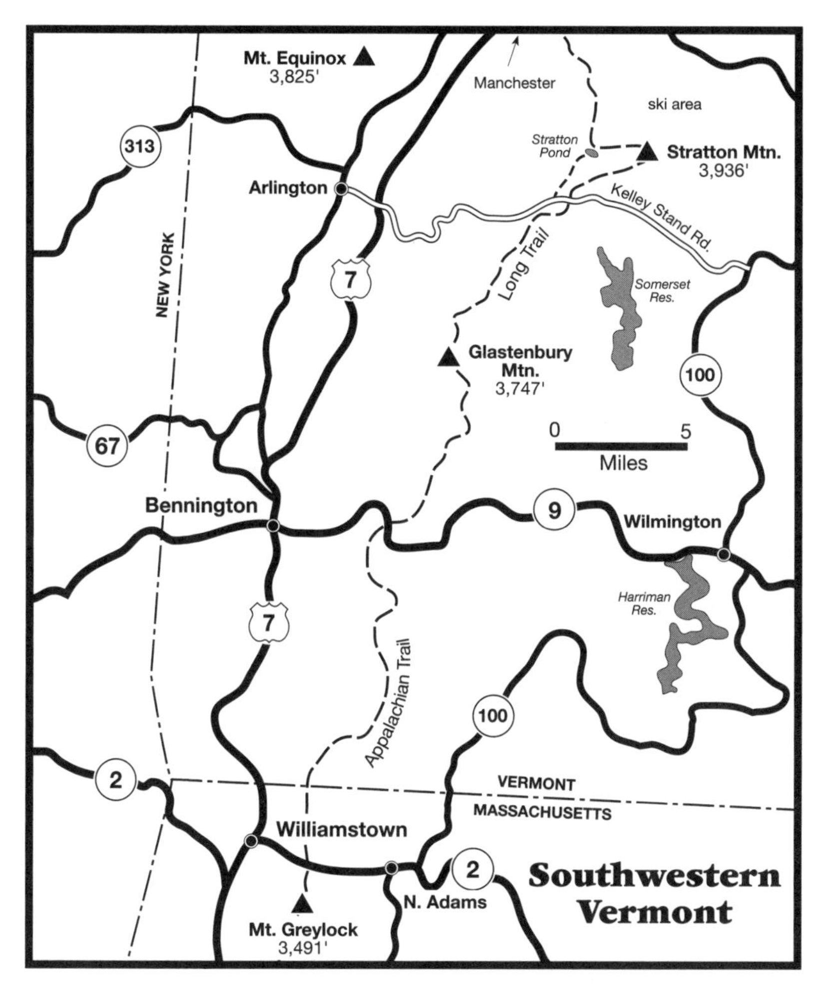

Approach: From Manchester, drive east on Route 30 past Bondville (Stratton Mountain access) to East Jamaica. Head south on VT 100 to West Wardsboro. Follow the Arlington-West Wardsboro Road (Kelley Stand Road) 7 miles west to a parking area at the Long Trail/Appalachian Trail road crossing.

Map: Vermont Atlas & Gazetteer, p. 25

38 • Mount Ascutney 3,150'

Rating: Moderate but steep
Time: 4.5 hours
Distance: 6.4 miles
Location: Near Windsor and south of White River Junction
Total climb: 2,400'
Summary: One of the best known mountain landmarks of Vermont, Mount Ascutney's views encompass a huge swath of VT and NH

Standing alone, far from Vermont's usual hiking venues, Mount Ascutney is fortunate to have its own excellent hiking trail system, with four different routes to the top. A great landmark, it is clearly visible from many Vermont and New Hampshire peaks. Mount Ascutney is a rather steep-sided mountain, and with a vertical difference of over 2,000', offers quite a solid hike. Geologically, it is a monadnock, and is made up of various granites. The presence of an unusual granite type (nordmarkite) on Ascutney has been very helpful in understanding New England's glacial flow patterns. The nordmarkite deposits around New England have beeen crucial in mapping the "boulder fan" south from Mount Ascutney. Thus it has been possible to effectively plot past glacial activity south of Ascutney. In the more recent past, Ascutney was the scene of quarrying and logging, but present activity is mostly recreational: hiking, skiing, hang-gliding, and camping. Ascutney State Park (two miles from US 5 on Route 44A) is open from Memorial Day to Columbus Day and offers camping and good trail access. From the Park, the paved Mountain Road (toll) reaches to the 2,750' level, providing hikers a higher starting point than afforded by the other trailheads. From the end of the road, the Slot Trail leads in only 0.7 mile to the summit tower.

The route we describe here starts from VT 44, a little east of the state park entrance. From the parking lot, the **Brownsville Trail** immediately climbs very steeply to the old quarry access, where it branches right on the mercifully low-angled road and follows it to the abandoned quarry site. After negotiating a somewhat rough and rocky section of trail, you settle into a steady climb on a well-maintained path. A short distance from the top, the Windsor Trail comes in from the left, and about 0.2 mile from the summit there is an obvious spur trail (right) to an open rock ledge, **Brownsville Rock**, with great views of the countryside below and mountains in

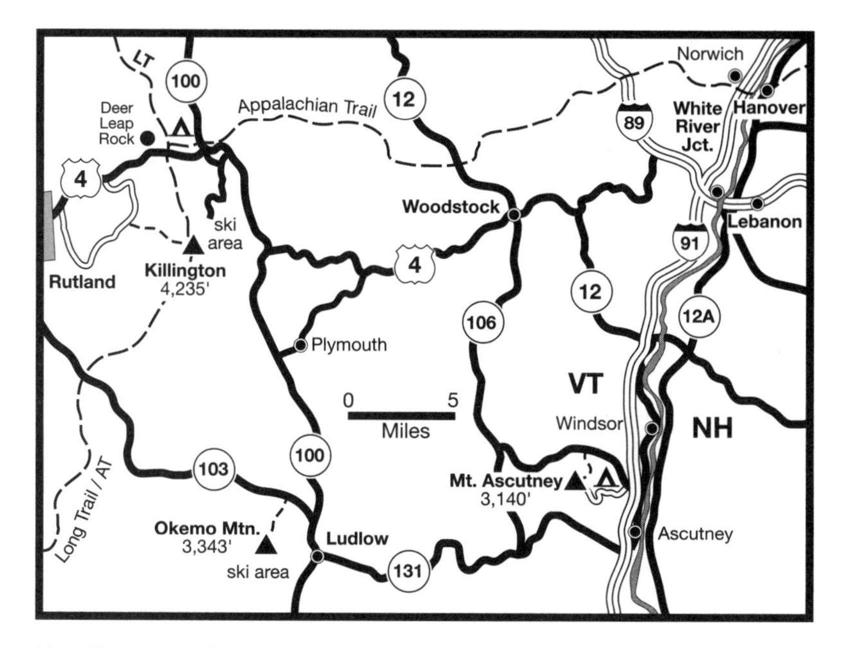

the distance. Continue to the summit with its observation platform. From here, on a clear day, much of Vermont's mountain landscape can be admired, from Stratton Mountain in the south, to nearby Killington and Okemo, as well as Camel's Hump and Mount Mansfield to the north. Because Ascutney is practically on the New Hampshire border, the eastern view encompasses a great swath of the Granite State. In clear conditions the Berkshires of Massachusetts can be seen.

Approach: Approaching from the south, use I-91 exit 8 (Ascutney), and drive north on US 5 about one mile to VT 44A. Head northwest on VT 44 three miles (passing the entrance to Ascutney State Park) to VT 44. Bear left and continue another mile to the trailhead parking lot on the left.

Maps: Vermont-New Hampshire Hiking (Map Adventures); Mount Ascutney Guide (Ascutney Trails Association); and Vermont Atlas & Gazetteer, p. 31

39 • Mount Abraham 4,006'

Rating: Moderate
Time: 4 hours
Distance: 5.2 miles
Location: Lincoln Gap, west of the village of Warren (Mad River Valley)
Total climb: 1,700'
Summary: A popular family hike to a high, open summit. It is spectacular during fall foliage.

This is a favorite first hike for families and a popular first mountain for kids. The summit is above treeline, and the climbing, although considerable, is more gentle than on Camel's Hump or Mount Mansfield. From the **Lincoln Gap** road, head north on the **Long Trail**, initially climbing over easy, up-and-down terrain, and reaching the **Battell Shelter** (lean-to) at 1.7 miles. Here the Battell Trail comes in from the left (west). The Battell Trail makes a two-mile relatively easy descent to Elder Road (off Quaker Street) in Lincoln. Continuing upward from the shelter on the Long Trail, climb over increasingly rocky terrain, and after a bit of scrambling on a few slabs, you soon reach the gentle dome that is the summit of Mount Abe. Below, the farms and houses of Lincoln seem surprisingly close. North along the spine of the Green Mountains, the ski runs of Sugarbush Ski Resort snake down Lincoln Peak and Mount Ellen.

While the majority of hikers return to Lincoln Gap the way they came up, longer hikes north along the Long Trail are commonly done. In particular the trek all the way to Appalachian Gap is a classic. See the description of the Monroe Skyline Traverse at right. Continuing as far as the top of Sugarbush South (Lincoln Peak) or Sugarbush North (Mount Ellen), and then dropping down ski runs are also popular variations.

Approach: From VT 100 at the village of Warren, take Lincoln Gap Road and make the very steep drive up to Lincoln Gap at 2,424'. There are a couple of parking areas just below the pass.

Maps: Vermont-New Hampshire Hiking (Map Adventures) and Vermont Atlas & Gazetteer, p. 39

Rime ice on the Monroe Skyline (Mt. Ellen, north of Mt. Abraham)

The 11.6-mile **Monroe Skyline Traverse** of a high, rugged section of the Green Mountains—from Lincoln Gap to Appalachian Gap—is a solid achievement for a day hiker. Two shelters along the way make the route workable as an overnight trip. From the summit of Abraham, continue 0.8 mile to Lincoln Peak (3,975'), and over Nancy Hanks Peak to the Castlerock Chairlift. There is little doubt as to what happens in winter: This is the top of the **Sugarbush Ski Area.** Continuing north along the narrow spine of the Green Mountains—it is heavily forested, thus virtually viewless—you reach **Mt. Ellen** (4,083') after another mile and a half, a total of 6.3 miles from Lincoln Gap. Mt. Ellen is the summit of Sugarbush North Ski Area. After taking in the superb views from Mt. Ellen, continue along the ridge and at about eight miles the Jerusalem Trail comes in from the left. Soon thereafter the 0.3-mile spur trail to **Glen Ellen Lodge** branches off to the right. The remaining 3.4 miles to Appalachian Gap take you over the top of General Stark Mountain (3,662') and across the summit of **Mad River Glen Ski Area.** Stark's Nest, the ski area's rustic warming hut at the top of the legendary single chairlift provides a place to sit and relax before your final 1.5-mile push to "App Gap."

40 • Snake Mountain 1,287'

Rating: Easy to moderate
Time: 2 hours and 30 minutes
Distance: 3.6 miles
Total climb: 950'
Location: 6 miles NW of Middlebury
Summary: Close-up views of Lake Champlain and the Adirondacks from a clifftop vantage point.

Visible for miles around, Snake Mountain rises a thousand feet above the low, rolling, dairy farm country of Addison County. The mountain is completely wooded except for the cliffs near the summit, the goal of this hike. The wide trail is what remains of the carriage road which once led to a summit hotel. The road is now completely impassable for cars. In fact the huge waterbars (transverse mounds of dirt) make it challenging for mountain bikers. It is very steep on the ascent and demands superior riding skills on the descent.

From the parking area walk the short distance to the gated dirt road which leads into the woods right where Wilmarth Road dead ends at Mountain Road. The route passes over easy terrain, rising slightly then dipping before arriving at a T-junction after less than a mile. Turn left here (note this for the return.) and get down to the business of climbing the mountain. After a relatively brief steep section (a few short switchbacks) the trail, and the terrain, is less demanding, and following a mixture of moderate climbs and mellow stretches, you work your way around to the west side of the mountain. In the fall and winter when the leaves are off the trees you will catch glimpses of Lake Champlain. After walking along the main spine of the mountain for 10-15 minutes, a clearing appears on the left. Follow a side path out to the rocks to enjoy the view from the top of the cliff. Farms spread out below you, and across nearby Lake Champlain the Adirondacks command your attention—especially in the late afternoon and early evening light. The drop-off is substantial, so be advised. The bare ledges and old foundation offer plenty of places to sit and relax. You may see ravens working off the wind currents at the cliff edge. This vantage point on Snake is a famous birdwatching site, especially during the spring and fall migrations. Descend by the same route.

Maps: Recreation Map & Guide to Addison County and Vermont Atlas & Gazetteer, p. 32 and 38

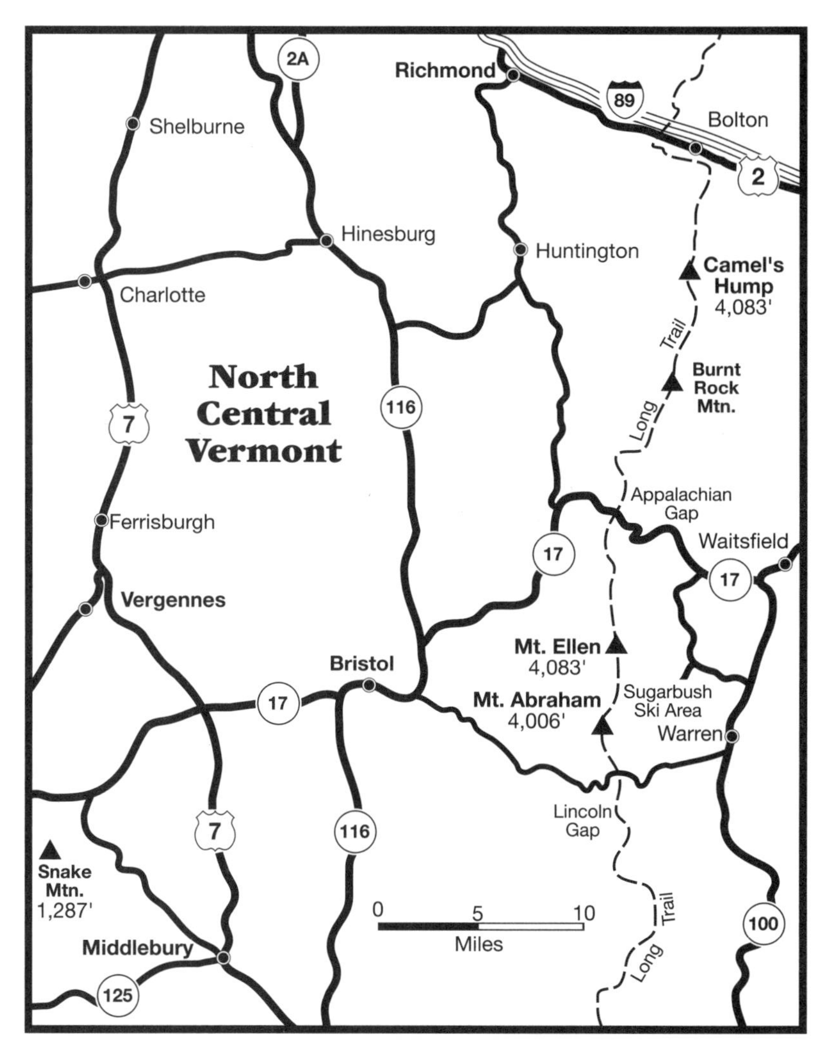

Approach: From Middlebury, follow VT 125 to VT 22A, and turn right (north) and continue 4.5 miles to Wilmarth Road. Turn right again and proceed to a T-intersection with Mountain Road. The parking area is a hundred yards or so to the left (north).

41 • Camel's Hump 4,083'

Rating: Moderately strenuous
Time: 6 hours
Distance: 5.7-mile loop
Location: South of Richmond, 25 miles east of Burlington
Total climb: 1,950'
Summary: Outstanding, rocky summit with panoramic views. The only undeveloped 4,000' mountain in Vermont.

The almost six-mile loop described below ascends the Forest City Trail, reaches the summit via the Long Trail, and descends on the Burrows Trail. Although simply going up and down the Burrows Trail is more expedient (shorter and less strenuous), the full loop version is the real classic here.

From the parking area enter the woods, and at the information kiosk immediately branch right on the **Connector Trail**. At 0.1 mile, after descending to cross an impressive little gorge, pick up the **Forest City Trail**. Head left and begin climbing, gradually at first and then more steeply, reaching the **Long Trail** just 200' north of **Montclair Glen Lodge**, a rustic cabin maintained by the Green Mountain Club.

You are now about 1.4 miles from your starting point, and it is 1.9 miles on to the top of the mountain. Head left on the Long Trail for Camel's Hump. After short climb to **Wind Gap** (2,800'), where the Dean Trail departs right towards Waterbury, the Long Trail gets down to business. Very steep climbing over irregular rocks eventually leads to open shoulders with good views. After an up-and-down section, the Long Trail deposits you at the base of the very steep southern aspect of Camel's Hump. After a long, merciless climb, you reach the base of the almost vertical south face. By contouring to the left, the route finds easier ground, and breaking out into the open, reaches the summit on exhilerating slabs. More mountain tops should be like this—nothing challenges your view! The view is one of the best: to the west Lake Champlain and the Adirondacks, to the north Mount Mansfield, and to the northeast the Worcester Range with New Hampshire's White Mountains in the distance. Immediately to the south, lie the mountains and ski areas of Mad River and Sugarbush. No roads, ski areas, or antennas detract from this great mountain spot.

Hikers approaching the summit of Camel's Hump

From the top, descend (north) on the rocky, and in places very steep, Long Trail for 0.3 mile to a grassy clearing. Head left from this clearing onto the 2.1-mile **Burrows Trail**. Although this four-way intersection is well-marked, be very careful to pick the right route. The heavily used Burrows Trail is often steep and rough on the upper part but mellows quite a bit as you approach the parking lot and return to your starting point. The title page of this chapter (page 115) shows the view of Camel's Hump from the west, perhaps the classic aspect of this Vermont icon.

Approach: From Burlington, take I-89 and US 2 to Richmond. From the traffic light in Richmond, drive south (right) through Huntington village to Huntington Center, 9 miles from Richmond. Turn left on Camel's Hump Road (Forest City Road), and continue 3.5 miles to the end.

Maps: Northern Vermont Hiking (Map Adventures) and Vermont Atlas & Gazetteer, p. 39-40

The Long Trail and the Green Mountain Club

Vermont's 265-mile Long Trail runs along the mountainous backbone of the state—the Green Mountains—from Massachusetts in the south to the Canadian border in the north. Conceived in 1910 and completed in 1930, the Long Trail is the oldest long-distance hiking trail in the U.S. In 1927, it was the inspiration for the Appalachian National Scenic Trail, the Appalachian Trail. The AT coincides with the Long Trail for one hundred miles in southern Vermont, before branching east to New Hampshire. Refered to as a "footpath in the wilderness," the Long Trail offers challenging hiking, much of it runs over steep and very rough terrain. A complete traverse of the Long Trail is the premier hiking goal in Vermont. Hikers typically take about three weeks to make a continuous, "end-to-end" trek, walking 10-15 miles per day. However most hikers elect to do the Trail in shorter sections, taking several years to complete the entire trail. Seventy lean-tos and primitive cabins provide shelter along the way. Hikers bring their own food, cookstoves, and camping gear.

The Long Trail is part of the 440-mile Long Trail System. This encompasses the many side trails which access the Long Trail, as well as the Long Trail itself. The side trails on popular mountains like Camel's Hump and Mount Mansfield are the most heavily used hiking trails in the state. It is estimated that the Long Trail System sees over 90% of the state's hiking activity. See the Vermont introduction for a brief overview of areas not included in the Long Trail System.

With 6,500 members (1999), the Green Mountain Club (GMC) is Vermont's primary hiking organization. It is also more or less synonomous with the Long Trail. As the officially designated guardian of the Long Trail, it is the Club's mission to maintain and protect the Trail. In recent years, major work has been done—it is ongoing—with landowners and government agencies to secure a permanent corridor for the Long Trail.

The Green Mountain Club's headquarters are located in Waterbury Center, about ten miles south of Stowe. In the main hiking season, from Memorial Day to Columbus Day, the Gameroff Hiker Center is open daily. Here GMC staff members sell maps and guide books and provide hiker assistance. In the off-season, this activity is handled directly by the main office. The nearest location of the Long Trail to the Club headquarters is the Mount Mansfield-Smugglers Notch area, about 15 miles distant. The Green Mountain Club publishes several guide books, including the definitive **Guide to the Long Trail**, and the Long Trail News, the quarterly membership magazine.

"The Belated Party on Mansfield Mountain" by Jerome Thompson, 1858
(The Metropolitan Museum of Art, Roger's Fund, 1969.)

As with most hiking and recreation organizations, the GMC is heavily dependent on its membership, both financially (dues and donations) and for volunteer time donated. This latter category facilitates such things as trail maintanence—there is a trail and shelter adoption program—and assistance with Club activities and events. The various committees can often use a helping hand. As always, at the basic level, if you are a regular user of hiking trails, consider joining your local club, or help by making a contribution to the ongoing effort to maintain trails.

42 • Mount Hunger 3,538'

Rating: Moderate
Time: 4 hours
Distance: 3.8 miles
Location: Worcester Range, southeast of Stowe
Total climb: 2,290'
Summary: A steep climb to an open summit with panoramic views. Blueberries in season.

Mount Hunger's location between Mount Mansfield and Camel's Hump and near Waterbury Reservoir offers the hiker one of the best summit views in the state. Even with a fair amount of haze the Presidential Range and other mountain groups in New Hampshire can be easily picked out. Although not the highest point on the ridge, Mount Hunger is the most visited summit of the Worcester Range. The Worcester Range is the impressive mountain wall on your right as you drive along Route 100 from Waterbury to Stowe.

From the parking area, the **Waterbury Trail** starts off gradually, but initially it is rocky with awkward footing. Soon settling into a steady, traversing climb, the trail makes two stream crossings before switching back to the left. There are some short, very steep sections before the trail breaks out into the open, just below the top. The bald, expansive summit area offers protected pockets to sit and relax. Enjoy the great view and contemplate future hikes. Traditionally, this summit has not been well marked, and since there are two other trails off the top, take care to ensure you descend on the same trail you ascended. It is also possible to continue over to Stowe Pinnacle—the **Skyline Ridge Trail**—and down into Stowe Hollow. See the description under Stowe Pinnacle.

The route from the east side—the Middlesex Trail—is the usual approach for folks from Montpelier. Its steep upper portion ascends a section of moderately steep slabs and is exhilerating under dry conditions.

Approach: From Waterbury (exit 10 on I-89), drive north on VT 100 to Waterbury Center, and turn right (in a dip) off Route 100. From the village green, drive north on Maple Street, and turn right on Loomis Hill Road. At a Y-intersection 2.7 miles from Waterbury Center, stay left; the trailhead is at 3.7 miles.

Maps: Northern Vermont Hiking; Map & Guide to Stowe and the Mt. Mansfield Region; and Vermont Atlas & Gazetteer, p. 46

Camel's Hump from Mount Hunger

Variation from Middlesex (east side): Somewhat longer than the Waterbury Trail, the **Middlesex Trail** is the standard route for folks approaching Mount Hunger from Montpelier. It is a more varied trail, and the upper section negotiates a series of slabs. This route is not recommended when icy! The signage leaves something to be desired, but the blue-blazed trail is excellent and recommended as a change for those who usually climb Mount Hunger from the Waterbury-Stowe side. The distance to the top is 2.8 miles. At 1.5 miles from the trailhead, the White Rock Trail branches left. (This side trail actually loops around the summit on the south side, making it possible to connect with the Waterbury Trail.) Plan on about four hours for this hike.

Aerial view of Mount Mansfield from the northwest Ed Rolfe

Backcountry Skiing

Mount Mansfield and its neighbors constitute a compact region of rugged, mountainous terrain with a vertical relief of 2,500'. For the most part these forested slopes present quite a challenge for conventional nordic skis, but they are perfect for the sturdier telemark equipment. A network of marked ski trails extends from Bolton Ski Area in the south (across both the east and west flanks of Mount Mansfield) to Smugglers Notch Ski Area in the north, and from Underhill in the west to the Stowe cross country areas of Trapp Family Lodge, Topnotch, Edson Hill, and Mount Mansfield. The Bolton to Trapps traverse (20 kilometers, difficult), the Overland Trail from Underhill to the Trapps trail network (3 to 4 hours, moderately difficult), and the Skytop-Burt Trail loop (2 to 3 hours, moderately difficult) are among the area's favorite tours. Vermont's 280-mile cross country ski trail, the Catamount Ski Trail, traverses the area using the Bolton-Trapps route and various ski area trail segments.

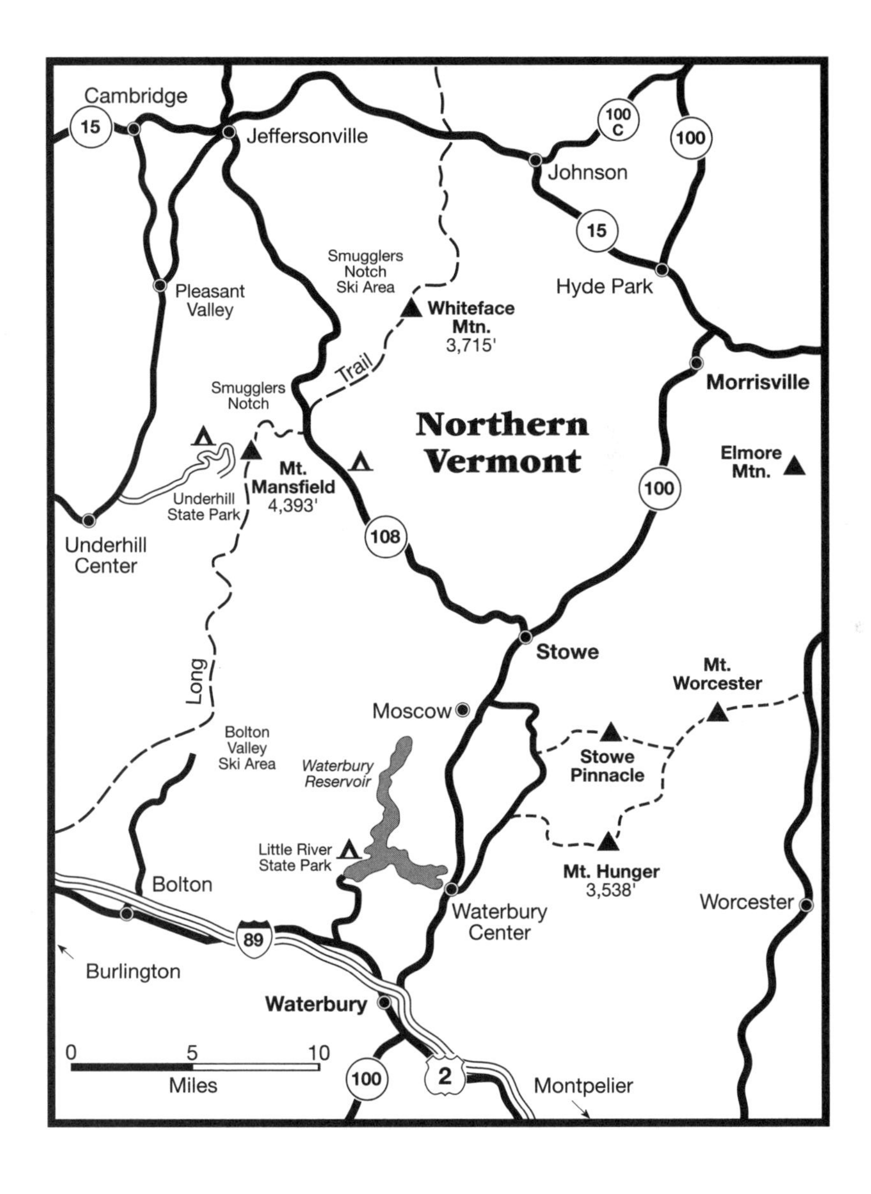
Cambridge
15
Jeffersonville
100 C
100
Johnson
15
Hyde Park
Smugglers Notch Ski Area
Pleasant Valley
Whiteface Mtn.
3,715'
Trail
Morrisville
Smugglers Notch
Northern Vermont
Elmore Mtn.
Mt. Mansfield
4,393'
Underhill State Park
100
Underhill Center
108
Stowe
Long
Mt. Worcester
Moscow
Bolton Valley Ski Area
Waterbury Reservoir
Stowe Pinnacle
Little River State Park
Mt. Hunger
3,538'
Bolton
Worcester
Waterbury Center
89
Burlington
Waterbury
0
5
10
Miles
100
2
Montpelier

43 • Stowe Pinnacle 2,740'

Rating: Easy to moderate
Time: 2.5 to 3 hours
Distance: 3 miles
Total climb: 1,520'
Location: Stowe

Summary: A popular Stowe hike to a somewhat unusual summit. Although short, this trip packs plenty of climbing.

Stowe Pinnacle is Stowe's moderate, short hike. If you feel like a hike, but aren't in the mood for a longer climb like Mount Mansfield, then the Pinnacle is a good choice. From the parking lot, head up through an overgrown field, soon entering woods. The initial portion of the heavily used **Pinnacle Trail** tends to be wet—it could benefit from a little trailwork. The trail soon gets drier, steeper, and rockier and after asking a fair amount of effort of you, brings you to a saddle where the grade eases momentarily. Here a short and informally marked spur trail (left) leads to a lookout over Stowe to Mount Mansfield. Continuing on the Pinnacle Trail, drop quite steeply before climbing equally steeply to reach the branch (left) that connects with the Skyline Ridge Trail. (The Skyline Ridge Trail climbs to the main ridge and connects Worcester Mountain with Mount Hunger.) Heading straight ahead, the top of the Pinnacle is only 0.2 miles farther on. You soon reach the open rock summit with its sweeping views to the south toward Waterbury and west to Mount Mansfield and Stowe. It is an unusual spot because directly behind you the main wall of the Worcester Range looms overhead. Return by the same route.

Approach: From Main Street in Stowe (opposite the church), take School Street, bear right at the fork and continue to Stowe Hollow. Follow Upper Hollow Road to the signed parking area for Stowe Pinnacle, on the left.

Maps: Northern Vermont Hiking; Map & Guide to Stowe and the Mt. Mansfield Region; 20 Day Hikes in the Mt. Mansfield Region; and Vermont Atlas & Gazetteer, p. 46

Stowe Pinnacle from Stowe Hollow

Skyline Ridge Trail

This is the name given to the trail which runs north along the spine of the **Worcester Range** from Mount Hunger to Worcester Mountain. The most popular section of the route is as follows. From the summit of Mount Hunger, follow the blue-blazed trail north along the ridge. After about two miles of somewhat rough up and down, follow the branch of the trail that descends steeply (left) towards Stowe Hollow. (The main branch continues north to Worcester Mountain.) When you meet up with the Stowe Pinnacle Trail, it is only 0.2 mile (left) and an easy climb to the open summit of the Pinnacle, a very worthwhile detour. It is 1.4 miles from the top of the Pinnacle down to the road in Stowe Hollow. The total length of this hiking route, from the base of the Waterbury Trail to Stowe Hollow, is about seven miles.

44 • Mount Mansfield 4,393'

Rating: Moderately strenuous
Time: 5 hours
Distance: 4.9-mile loop
Total climb: 2,800'
Location: West of Stowe
Summary: The standard route up the Chin, the highest point on Vermont's highest mountain.

The premier hiking mountain of Vermont, Mount Mansfield has ten more or less distinct routes to the top or at least to its summit ridge. The following route is perhaps the most popular. From VT 108, follow the well-marked (white blazes) and well-maintained **Long Trail** as it ascends moderately through woods. At 1.7 miles—a little over an hour—you will come to **Taft Lodge**. Recently rebuilt (1996), this solid log cabin is an important overnight stop for Long Trail hikers; there is bunk space for 24. During hiking season, a GMC caretaker is in residence; the rest of the year, the cabin is closed. From the lodge, it is only 0.6 mile to **the Chin**, but the trail climbs another 750' and is exposed in a few places near the top. Two trails join the LT from the right on this segment, first Hell Brook Cut-off, then Hell Brook Trail itself.

Mt. Mansfield is a two mile ridge, and from the top, much of the interesting view is south along the relatively level summit ridge to the Nose, the other high point of the ridge. At 4,062', the Nose can

Mount Mansfield from Stowe, the Nose on the left, Chin on the right

Smuggler's Notch from Mount Mansfield

be considered a 4,000'-er in its own right. With Lake Champlain and Burlington to the west, Smugglers Notch to the northeast, the ski runs of Stowe Mountain Resort at your feet, Stowe sprawling to the east, Mount Hunger and the Worcester Range to the southwest, and Camel's Hump and the more distant peaks fading away to the south, there is indeed alot for the eye to take in. This fine rock summit maintains a good mountain feel despite the encroachments of mankind.

To descend, either return the way you came up (by heading north on the Long Trail), or head south on the Long Trail 0.2 mile to where the **Profanity Trail** comes in from the left. This trail provides a direct route back down to Taft Lodge and is much less exposed to the elements and drop-offs. It is 0.7 mile back to the lodge and from there, another 1.7 on down the gradual grades of the Long Trail back to the road and your starting point.

Approach: From Stowe, 10 miles north of the I-89 exit at Waterbury, drive up Mountain Road (VT 108) 8.5 miles to where the Long Trail meets the highway on the left and park.

Maps: Northern Vermont Hiking; Mount Mansfield Region (GMC); 20 Day Hikes in the Mt. Mansfield Region

45 • Mount Mansfield via Sunset Ridge

Rating: Moderately strenuous
Time: 5 hours
Distance: 6.6 miles
Total climb: 2,550′
Location: In Underhill, east of Burlington

Summary: One of the finest hikes in Vermont, a prolonged climb on an open ridge with sweeping views of Lake Champlain and the Adirondacks.

As mentioned for the previous hike, Mount Mansfield (4,393') is a mountain of many trails. We give the most popular route on the west side here, as well as a major loop variation using another west side favorite. From **Underhill State Park**, walk up the (gated) **CCC Road** for a mile. This well-maintained, gravel road is a legacy of the Great Depression. It was, as its name suggests, one of the projects completed by the Civilian Conservation Corps. Where the CCC Road turns sharply right, bear left on the **Sunset Ridge Trail**. Initially it runs over very easy ground, crossing a couple of streams on bridges and passing the base of the Laura Cowles Trail, a very direct route to the summit ridge. The Sunset Trail then steepens, climbing and traversing as it works its way up to the ridge. A few scrambly sections bring you out onto the broad, open ridge, and the route to summit is laid out before you. The trail ducks in and out of scrubby growth but is increasingly out in the open, with most of the walking on bare rock. Cairns and paint blazes on the rocks are used to mark the route.

Upon reaching the base of the summit pyramid, the route skirts right, and after reconnecting with the Laura Cowles Trail, reaches the **Long Trail**. At this point, head left on the Long Trail (note the Profanity Trail which drops down to Taft Lodge from this same intersection), and as you climb up easy slabs, you reach the summit in a few minutes. The panoramic view from the top sweeps across the mountains of the Adirondacks and northwestern New England. In afternoon light Lake Champlain's 100-mile length shimmers in the west. Descend by the route you came up, paying close attention at the various trail junctions.

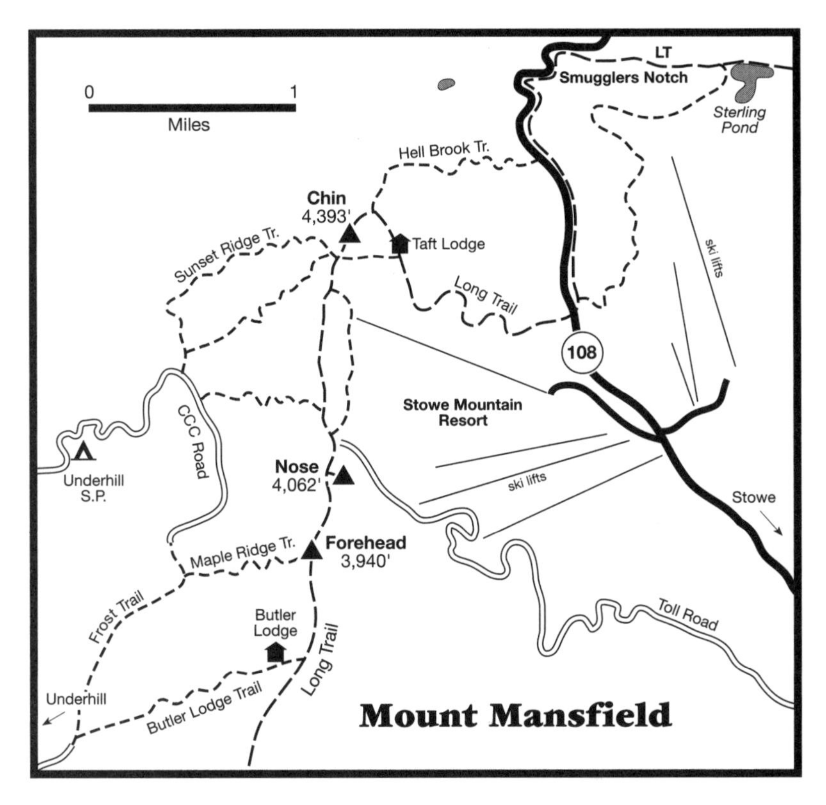

Maple Ridge variation: The following loop hike is the classic tour of Mount Mansfield's two prominent west ridges. You ascend Maple Ridge, traverse the mile and a half long above-tree line ridge connecting the two summits, and descend Sunset Ridge. Start out from Underhill State Park as described above, but at the junction with the CCC Road and Sunset Ridge Trail, continue on the **CCC Road** to its end, at 2.1 miles. Here pick up the **Maple Ridge Trail** and climb steeply to the ridge proper, where the Frost Trail comes in from the right. The view unfolds as you climb, while the cairn-marked trail twists and turns, navigating over and around improbable rock formations. This is unique terrain that offers spectacular

Ravens on the summit of Mount Mansfield

views. Some of the short cliff sections may be quite difficult for dogs. About 1.5 miles from the CCC Road, you reach the broad, semi-open dome of the **Forehead**, and the **Long Trail**. From here, carefully follow the white-blazed Long Trail north (left) two miles to the true summit.

Of the many distractions along this next section—road crossings, frequent side trails, car and visitor traffic from the Toll Road, the opportunity to climb the **Nose** (4,062') is perhaps the most noteworthy. About a half mile from the Forehead, the Triangle Trail branches right and offers a fun scramble up Mansfield's second summit, giving a unique perspective on the mountain. (See the illustration on page 129.) Now return to the Long Trail and continue out onto the open summit ridge to enjoy this high moun-

Aerial view of Mount Mansfield from the south Ed Rolfe

tain walk. Please walk only on the trail (or rocks); the arctic-alpine vegetation does not tolerate being tromped on! A little over a mile from the Nose, the Sunset Ridge Trail departs left; this is your descent route. The **Chin**, the high point of the trip, is 0.2 mile farther. From the summit return to the **Sunset Ridge Trail**. Head right down this most spectacular of ridge walks in Vermont, returning to the CCC Road in 1.1 miles. From here stroll the easy mile back down to Underhill State Park and your starting point.

Approach: From Burlington, follow VT 15 to Underhill (Flats). Bear right on River Road and continue three miles to Underhill Center. Here bear slighty left on Pleasant Valley Road one mile to Mountain Road on the right. Follow this 2.7 miles to Underhill State Park. A modest day usage fee is charged.

Maps: Northern Vermont Hiking; Mount Mansfield Region (GMC); and Vermont Atlas & Gazetteer, p. 45-46

46 • Mount Pisgah 2,751'

Rating: Moderate
Time: 3 hours
Distance: 3.5 miles
Location: North of St. Johnsbury, in the Northeast Kingdom
Total climb: 1,450'
Summary: Pleasant climb to one of Vermont's most dramatic mountain viewpoints, the clifftop view of Lake Willoughby, 1,000' below.

Mount Pisgah is a ridge that runs north to south, paralleling beautiful **Lake Willoughby**, a land-locked fjord. There is both a North Trail and a South Trail. Linking the two trails together to make a traverse of the mountain makes an interesting trip; a road section of three miles along Route 5A completes the loop. The route described here uses the South Trail.

From the parking lot, cross the highway and follow the well-maintained **South Trail** as it navigates boggy terrain on a series of bridges. The trail then ascends very steeply, and passes **Pulpit Rock** after 0.9 mile. The short spur down to Pulpit Rock is steep, and the loose, gravely surface combined with the considerable dropoff, makes it somewhat dangerous. So if you climb down for the view—of Lake Willoughby below and across to Mount Hor—be very careful. This section of the trail traverses an extremely steep slope; it seems a wonder the dense forest was able to establish itself here. Continuing up the mountain and after a fair amount of climbing, the route leads up a small slab, where there is a good view south to Burke Mountain. Pisgah's wooded summit is just a short distance beyond. From the top, take a few minutes to descend a short distance on the North Trail, where you can pick up the side trail (left) to the stupendous clifftop vantage point. This is the high point of the hike. Lake Willoughby is literally at your feet, about one thousand feet below. The cliff is the domain of ravens and in winter, of occassional ice climbers. Return by the route you came up.

Although not a high mountain, even by New England standards, Pisgah is a prominent feature and its steep-sided dome shape is easily identified from many miles away. There are other popular hikes in the area. **Burke Mountain** (3,267') and **Wheeler Mountain** (2,371') come to mind. With its crisp granite slabs, Wheeler offers the hiker an ever so brief taste of rock climbing.

Young hikers storm the mountain
David Goodman

Approach: From St. Johnsbury, drive north through Lyndonville to the village of West Burke. From here, continue north on VT 5A for 6 miles towards Lake Willoughby and the trailhead parking at the base of the CCC Road, on the left side of the highway just south of the lake.

Maps: Northern Vermont Hiking (Map Adventures) and Vermont Atlas & Gazetteer, p. 54

New Hampshire

Southern & Central New Hampshire

Mount Monadnock (3,165') in the far south and **Mount Cardigan** (3,121') near Hanover, about mid-state, are the two best known hiking mountains in New Hampshire outside of the White Mountains. Both mountains have a good selection of routes and open summits. **Mount Kearsarge** and Mount Sunapee—both near Mount Cardigan—also see a lot of hiking activity. Two local favorite hiking destinations, **Smarts Mountain** (3,240') and Mount Cube (2,909'), lie along the Appalachian Trail a little north of Hanover. The Dartmouth Outing Club looks after most of the trails in the area near and immediately north of Hanover, including the important trail network on Mount Moosilauke. Moosilauke (4,802') is covered in the next section, the White Mountains. To the east, **Mount Major** (1,784') with its sweeping view of Lake Winnipesaukee, is the hike we have chosen to represent the Lakes Region. Other popular hikes in this area are Belknap and Gunstock (near Guilford) and the Squam Range (Mount Percival). The very short hike up West Rattlesnake gives a great view over Squam Lake.

Returning to the southernmost part of the state, other hiking areas of note are the twin summits of Pack Monadnock (2,288'), near Peterborough, and west and southeast of Manchester, respectively, the Uncanoonucs and Pawtuckaway State Park. The southern part of the state has no fewer than three long-distance hiking trails. The 21-mile Wapack Trail runs from Watatic Mountain (Ashburnham, Mass.) north along highpoints to the Pack Monadnocks. The 160-mile **Metacomet-Monadnock Trail** starts in Connecticut and runs through Massachusetts, crossing Mount Tom (Northampton), to end on Mount Monadnock. Lastly, the 49-mile Monadnock-Sunapee Greenway continues north where the Metacomet-Monadnock Trail leaves off, linking Mount Monadnock with Mount Sunapee.

Photo previous page: Aerial view of Mt. Washington from the east: Tuckerman Ravine on the left, Huntington Ravine on the right.

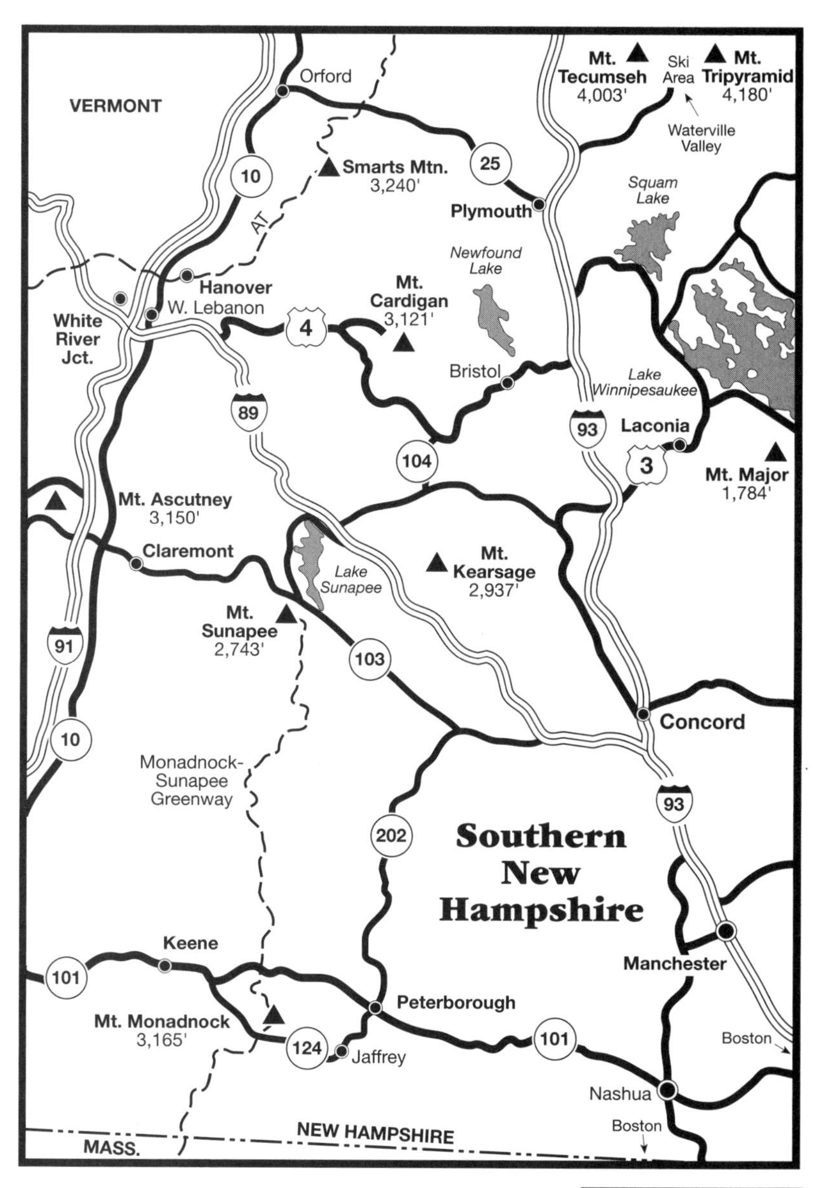
Southern New Hampshire
VERMONT
Orford
Mt. Tecumseh 4,003'
Ski Area
Mt. Tripyramid 4,180'
Waterville Valley
Smarts Mtn. 3,240'
25
10
Plymouth
Squam Lake
AT
Newfound Lake
Hanover
W. Lebanon
White River Jct.
Mt. Cardigan 3,121'
4
Bristol
Lake Winnipesaukee
89
93
Laconia
104
3
Mt. Major 1,784'
Mt. Ascutney 3,150'
Claremont
Lake Sunapee
Mt. Kearsage 2,937'
Mt. Sunapee 2,743'
91
103
Concord
10
Monadnock-Sunapee Greenway
93
202
Keene
Manchester
101
Peterborough
Mt. Monadnock 3,165'
124
Jaffrey
101
Boston
Nashua
Boston
NEW HAMPSHIRE
MASS.

47 • Mount Monadnock 3,165'

Rating: Easy to moderate
Time: 3 hours
Distance: 4.4 miles
Location: Southern New Hampshire, southeast of Keene
Total climb: 1,800'
Summary: Although a relatively low mountain, Monadnock offers more climbing on bare rock than most 4,000'-ers.

With about 125,000 visitors each year, Mount Monadnock is probably the most climbed mountain in the United States. It is even claimed to be the second-most climbed mountain in the world, after Japan's Mount Fujiyama (400,000/year). The bare rock of the upper mountain does make this one of the most exciting summits in New Hampshire. Only 80 miles from Boston, it is the closest, best choice for a large number of hikers. Although barely over 3,000', it is not a trivial climb, and hikers in excellent condition will be doing well to make it to the top in under an hour.

There are trails on every side of Mount Mondanock, and several loop trips are possible. Most hikers start from the state park headquarters area, and the most popular trail, by far, is the **White Dot Trail**. To do this route, follow the wide and rocky path—yes, it is marked with white dots—over easy terrain, passing the branch left (0.5 mile) to the **White Cross Trail**. At 0.7 mile, you come to **Falcon Spring**, an important trail intersection. Here **Cascade Link Trail** branches right, providing a longer route to the summit. To do the standard route, continue straight. From here onward, the trail steepens, requiring some use of hand and footholds. On bare, dry rock this is fun stuff, although in a few places the surface is slippery, worn smooth by the literally millions of feet that have trod the rock over the years.

The upper third of the route is almost completely out in the open, and it is a joy, one of the more exhilarating climbs in New England. Scrambling up the sloping ledges—plenty steep for many hikers—provides an exciting glimpse of the bare rock world of mountaineers. The summit beckons, and with good visibility, Boston's skyline stands out nicely, 60 (straight-line) miles to the southeast. The White Cross Trail rejoins the White Dot Trail 0.3 mile from the top. After enjoying this remarkable place, descend the way you came up, again following the white dots. For a slightly

The summit of Monadnock

longer and more scenic variation, descend on the White Cross Trail; it rejoins the White Dot Trail at Falcon Spring.

Approach: From Jaffrey, drive west on NH 124 for 2 miles, turn right and follow the Monadnock State Park signs 2 miles farther. Jaffrey is south of Peterborough, near the Massachusetts border.

Maps: Monadnock State Park (State Park); Mount Monadnock (AMC); and New Hampshire Atlas & Gazetteer, p. 20

48 • Mount Cardigan 3,121'

Rating: Easy
Time: 2 hours
Distance: 3 miles
Location: East of Lebanon and Hanover, in the town of Orange
Total climb: 1,220'
Summary: A short climb to a fine, open summit. A traditional first mountain for young hikers.

Similar to Mount Monadnock (Hike #47), Mount Cardigan is a small mountain with a large reputation. Because of their open summit rocks, both offer an introduction to the stark beauty of mountains. For kids, Mount Cardigan is one of the best known "first hikes" in the state; thus, it is a great favorite with families. For locals who would rather be "in the mountains" it at least makes for a good training outing. Cardigan supports quite a number of trails, especially on the east side.

The route we have chosen, the easiest on Cardigan, ascends the west side of the mountain. (See below for longer and more difficult routes.) From the **Cardigan State Park** picnic area, the orange-blazed **West Ridge Trail** ascends at an easy angle and offers a pleasant and direct route to the summit. After a half mile, the South Ridge Trail branches off to the right. After passing two more trail branches (on the right), you finish the climb on low-angle slabs, the route marked with cairns and paint blazes. From the summit's bare rock dome, the views are panoramic and range from Mount Washington in the far distance to the interesting minor summit of **Firescrew** (3,064') just to the north. The little jaunt over to Firescrew is well worth the extra effort. The fire tower is manned during the summer season and visitors are welcome. Descend by the same route or by the following easy variation: Follow the **Clark Trail** south off the well-signed summit, encountering the **South Ridge Trail** after 0.2 mile. Head right on it back down to the West Ridge Trail and on to the parking area.

Approach: From Canaan on US 4 (exit 17, I-89), drive north 0.5 mile on NH 118. Turn right, and following signs, drive four miles to Cardigan State Park and the trailhead.

Maps: Mount Cardigan (AMC); Outdoor Map of New Hampshire (Topaz); and New Hampshire Atlas & Gazetteer, p. 38

Summit of Cardigan — Robert Kozlow

The Holt Trail: On Cardigan's east side, a fan-shaped network of trails radiates out from **Cardigan Lodge**, with the **Holt Trail** as its central thread. Starting from the lodge, it runs over easy ground, reaching **Grand Junction** at 1.1 miles and an elevation of 1,700'. Here, the standard route veers left and continues on the **Cathedral Forest Trail**, reaching the summit on the **Clark Trail**, for a total of 2.6 miles. However, hikers that stick with the Holt Trail above Grand Junction are in for a flashy finish! Just beyond the trail junction, you ascend an extremely steep gully. This then gives way to open ledges on the steep upper face of the mountain. Using cracks and ledges, clamber to the top. There is some exposure here, and the route is emphatically not advised if the rock is wet or snow-covered. The upper Holt Trail is one of the half dozen most difficult routes in New Hampshire. Descent is via the ascent route described above or to the north via the somewhat longer Mowglis-Firescrew-Manning combination.

49 • Smarts Mountain 3,240′

Rating: Moderate
Time: 5 hours 30 minutes
Distance: 7.8 miles
Total climb: 2,400′
Location: North of Hanover and just east of Lyme
Summary: A solid hike with good views. Done as a day hike or as an overnight.

The mountainous terrain north of Hanover—the Middle Connecticut River Mountains—is a prelude to the higher summits of the White Mountains. There are a number of interesting hikes here. The popular **Lambert Ridge Trail** ascends Smarts Mountain from the south, providing a significant climb with good viewpoints and a tower at the summit. This route is also a segment of the **Appalachian Trail**. From the road, ascend moderately through hardwoods on a good trail, reaching a viewpoint after a half hour. After another mile (now at 1.8 miles from the car), there's an enticing view of the summit. Descend briefly before tackling the steeper upper mountain. At the summit area the DOC's (Dartmouth Outing Club) tent platforms and shelter are popular camping spots, and the views from the old fire tower are excellent. Return the way you came up.

From the top of Smarts, **Mount Cube's** rocky outcrop of a summit is about eight miles north along the Appalachian Trail. Thus a point-to-point traverse of about 15 miles is quite feasible, since from the summit of Cube (2,910') the AT reaches NH 25A after a 3.4-mile descent. However, the vast majority of hikers will make their ascent of Cube directly from NH 25A. This favorite hike is about five hours and is 6.8 miles round trip.

Approach: From Lyme (north of Hanover), leave NH 10 and drive east to the Dartmouth Skiway, the College's small alpine ski area. At the Skiway bear left on Dorchester Road and continue 1.6 miles to a small parking area on the left.

Maps: Vermont-New Hampshire Hiking (Map Adventures) and New Hampshire Atlas & Gazetteer, p. 38

50 • Mount Kearsage 2,937'

Rating: Easy
Time: 1 hour 45 minutes
Distance: 2.2 miles
Total climb: 1,100'
Location: Winslow State Park, about 10 miles east of Lake Sunapee and just north of I-89
Summary: A short, steep hike to an open summit with terrific views.

The accessible summit of Mount Kearsarge is a popular destination for a summer picnic. Somehow, the various communications antennas don't seem to detract from the experience of the rocky, open summit. In clear weather Cardigan, Moosilauke, Franconia Ridge, Mount Washington, and many other mountains are visible. Slightly lower Mount Sunapee, with its ski runs, is only 12 miles to the southwest as the crow flies. Mount Kearsarge has two trails and two state parks: the half-mile route from the south (from Rollins State Park) and the longer **Wilmot Trail** (also called the Northside Trail) from **Winslow State Park**, described here.

From the upper end of the picnic area, pick up the trail—it's well-worn and hard to miss. A little over halfway, after a short, very steep section, the grade eases, the trail leads across smooth rock slabs, and the view gradually opens up. Total distance to the summit is only 1.1 mile. Descend by the same route.

Approach: From I-89 exit 10, follow the signs to Winslow State Park (six miles). Turn left on Kearsarge Valley Road then right on Kearsarge Mountain Road and follow it to the state park.

Maps: Outdoor Map of New Hampshire (Topaz) and New Hampshire Atlas & Gazetteer, p. 34

51 • Mount Major 1,784′

Rating: Easy with some moderately steep slabs near the top
Time: 2 hours 30 minutes
Distance: 3 miles
Total climb: 1,180′
Location: Southern end of Lake Winnipesaukee, about 25 miles northwest of Rochester
Summary: Beautiful lake views from the broad, bare-rock summit.

The Lakes Region is an immensely popular summer vacation spot. Since none of the higher summits are in the immediate vicinity, nothing major at any rate, Mount Major receives a lot of attention. It is an exciting hike to an open summit with sweeping views of Lake Winnipesaukee, central New Hampshire, and into Maine. Although it is a short hike and popular with families, the mountain is quite steep in a few places. Starting out from the parking area, the trail coincides with a jeep road. The trail soon branches off (right) before rejoining the jeep road. After a brief level section, the trail departs left from the jeep road and climbs steadily to the summit. As you ascend rock slabs, views of the lake begin to open up. There are a few very short slab sections that will require extra caution with small children, especially on the descent. The huge, wide-open top is more of a plateau than a pointed summit. If you've gotten sweaty on the way up, the old stone enclosure will provide relief from the cooling breeze. Take the same route down.

Approach: From the village of Alton Bay, at the extreme southeast corner of Lake Winnipesaukee, drive north on NH 11 4.2 miles to the large parking area.

Maps: Outdoor Map of New Hampshire (Topaz) and New Hampshire Atlas & Gazetteer, p. 36

West Rattlesnake (1,260') is the popular short hike at the northern edge of the Lake Region. While Major looks out across Lake Winnipesaukee, the Rattlesnakes (there is an East Rattlesnake as well) command a sweeping view of Squam Lake. The trailhead for West Rattlesnake is on NH 113, a few miles east of Holderness. The 0.8-mile Bridle Path climbs only 450' to reach the south-facing ledges on West Rattlesnake's summit.

Photo right: Squam Lake from Rattlesnake
Robert Kozlow

The White Mountains

The term "White Mountains" is sometimes used to refer to all of New Hampshire's mountains, but it is more precise to equate the White Mountains with the White Mountain National Forest. At any rate, we are concerned here with the mountainous region that begins in the south in the Lakes Region. It extends northward in a broad fashion, past Waterville Valley and Mount Chocorua, across the Kancamagus Highway through Franconia and Crawford Notch before encompassing the Presidential, Carter, and Baldface Ranges, and exiting into Maine with the Mahoosucs.

Like the rest of our eastern mountains, the "Whites" are heavily forested. Below 3,000' the forest is deciduous, while above 3,000' spruce and balsam fir reign. Tree line occurs a little higher here than in Vermont, at about 4,500'. The mountains' glacial origins are obvious: Crawford Notch and Great Gulf are classic examples of the U-shaped valley, while Tuckerman Ravine and King Ravine are glacial cirques.

The principal hiking areas are **Waterville Valley** (Osceola, Tripyramid), the **Pemigewasset Wilderness** (the Bonds), the **Sandwich Range** (Whiteface, Chocorua), **Franconia Notch State Park** (Lafayette, Lincoln, the Kinsmans), the **Twin Range** (Garfield, South Twin), the **Zealand area** (the Bonds), **Crawford Notch State Park** (Mount Willard, Webster, Jackson), the **Southern Presidentials** (Washington, Monroe, Eisenhower, Pierce), the **Northern Presidentials** (Adams, Madison, Jefferson), the **Carter Range** (Wildcat, Carter Dome, Shelburne Moriah), the **North Conway area** (Moats, Kearsarge North, Doublehead), and the **Mahoosuc Range** (Carlo, Goose Eye).

The Appalachian Mountain Club maintains a string of eight alpine-style, full-service huts in the area. The huts are either on or very near the Appalachain Trail. The Club's field office and hiker facility are at Pinkham Notch at the foot of famed Tuckerman Ravine. The U.S. Forest Service has four district offices in the White Mountain National Forest, with visitor centers located in Conway and a few miles north of Gorham.

Franconia Ridge: Hikers approaching Mount Lincoln, Liberty and Flume in the background
Robert Kozlow

52 • Welch and Dickey

Rating: Moderate, one steep slab
Time: 3 hours
Distance: 4.5 miles
Location: At the entrance to Waterville Valley
Total climb: 1,830′
Summary: Variety of terrain with unusual mountain views. About half the hike is on bare rock.

These two lowly mountains take you across more exposed rock than the rest of the hikes in the Waterville Valley area combined, including Tripyramid! In fact, about half of this varied loop is on granite slabs and exposed bedrock. **Welch Mountain** (2,590') and **Dickey Mountain** (2,734') are situated at the entrance of Waterville Valley, and because of the general openness of the route, great views (of Waterville Valley's compact mountain environment) are to be had. From the trailhead, initially stay right—on **Welch Mountain Trail**—and ascend through woods, reaching a large open shoulder about midway up Welch Mountain. From here the trail steepens, threading its way through stands of jack pine (very unusual in New Hampshire) and blueberry bushes, at one point ascending a steep 100-foot slab before reaching the spectacular summit ledges of Welch at two miles. About 20 minutes of walking and scrambling lead to the higher but less interesting (the views are somewhat obstructed) summit of Dickey.

You can return from here by the way you came, but it is more fun to continue around the loop. With this in mind, stay on the trail down the backside of Dickey, descending on low-angle aprons of granite, carefully following the yellow blazes and cairns. This is the **Dickey Mountain Trail**. After a while you will find yourself walking along the top of a cliff with an unusual view across a deep basin back to the summits of Dickey and Welch. Eventually this fun stuff comes to an end, and you enter the woods and make your final descent on the pleasant trail, soon returning to the trailhead.

Approach: From Campton (exit 28, I-93), drive six miles on NH 49 toward Waterville Valley, and turn left on to Upper Mad River Road, before the entrance to Waterville Valley itself. At Orris Road (0.7 mile) turn right, reaching the trailhead parking area on the right at 1.3 miles.

Winter hiking on Dickey Mountain

Maps: Trail Map and Guide to the Sandwich Range Wilderness (WODC); Hiking Trails in the Waterville Valley Area (WVAIA); Crawford Notch-Sandwich Range (AMC); and New Hampshire Atlas & Gazetteer, p. 39

53 • Mount Tripyramid 4,180′

Rating: Strenuous and difficult
Time: 7 hours
Distance: 11-mile loop
Total climb: 2,900′
Location: Waterville Valley

Summary: North Peak's slide, a moderately angled slab of exposed bedrock, is one of New Hampshire's hardest hikes.

Waterville Valley is almost completely surrounded by mountains. This ring of peaks includes a number of 4,000'-ers: Mount Tecumseh, Mount Osceola and its East Peak, and last but by no means least, steep-sided Mount Tripyramid. The latter is so named because of the three highpoints along its narrow ridge. It offers a very challenging loop hike. Both the north (the highest point) and south summits have extensive slide sections. While the South Peak's slide is mostly scree (loose rock), the smooth rock of the long ramp which drops off the north summit is more intimidating; it is better ascended than descended. Since moving safely on this slab depends on good boot friction, it should not be attempted in rainy or snowy conditions.

From the parking area, walk 3.6 miles up **Livermore Road**, a beautifully maintained woods road, to the **North Slide Trail**. After a short passage through dense woods, you arrive at the base of the imposing **North Slide**. Take your time climbing up the slabs, and enjoy the view because there isn't much of one from the top. Under normal, dry conditions it takes about 30 minutes to ascend the slide. Exiting left at the top, you immediately reach the summit of **North Peak** (4,180') with its somewhat obscured views. Continue along the narrow and heavily wooded ridge to **Middle Peak** (4,140') and on to **South Peak** (4,090'). Note that South Peak does not satisfy the requirements for "offical" 4,000'-er status, as the connecting ridge with Middle Peak does not drop down low enough. From South Peak, descend the **South Slide**, staying right at the junction with the Sleeper Trail. The loose rock and scree of South Slide may be a little disconcerting, but most will find it to be easier and safer than the North Slide's relatively smooth slab. At the base of the slide, stay on South Slide Trail to Livermore Road, then head left and stroll back to the parking lot.

If you want to climb the North Peak but would like to avoid the North Slide, the recommended route is to climb South Peak via the

Mount Tripyramid, North Slide on the left James Bond aerial photo

descent route given above. Next, traverse the ridge over Middle to North Peak, before returning the way you came up, via the South Peak Slide.

A loop option (avoiding North Slide) would be to walk a little farther on Livermore Road to the Scaur Ridge Trail and then take Pine Bend Brook Trail on to the summit of North Peak; this bypasses North Slide. Continue across Middle Peak and on to South Peak as described above. Consult one of the detailed maps below for route planning.

Approach: From Waterville Valley Resort (exit 28, I-93 at Campton), drive through the resort area, following signs to the Livermore Road Trailhead.

Maps: Trail Map and Guide to the Sandwich Range Wilderness (WODC); Hiking Trails in the Waterville Valley Area (WVAIA); Crawford Notch-Sandwich Range (AMC); and New Hampshire Atlas & Gazetteer, p. 40

54 • Mount Potash 2,660′

Rating: Easy to moderate
Time: 3 hours
Distance: 4.4 miles
Total climb: 1,400′
Location: Kancamagus Highway, opposite the Passaconaway Campground and a few miles west of Mount Chocorua
Summary: Moderate climb on an interesting trail. Good views from the semi-open summit.

Potash is popular with families: not too long and not much steep climbing. However, two brief sections require caution where the trail runs along the top of very steep slabs. Starting from the parking area (set back from the highway), follow signs for the **Mount Potash Trail**. After negotiating a few sharp turns—all marked—the yellow-blazed trail settles down. Five minutes of easy walking brings you to a wide, shallow stream. There is no bridge, but if the water level isn't unduly high, it's not difficult to hop across on rocks. The trail now climbs moderately through a typical open forest of mixed tree species. Soon you cross a woods road, and after another ten minutes or so, you enter an area of beautiful spruce and hemlocks. Tree roots intertwined with the trail's coarse granite boulders provide a pleasant visual distraction as you climb steadily. After briefly leveling off, the trail abruptly comes out on top of a ledge that drops away steeply, giving you your first views. Mount Passaconaway (4,043') looms overhead. Faint yellow blazes lead the way, guiding you back into the woods for more rocks and roots. After another 15-20 minutes, with steep climbing in places, you once again emerge to views from the top of a south-facing ledge. The trail has now worked its way around to the back of the mountain, and the final ascent is on the south side. Climb up a ramp of granite, moving off it to the right for the final clamber to the ledgy summit.

Low spruces cluster here and there on the top, but there is a nice open feeling, and it's easy to see in most directions. Besides Passaconaway and Whiteface to the south, there is a good view of Carrigain and to the right and farther away, Mount Washington. Closer at hand, the forested landscape shows signs of logging activity here and there.

Mt. Carrigain from the summit of Mt. Potash

Also on the south side of the highway, about two miles farther east, is popular **Sabbaday Falls**. From the well-marked parking area an easy fifteen-minute walk brings you to picturesque chutes and basins scoured out of the granite bedrock.

Approach: From Conway, (NH 16) drive west on the Kancamagus Highway 13.5 miles. The trailhead parking area (sign for Downes Brook Trail) is in to the left (south side).

Maps: Trail Map and Guide to the Sandwich Range Wilderness (WODC); Crawford Notch-Sandwich Range (AMC); Trail Map and Guide to the White Mountain National Forest (DeLorme); and New Hampshire Atlas & Gazetteer, p. 44

55 • Mount Chocorua 3,475′

Rating: Moderately strenuous
Time: 6 hours 30 minutes
Distance: 9 miles
Total climb: 2,800′
Location: South of Conway

Summary: There are many routes on this favorite mountain, none of them easy. Great views from the wide-open summit.

Without a doubt Chocorua is one of the most popular mountains in New England and justifiably so. Its striking, rocky spire has been painted and photographed innumerable times. The route chosen here, the **Piper Trail**, is admittedly one of the longer trails but is also one of the more interesting. (See the comments below for a shorter route.) Beginning just off NH Route 16 on the mountain's east side, the Piper Trail starts out on easy terrain following an old logging road. Soon after crossing into the National Forest, the Weetamoo Trail branches left (at 0.8 mile), and at 1.4 miles, the Nickerson Ledge Trail leads off to the right. After climbing past a view towards Carter Ledge, the trail steepens and climbs in a switchbacking fashion reaching the steep spur trail (0.2 mile) up to **Camp Penacook** at 3.1 miles. The open shelter and tent platform together can accommodate 14-16 people. At this point, the glimpses through the trees of the rocky summit soaring high overhead are a little daunting, but carry on! Continuing now mostly on exposed bedrock—stone stairs lead the way—the trail leads steeply up to the summit ridge.

Head left along the ridge walking and climbing over open ledges to reach the top, 4.5 miles from your starting point. Although not above the natural tree line, Chocorua's large summit area is bare rock, and you are completely exposed to the elements. Remember that lightning storms are a particular hazard on warm summer afternoons. On the plus side, Chocorua's views are fantastic; it is near the entrance of Mount Washington Valley, and Mount Washington itself is 22 miles due north. Dozens and dozens of mountains can be seen. Immediately to the west of Mount Chocorua, the Sandwich Range leads away toward Waterville Valley. Descend the same way you came up, carefully checking signs to make sure you take the correct trail.

An optional route, one requiring less effort and time, is the **Champney Falls Trail**. This trail climbs 2,250 feet and is 3.8 miles

Approaching the summit of Chocorua
Richard Bailey

to the top. This trail begins from a large hiker parking lot on the Kancamagus Highway about ten miles west of Conway.

Approach: From Conway, drive south on NH 16 6.5 miles to the Davies Campground and General Store, and use the hiker parking area (WMNF) behind the store. There is a nominal parking fee.

Maps: Trail Map and Guide to the Sandwich Range Wilderness (WODC); White Mountains Hiking; Crawford Notch-Sandwich Range (AMC); and New Hampshire Atlas & Gazetteer, p. 40

56 • Mount Whiteface and Mount Passaconaway

Rating: Strenuous
Time: 8 hours
Distance: 12-mile loop
Location: A few miles north of Center Sandwich and just west of Mount Chocorua
Total climb: 3,800'
Summary: A varied trail leads to spectacular views of the Lakes Region. The loop over both summits is fairly demanding.

Mount Whiteface and Mount Passaconaway are often climbed together, although the ridge joining them dips 800' and is over two miles long. Perhaps the reason for pairing them is that there are no significant neighbors. The **Blueberry Ledge Trail** provides an exciting and challenging route up the south side of Mount Whiteface (4,020'), and the loop, including slightly higher Passaconaway (4,043'), is an excellent hike and a full day's work. From the hiker parking area, walk up **Ferncroft Road** and following signs, cross the river and pick up the trail. It climbs gently to moderately and reaches an open area (good views south) at 1.6 miles where the Blueberry Ledge Cutoff rejoins from the right. The trail is steeper from here onward but is always varied and enjoyable. After passing a fine lookout with views into the impressive basin between Passaconaway and Whiteface, the trail ascends a very narrow, steep ridge. The exciting finale up slabs and ramps ends at a spectacular viewpoint—the Lake Region is at your feet—just below the south summit of Whiteface.

Continue across the wooded main summit on the **Rollins Trail** and make the traverse over to Passaconaway (800'-descent) reaching **Dicey's Mill Trail** after 2.3 miles of somewhat rough up and down travel. Head left up Dicey's Mill Trail for 0.9 mile to the top of Mount Passaconaway. After locating the viewpoint just beyond the summit, return on Dicey's Mill Trail all the way back to Ferncroft Road, a distance of 4.3 miles. Dicey's Mill Trail is the standard ascent route for Mount Passaconaway from Ferncroft should you want to forgo Whiteface and do only Passaconaway. It should be noted that the **Wonalancet Out Door Club** (WODC),

Mount Whiteface from Ferncroft

spearheaded by local residents, very ably maintains the trails in this region. They produce an excellent topographic map of the area, referenced below.

Approach: From Center Sandwich, follow NH 113 and 113A north 10.7 miles to Wonalancet. Turn left on Ferncroft Road; the hiker parking area is 0.5 mile on the right.

Maps: Trail Map and Guide to the Sandwich Range Wilderness (WODC); Crawford Notch-Sandwich Range (AMC); and New Hampshire Atlas & Gazetteer, p. 40

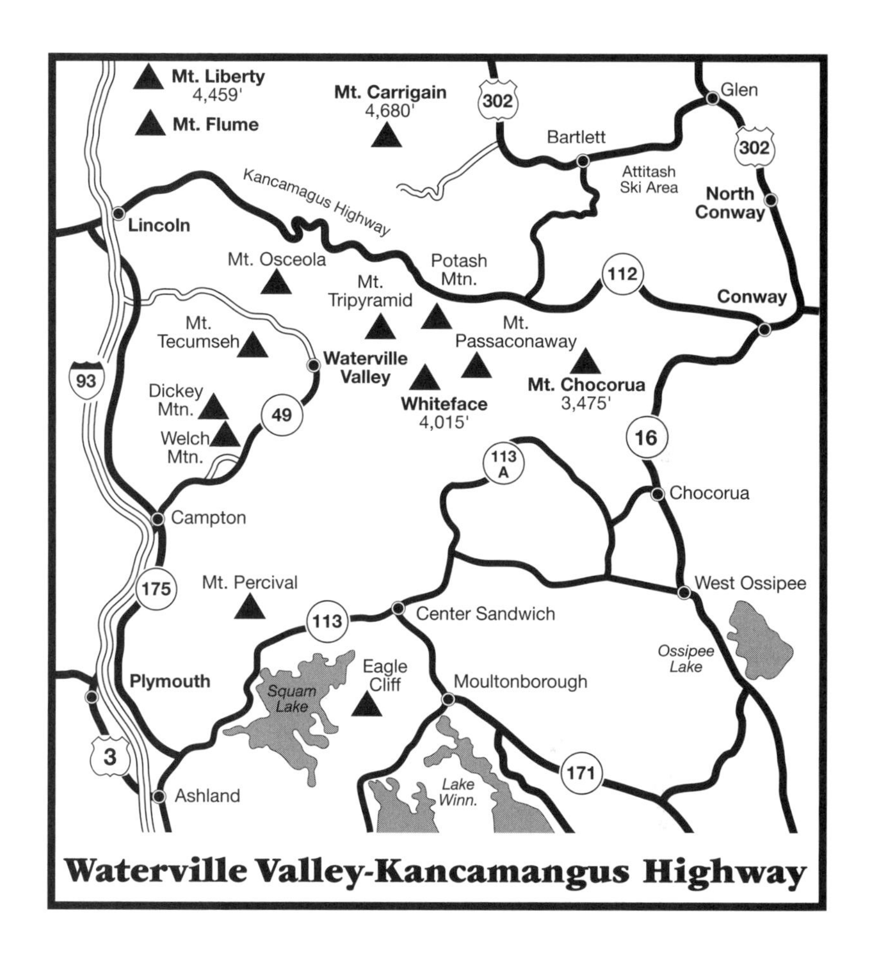

Photo left: Arethusa Falls

57 • Mount Moosilauke 4,802′

Rating: Strenuous
Time: 7 hours
Distance: 7.6 miles
Total climb: 3,100′
Location: About ten miles west of Lincoln and I-93
Summary: Steep climb along a rushing stream with unusual trail work. Summit is a huge, grassy dome.

Moosilauke's high, broad dome is easily recognized from many miles away. Standing somewhat isolated, it is the southern outpost of the White Mountain high summits; the first of the 4,000'-ers as you approach from the south. There are six routes up the mountain, from all sides, none of them easy. The Appalachian Trail (AT) traverses Moosilauke from south to north, and man-sized cairns mark its route across the expansive, grassy summit. Moosilauke is sacred turf for Dartmouth College, whose **Dartmouth Outing Club** (DOC) maintains the trails in these parts. Most of the college's activity is centered around **Ravine Lodge** on the east side of the mountain. Although a number of important hiking trails start from Ravine Lodge, the lodge itself is not open to the public.

Starting from **Kinsman's Notch**, the **Beaver Brook Trail** is an interesting, somewhat longer route (with less traffic) than the trails from Ravine Lodge. This trail is the AT heading south. It climbs steadily and at times very steeply along a plunging brook, with well-placed rungs and steps (wood blocks bolted to the rock) providing adequate foot and hand holds on the smooth slabs. After about one and a half hours you come to the 200' side trail (right) to Beaver Brook Shelter, where there is a view of distant Mount Washington. After cresting the main ridge, the trail contours across Mount Blue. Keep an eye out for raven acrobatics in wild Jobildunk Ravine, which drops away to your left. The final ten minutes of walking are across Moosilauke's open summit; follow the large cairns. Not surprisingly, the view is a full panorama. A partial run down would be that it sweeps from Mount Washington and the Presidential Range to the nearer Franconia Notch area to the low mountains along the Connecticut River, before presenting you with a huge chunk of the Vermont landscape.

Since there are a number of trails converging on the summit, use care when you start your descent: head north on the white-blazed

Beaver Brook Trail in winter Laurie Caswell

Appalachian Trail, again following the procession of huge cairns across the summit plateau.

Approach: Approaching from the east, follow NH 112 west from North Woodstock/Lincoln (I-93, exit 32) to Kinsman Notch and the trailhead. From the west, from North Haverhill, take NH 116, then NH 112 to Kinsman Notch.

Maps: Moosilauke-Kinsman (AMC); Vermont-New Hampshire Hiking; Outdoor Map of New Hampshire (Topaz); and New Hampshire Atlas & Gazetteer, p. 43

58 • Lonesome Lake

Rating: Easy to moderate
Time: 2.5 hours
Distance: 3.4 miles
Total climb: 1,000′
Location: Franconia Notch
Summary: Moderate climb to a mountain lake and an Appalachian Mountain Club hut.

One could argue that Franconia Notch is home to New Hampshire's most exciting, most alpine, and most dynamic landscape. While the summits here are not as high as the Presidentials, their slide-scarred flanks soar skyward more steeply. As far as actual cliffs are concerned, Cannon Cliff's thousand vertical feet of granite is unequaled in New Hampshire, in fact in the Northeast. The next hike description covers the showcase hike of the Notch, the Franconia Ridge Traverse.

This description covers the immensely popular hike to Lonesome Lake. Since it's only 1.5 miles to the lake and 0.2 mile on to the AMC's **Lonesome Lake Hut** (open to the public during the hiking season), this trip is great for families. The pleasantly graded path, the **Lonesome Lake Trail**, begins at **Lafayette Place Campground**. Although not reached without a fair amount of climbing (1,000'), the lake and hut are adequate reward for your effort. The views across Franconia Notch are among the best mountain views in New Hampshire, especially late in the fall. An 0.8-mile loop trail (soggy along the west side) traces the shoreline, giving more views over to Franconia Ridge. Descend the way you came up, by the Lonesome Lake Trail.

For those who want to climb **Cannon Mountain**, continue on Lonesome Lake Trail, which ends at **Kinsman Ridge Trail** after one mile. Here, bear right, and continue over steep, rather difficult terrain to the summit (2 miles from the lake) with its observation deck and superb views. The top of the ski area and tram are just below. Return by the same route, or continue on the Kinsman Ridge Trail and descend to the Cannon Tramway parking area.

Approach: From Lincoln, (exit 32) continue north for 8 miles on I-93 to Lafayette Place. From the north, Lafayette Place is two miles south of Cannon Mountain Ski Area.

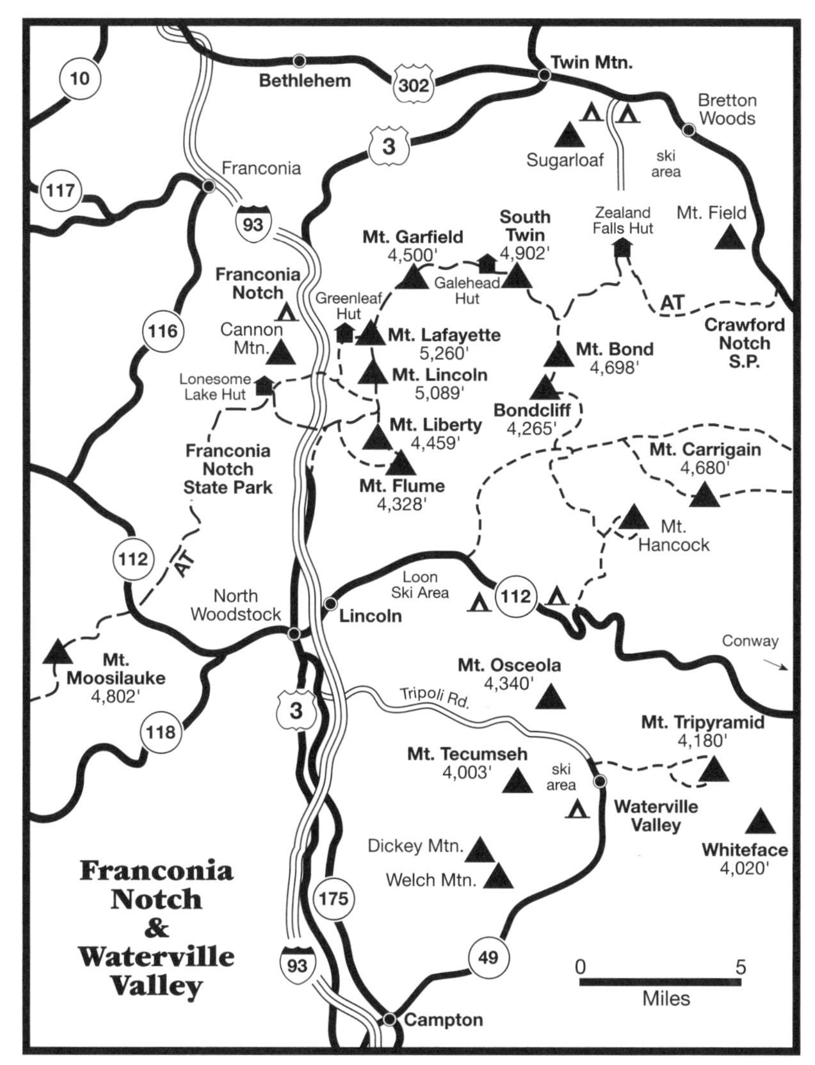

Maps: White Mountains Hiking; Moosilauke-Kinsman (AMC); Trail Map & Guide to the White Mountain National Forest (DeLorme); and New Hampshire Atlas and Gazetteer, p. 43

59 • Franconia Ridge Traverse

Rating: Strenuous; alot of climbing
Time: 7 hours
Distance: 9-mile loop
Total climb: 3,850′
Location: Franconia Notch

Summary: A long climb to an exciting, alpine-style ridge. Steep descent off Mount Lafayette past Greenleaf Hut.

This may be it, the best hike in the East! While never difficult in a technical sense, this route has you on steep slopes the entire time, climbing, traversing, and descending. It's a wonderful introduction to the alpine world. Start walking from the parking area at **Lafayette Place**, and staying to the right, pick up the **Falling Waters Trail**. It winds upward alongside a stream, crossing and re-crossing it and passing several small waterfalls. On the upper section of the steep mountainside, you pass through a typical dense spruce-balsam forest before reaching tree line, just below the summit of **Little Haystack** (4,760') at 3.2 miles. With the serious climbing under your belt, so to speak, you can now enjoy this fantastic ridge as you continue toward the trip's high point, Mount Lafayette (5,260').

Approaching the summit of Mount Lafayette

Franconia Ridge from Mt. Lincoln Robert Kozlow

The next 1.7-mile stretch is the best part of the circuit. Head north (left) along the mostly open ridge on the white-blazed **Appalachian Trail**, reaching the top of **Mount Lincoln** (5,089') at 3.9 miles from the highway. The ridge is high and narrow (but not precariously so) with long, very steep slopes on either side, especially to the west. The views down into Franconia Notch on your left and into the Pemigewasset Basin on your right are stunning, but with these fine open views comes exposure to the elements. You are entirely out in the open except for some shrubby growth south of Lafayette's summit. Do not venture out on the ridge if the weather is threatening, as there is no feasible escape route from the middle of the ridge. From Lincoln's summit, the trail drops down about a hundred feet, traverses easy terrain, and after passing through a brief pocket of spruce, completes the final 400'-climb to the bare summit of **Mount Lafayette**.

Once on top of Lafayette (at 5 miles), rocks and an old stone foundation provide good places to sit and relax, as well as protection from the breeze, if needed. After resting and taking in the view, descend on the **Greenleaf Trail** (not the AT) as it heads left (west) off the summit. Marked with cairns, it drops down steep,

Franconia Range and Lonesome Lake Robert Kozlow

open slopes 1.1 miles to **Greenleaf Hut** at the tree line. This charming alpine refuge is maintained by a "croo" from the AMC and during the season offers snacks for day hikers as well as full meals and lodging. Reservations are required for overnight stays—call the AMC at Pinkham Notch.

From the hut, follow **Old Bridle Path** down a narrow and rather precipitous ridge. There are occasional exciting views into wild, inhospitable Walker Ravine with Franconia Ridge looming high overhead. The angle gradually slackens as the hike eases to a close, rejoining Falling Waters Trail just above Lafayette Place. Because of its accessibility and appeal, there are hikers on the ridge most days of the year. The circuit is done in either direction.

Approach: From Lincoln, (I-93, exit 32) continue north 8 miles on I-93/US 3 to the Lafayette Place parking areas. From Cannon Mountain Ski Area in Franconia Notch, drive south two miles.

Maps: Moosilauke-Kinsman (AMC); White Mountains Hiking; Trail Map & Guide to the White Mountain National Forest (DeLorme); and New Hampshire Atlas and Gazetteer, p. 43

Photo right: Aerial view of Franconia Notch & Franconia Ridge James Bond

Franconia Notch Attractions

Franconia Notch has been a tourist destination for many years. In fact, when Thomas Jefferson was president, his likeness with the Old Man of the Mountain was noted. While Franconia Notch's various rock and stream formations easily justify a visit, it is the mountain grandeur of the place that makes the strongest impression. Soaring mountainsides crowd together, leaving little room for passage along the valley floor. Think of it as a Swiss Alp sampler; it is home to some of the most spectacular hiking in the East.

The "Old Man of the Mountain" is the most famous natural feature in the Notch and the New Hampshire state symbol. The 40'-high craggy face can be seen from Profile Lake, just south of Cannon Mountain Ski Area. (Note: The Old Man is no more! On May 3, 2003, the rocks forming the face broke loose from the cliff.) The Flume is an 800'-long gorge, fed by a gushing waterfall. A system of boardwalks allows for close-up viewing. The Basin is a 30-foot wide pothole, scoured out of smooth granite. It takes only a few minutes to walk down to it. The Park provides an excellent topographic map (free) showing all the trails.

60 • Franconia Notch to Crawford Notch

Rating: Strenuous
Time: 2 to 3 days
Distance: 21 miles
Total climb: about 7,000'
Location: Franconia Notch to Crawford Notch

Summary: One of the most rugged and spectacular sections of the entire Appalachian Trail. The AMC's Greenleaf, Galehead, and Zealand Falls Huts dot the route.

The 21-mile traverse from Franconia Notch that skirts the northern edge of the Pemigewasset Basin—along the Garfield and Twin Ranges—is one of three big traverses in the White Mountains. Although less exposed to wind and weather than the Presidential Range Traverse (Hike #69), it seems to be perceived as more demanding and is not often attempted as a one-day hike. As a multi-day trip it serves as great training for longer expeditions. Its final portion coincides with the Bond Traverse (Hike #62).

From **Lafayette Place** in Franconia Notch, make the steep climb on the **Old Bridle Path** to **Greenleaf Hut**, a distance of 2.9 miles. Spending the night here makes good sense if you started late in the day or if you plan to use three days for the trip. A short way past the hut, the route (now the Greenleaf Trail) climbs out of the trees and works its way up steep, spectacularly open slopes to the summit of **Mount Lafayette** (5,260'). The views from here are among the best: across Franconia Notch to the Kinsmans and Cannon Cliff, south along Franconia Ridge (see photo), and across the Pemigewasset Basin to the Bonds.

From here to Zealand Falls Hut you are on the white-blazed **Appalachian Trail**. Head north along the Garfield Ridge Trail as it arcs east across the narrow Garfield Range, grazing the summit of **Mount Garfield** (4,500'), before descending steeply toward Galehead Hut. It is 7.7 miles between these two huts. From the hut, a very steep climb (0.8 mile) on **Twinway** leads to the open summit of **South Twin** (4,902'). Fantastic views here! The Twinway trail then runs across a broad, plateau-like ridge to **Mount Guyot** (4,580')—the Bondcliff Trail comes in from right just below the summit. (From here down to Zealand Hut, the Bond Traverse coincides with this route.) Descend off the main ridge, passing the 0.1-mile spur trail (left) to viewless **Zealand Mountain** (one of the

Galehead Hut Robert Kozlow

least interesting of the 4,000' peaks), before coming to the short side trail (right) to the **Zeacliff** overlook—very noteworthy indeed! Views of the Pemi region and across to Mount Carrigain are outstanding (see photo, Hike #65). From here descend through a fine woods to **Zealand Falls Hut**. It is seven rugged miles from Galehead to Zealand Hut.

At the trail junction 0.2-mile below Zealand Hut, several options present themselves. The **Zealand Trail** brings you to the **Zealand Road** trailhead in 2.6 miles; from here it is another 3.5 miles to Route 302. Alternatively, a combination of the Zealand, A-Z, and Avalon Trails brings you to **Crawford Notch** in 6.1 miles. Call the AMC at Pinkham Notch to make hut reservations.

Approach: From Lafayette Place, two miles south of the Cannon Mountain Ski Area exit, in Franconia Notch.

Maps: Franconia-Pemigewasset (AMC); Trail Map & Guide to the White Mountain National Forest (DeLorme); and New Hampshire Atlas and Gazetteer, p. 43-44

61 • Mount Garfield 4,500′

Rating: Moderately strenuous
Time: 6 hours 30 minutes
Distance: 10 miles
Location: East of Franconia Notch, and south of Twin Mountain
Total climb: 3,100′
Summary: Unique views of the Pemigewasset Wilderness, the Bonds and Franconia Ridge from an isolated, rocky summit.

Mount Garfield is the somewhat bulky, prominent peak on the ridge—called the Garfield Ridge—that runs east from Mount Lafayette to North and South Twin. Its sharp, rocky summit offers dramatic views south down into the basin of the **Pemigewasset Wilderness**. To the west, the eye is drawn upward to higher Mount Lafayette and the Franconia Ridge, while to the east, the Bonds and the Twin Range further define this interesting vantage point. The summit feeling on Garfield is similar to that on Mount Haystack in the Adirondack High Peaks: you on a pointed summit with the mountain falling away at your feet, yet nearby, higher summits loom overhead.

From the parking area, the **Garfield Trail** climbs gently through a mixed forest, but it steepens just before reaching the **Garfield Ridge Trail** (which is the Appalachian Trail) at 4.8 miles. Upon reaching the AT head right—the left fork leads to Galehead Hut—and climb quite steeply to the dramatic, open summit at about five miles from the car. An old stone foundation provides good protection from the wind. Hopefully the weather and clouds will cooperate, and you will be able to fully appreciate the complex mountain scene before you. To descend, use the route you came up.

Approach: From Franconia Notch, drive six miles north on US 3 and turn right on Gale River Loop Road. The parking area is on the left at 1.2 miles. WMNF fee area.

Maps: Moosilauke-Kinsman (AMC); Trail Map & Guide to the White Mountain National Forest (DeLorme); and New Hampshire Atlas and Gazetteer, p. 43

Aerial view of Mount Garfield James Bond

Nearby **South Twin** (4,902') is also a classic. It is covered briefly in the previous hike description. To do it as a day hike, take the **Gale River Trail.** (The trailhead is located 1.6 miles in on Gale River Road which branches off US 3, 5.5 miles north of the Franconia Notch exit of I-93.) When you reach the Appalachian Trail, head left to Galehead Hut, 4.6 miles from your starting point. From the hut the AT climbs very steeply for 0.8 mile to the open summit of South Twin. The panoramic view takes in Franconia Ridge, the Pemigewasset Basin, Mount Garfield, the Bonds, North Twin, and in the distance, Carrigain and the Presidential Range. Energetic souls can do four (or more) 4,000' summits on this trip. North Twin (4,761') is about a mile to the north over fairly easy terrain, and Galehead Mountain (4,024') is located about 15-20 minutes from Galehead Hut on a spur trail. If you include Mount Garfield on this ambitious program, you have four summits.

62 • Traverse of the Bonds

Rating: Strenuous
Time: 2 days
Distance: 20 miles
Total climb: 3,700′
Location: Eastern rim of the Pemigewasset Wilderness basin, between Zealand Notch and the Kancamagus Highway
Summary: A high ridge walk in a wilderness region. Remote and exposed with unusual views of the alpine landscape.

This route can be done in either direction; it is presented here from north to south. More remote than the Presidential Traverse (#69) or the Franconia-Crawford Notch Traverse (#60), much of the trail is rougher, and there are no huts conveniently placed along the way.

From the **Zealand Road** trailhead, hike over easy terrain on mellow **Zealand Trail** to **Zealand Falls Hut**, a distance of 2.8 miles. From the hut, continue on **Twinway** (AT, white-blazed) to **Zeacliff** at 1.3 miles. Here a short spur trail leads left to one of the best views in the White Mountains, a huge swath of the Pemigewasset Wilderness, including majestic Mount Carrigain and Carrigain Notch. After passing the spur trail to Zealand Mountain three miles from Zealand Hut, you reach the flatish summit of **Mount Guyot** (4,580'). Just beyond, the Bondcliff Trail heads left (south) from Twinway.

Leaving the Appalachian Trail/Twinway, walk south on the **Bondcliff Trail** descending over open, moderate terrain. After about a half mile, a 0.2-mile spur trail leads left to the **Guyot Campsite** and its open log shelter. Since you have done most of the climbing by now, this is a good spot to camp. Returning to Bondcliff Trail, it is 0.2 mile to the 0.5-mile side trail (right) to **West Bond** (4,540')—a mandatory digression for serious peakbaggers! **Mount Bond** (4,698') is another 0.6 mile south along Bondcliff Trail. From the open summit of Bond, the lower summit of **Bondcliff** (4,265') is quite prominent. It takes about 30 minutes to make the descent and traverse over to Bondcliff's spectacular clifftop summit. See the photo at right.

Initially, the trail descends steeply from Bondcliff, reaching the **Wilderness Trail** after 4.4 miles and a drop of 2,650 feet. You have now descended to the East Branch of the Pemigewasset River, and it is an easy, somewhat monotonous, 4.7-mile march (the remain-

On Bondcliff
Robert Kozlow

ing descent is only 450') to the trailhead at **Lincoln Woods** on the **Kancamagus Highway**. On a warm day, making the short side trip to take a dip at Franconia Falls (about three miles before you reach Lincoln Woods) is a refreshing diversion.

This trip gives you the opportunity to climb four 4,000-footers: Zealand, West Bond, Mount Bond, and Bondcliff.

Approach: From Twin Mountain, north of Franconia Notch, drive east 2.3 miles on US 302 to Zealand Road, turn right and continue 3.5 miles to the end of the road and the trailhead. The southern trailhead is Lincoln Woods, four miles east of Lincoln.

Maps: Franconia-Pemigewasset (AMC); Trail Map & Guide to the White Mountain National Forest (DeLorme); and New Hampshire Atlas & Gazetteer, p. 43-44

63 • Middle Sugarloaf 2,539'

Rating: Easy
Time: 2 hours
Distance: 2.8 miles
Total climb: 900'
Location: In Twin Mountain, off Zealand Road, just south of US 302
Summary: Excellent views of the Presidential Range from this very accessible summit.

Thanks to a forest fire many years ago, Middle Sugarloaf and North Sugarloaf are both bare summits and thus offer great views. Starting out quite gently from Zealand Road, the Sugarloaf Trail soon steepens before attaining the col between North and Middle Sugarloaf. Trails lead to each summit. Since the view is better from Middle Sugarloaf, head left, making the final push to the top for a total climb of about 900'. The final section is quite steep. From the top, you can see most of the Presidential Range, even Mount Adams, far to the north. Somewhat lower North Sugarloaf (2,310') gives a different perspective, and the short jog over and back adds about 0.6 mile to the round trip. The trail to North Sugarloaf crosses a pegmatite dike where large quartz and mica crystals may be collected. Both North and Middle Sugarloaf are quite prominent from US 302 in the Twin Mountain area.

Approach: The trailhead is one mile in on Zealand Road. Zealand Road runs south from US Route 302, at the USFS Zealand Campground, 2.3 miles east of Twin Mountain.

Maps: Trail Map & Guide to the White Mountain National Forest (DeLorme) and New Hampshire Atlas and Gazetteer, p. 44

On Sugarloaf   Ned Therrien

Hiker facilities at Crawford Notch

Reminders from bygone days, the picturesque old train depot known as Crawford's and another historic structure now known as the **Crawford Notch Hostel** serve hikers and other visitors to the area. The buildings are located four miles east of Bretton Woods on US 302 at the height of land in Crawford Notch. During hiking season the depot is a staffed information center; you can buy maps, books, and snacks. The nearby hostel provides basic accommodation year-round. The two bunkrooms have space for 24 and guests bring their own sleeping bags and food. Cooking is a do-it-yourself affair in the hostel's kitchen.

The **AMC Hiker Shuttle** services the area, making it convenient to do long one-way hikes to or from Crawford. For example, you could start hiking from Pinkham Notch or Appalachia and do a several-day traverse of the Presidentials ending at Crawford Notch. You could then use the Shuttle to bring you back to your starting point. For the shuttle schedule contact the Appalachian Mountain Club at Pinkham Notch.

64 • Mount Willard 2,850'

Rating: Easy
Time: 1 hour 30 minutes
Distance: 2.8 miles
Total climb: 925'
Location: Crawford Notch

Summary: A gentle climb terminates abruptly on top of a major cliff with breathtaking views of the valley far below.

Looking for a short hike on easy terrain that leads to a dramatic view? Mount Willard may be your best bet. It is also a great stretch-your-legs hike if you are just driving through the area. Even serious hikers should do this one because among New England's "notches", Crawford Notch is unique. The notch itself is quite narrow, with barely enough room for the two-lane highway and railroad line to squeeze between rock buttresses. What makes this notch one of a kind, however, is the transition of the valley floor. From the (north)west, the approach is a gentle climb across a high, broad valley, but as soon as you pass through the portal, you plunge steeply over a headwall and drop 600' into a textbook example of a U-shaped glacial valley. Having a look at this is what the Mount Willard hike is all about.

From Crawford's, start on the **Avalon Trail**, but branch left after only 0.1 mile on the **Mount Willard Trail** which leads—at times along the remnants of an old carriage road—to the clifftop ledges high above Crawford Notch. From here, both the highway along the valley floor and the railroad part way up Mount Willey's flank highlight the great glacial trough that winds away to the southeast. The Saco River drains this valley. Use care at the edge—the sloping ledges can give a false sense of security. Stay well away from the edge, as there is no protection from the drop-off, and be especially careful with small children. Return by the same route.

Approach: Park at Crawford Notch at "Crawford's", the renovated train depot, once again in use by the North Conway Scenic RR and the AMC. Crawford Notch is on US 302, nine miles west of Twin Mountain.

Maps: Crawford Notch State Park map (free); White Mountains Hiking; Crawford Notch-Sandwich Range (AMC); Trail Map & Guide to the White Mountain National Forest; and New Hampshire Atlas and Gazetteer, p. 44

Crawford Notch's glacial valley as seen from Mount Willard

Appalachian Mountain Club

The Appalachian Mountain Club, the "AMC", is the primary hiker organization in the Northeast. Its 80,000 members make it the largest predominately hiker organization in the U.S. It is a recreation and conservation group whose activities include canoeing, backcountry skiing, rock climbing, and biking. The AMC offers classes in outdoor activities ranging from introductory camping to mountain leadership skills. Regional chapters oversee the maintanence of about 1,200 miles of Maine and New Hampshire trails. Open to the public and conveniently spaced along the Appalachian Trail in New Hampshire, the AMC's eight alpine-style huts provide shelter, bunks, and meals. The Club's **Pinkham Notch Visitor Center** (Pinkham Notch Camp), at the base of Mount Washington's Tuckerman Ravine, is a hiker's mecca: A classic starting point for hikers, ice climbers and spring skiers. By joining the AMC—or another hiking organization—you participate in the stewardship of our natural areas and help foster environmentally sound recreation activities.

65 • Mount Carrigain 4,680'

Rating: Moderately strenuous
Time: 7 hours
Distance: 10 miles
Total climb: 3,250'
Location: South of Crawford Notch
Summary: A high, remote mountain. Most of the major White Mountain peaks can be seen from its summit.

Located on the eastern edge of the Pemigewasset Wilderness, between Crawford Notch and the Kancamagus Highway, Mount Carrigain is a fairly remote mountain. Its long, forested approach is reminiscent of some of the Adirondack High Peak climbs. Although not terribly far in—about five miles—there is a definite feeling of isolation and remoteness about Carrigain. The summit observation platform gets you above the low rim of trees, and you can study the panoramic views to your heart's content. Most of New Hampshire's 4,000' summits can be picked out.

From the parking area on **Sawyer River Road**, the **Signal Ridge Trail** starts out along a rushing stream (great for cooling off on a hot day), crosses a grassy logging road at 1.4 miles and meets the Carrigain Notch Trail after 1.7 miles. Continue straight on Signal Ridge Trail, passing through a swampy area. A long, steady climb soon gets underway. There are good intermittent views, especially when the leaves are off the trees. At 4.5 miles, the trail surmounts Signal Ridge just below the summit. The top is now in plain view, only a half mile away. The final steep climb is in a dense spruce-balsam woods. Climb the low observation platform for the unobstructed view. Descend by the same route.

An interesting and somewhat longer descent route is to follow the **Desolation Trail** (northwest) off the summit. This descends steeply, at times extremely so—although with generally quite good footing—to a trail junction with the Carrigain Notch Trail. From here there are several options, but the logical way back to Sawyer River Road is to head right on Carrigain Notch Trail. (Note: Heading right on **Carrigain Notch Trail** soon brings you to Stillwater Junction where you have two options: The Wilderness Trail leads toward the Kancamagus Highway, and the Shoal Pond Trail heads north to the Zealand area.) Carrigain Notch Trail climbs very gradually into Carrigain Notch, before descending equally benignly, returning you to the Signal Ridge Trail. Now head left and return to your car. This variation adds a total of 3.5

Mount Carrigain & Carrigain Notch Ed Rolfe

miles and 2 hours to the trip. The accompanying photo shows the terrain covered by the alternate descent route. In the photo above, Carrigain Notch is the deep depression to the left of Carrigain's summit.

Approach: From North Conway, drive to Bartlett (on US 302) and continue 3.7 miles to Sawyer Road, on the left. Follow Sawyer Road 2 miles to the trailhead parking area, on the left.

Maps: Crawford Notch-Sandwich Range (AMC); Trail Map & Guide to the White Mountain National Forest (DeLorme); and New Hampshire Atlas and Gazetteer, p. 44

The Presidential Range

Northernmost of New Hampshire's hiking areas, the Presidential Range rises majestically above its surroundings, dominating the landscape. High and exposed, the Range has the most extensive above-tree line region in the eastern United States, exciting stuff for East Coast dwellers. However, with the high, open terrain comes full exposure to the elements. This is not to be taken lightly: strong winds are commonplace, and the weather here can be life threatening, even in summer. Its four main summits are one to two thousand feet higher than other mountains in the area. Bounded on the south by **Crawford Notch** and Route 302, the range begins as three ridges which converge just south of **Mount Washington** (6,288'). North of Washington's barren summit cone, the ridge is high and narrow with steep flanks falling away on either side. Continuing northward, **Mount Jefferson** (5,712') comes next, then **Mount Adams** (5,774'), and lastly **Mount Madison** (5,367'). From Madison the terrain drops away 4,000' on three sides. This 6-mile ridge, from Washington to Madison, is one of the great walks of the eastern U.S.

The **Appalachian Trail** runs along the entire ridgeline. From its starting point in Crawford Notch, it gains almost 5,000 vertical feet on its ascent of Mount Washington. Along the way, ten side trails work their way up the glaciated flanks: some follow ravines or sharp ridges, while others ascend precipitous cirque headwalls. This is a hiker's eldorado and has been for over 100 years. Most of the trails here, Crawford Path, Caps Ridge, Gulfside, Six Husbands, Valley Way, Lowe's Path, Air Line, Tuckerman Ravine, to name a few, are among the great classics in New Hampshire. Three Appalachian Mountain Club huts lie on or near the AT in the Presidentials, providing the option for a more "civilized" traverse of the Range. In addition to these full-service huts, the Randolph Mountain Club maintains two self-service cabins high on the west flank of Mount Adams.

The definitive map of the Presidential Range is "Mount Washington and the Heart of the Presidential Range" by Bradford Washburn and published by the AMC and the Museum of Science (1:20 000 scale, 50 feet contours).

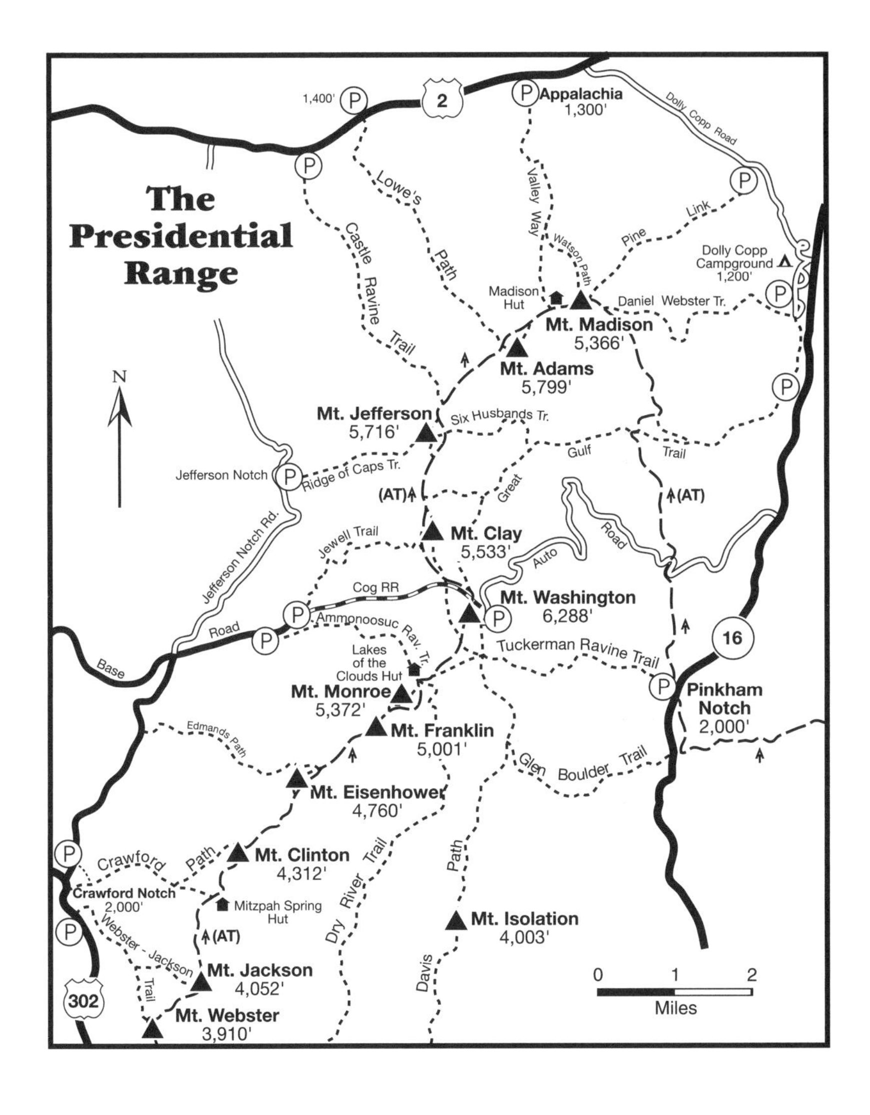
The Presidential Range
1,400'
2
Appalachia
1,300'
Dolly Copp Road
Lowe's Path
Castle Ravine Trail
Valley Way
Watson Path
Pine Link
Dolly Copp Campground 1,200'
Madison Hut
Mt. Madison
5,366'
Daniel Webster Tr.
Mt. Adams
5,799'
N
Mt. Jefferson
5,716'
Six Husbands Tr.
Gulf
Trail
Jefferson Notch
Ridge of Caps Tr.
Great
(AT)
Jefferson Notch Rd.
Mt. Clay
5,533'
Jewell Trail
Road
Auto
Cog RR
Mt. Washington
6,288'
Ammonoosuc Rav. Tr.
Road
Base
Lakes of the Clouds Hut
Tuckerman Ravine Trail
16
Mt. Monroe
5,372'
Pinkham Notch
2,000'
Edmands Path
Mt. Franklin
5,001'
Glen Boulder Trail
Mt. Eisenhower
4,760'
Crawford Path
Mt. Clinton
4,312'
Dry River Trail
Davis Path
Crawford Notch
2,000'
Mitzpah Spring Hut
Webster - Jackson Trail
Mt. Isolation
4,003'
Mt. Jackson
4,052'
302
Mt. Webster
3,910'
0
1
2
Miles

66 • Webster Cliff

Rating: Moderately strenuous
Time: 5 hours
Distance: 6.6 miles (short version)
Total climb: 2,700′
Location: East of Crawford Notch

Summary: A steep section of the Appalachian Trail yields a cliff-edge walk with views of Crawford Notch far below.

The dramatic glacial valley that flows south from Crawford Notch is cradled between Mount Willey on the west and Mount Webster on the east. Both mountain flanks are extremely steep, with Webster the more precipitous of the two (see photo at right). The hike described here gains the long ridge of Webster on relatively easy, although very steep terrain and then climbs along the semi-open ridgeline, providing some of the more exciting views in the White Mountains.

From the highway, the **Webster Cliff Trail** (it is also the Appalachian Trail) ascends the very steep south side of Mount Webster, reaching the first good viewpoint at 1.8 miles. The trail then works its way up and along the top of Webster Cliff with breathtaking views down into Crawford Notch and across to the Willey Range. You reach the rocky summit of **Mount Webster** (3,910') at 3.3 miles. From here the open summit of Mount Jackson (4,052') is an optional, and generally easy, 1.4 miles farther. Beyond **Mount Jackson**, the Webster Cliff Trail continues to **Mizpah Spring Hut** at 5.7 miles.

Most hikers descend the way they came up, but it is also possible to descend directly to Crawford Notch. Two options present themselves. From the summit of Webster, continue only a few minutes—0.1 mile—on the Webster Cliff Trail, where the **Webster-Jackson Trail** comes in from the left. Descend on this (the Webster arm) 2.4 miles to Crawford Notch. Alternatively, continue on Webster Cliff Trail to the summit of Jackson where there are close up views of Mount Washington. From here drop down the Jackson arm of the Webster-Jackson Trail, arriving in **Crawford Notch** after 2.6 miles. From Crawford Notch it is then four miles along Route 302 back to your car. Arrange transportation or plan to take the AMC Shuttle for this segment.

Webster Cliff from Route 302 in Crawford Notch

Approach: Trailhead parking is on US 302, four miles south of Crawford Notch and one mile south of the Willey House Recreation area. Crawford Notch is between Bretton Woods and Bartlett.

Maps: White Mountains Hiking; Presidential Range (AMC); and Trail Map and Guide to the White Mountain National Forest.

67 • Mount Eisenhower 4,760'

Rating: Moderate
Time: 5 hours
Distance: 6.6 miles
Location: Bretton Woods, just north of Crawford Notch
Total climb: 2,800'
Summary: A classic trail leads to a panoramic view. Mount Washington is only three miles away.

When viewed from Route 302 in Bretton Woods, Mount Eisenhower is a graceful, rounded peak, the most distinctive of the chain of summits that runs south from Mount Washington. While the Appalachian Trail (here Crawford Path) traverses Eisenhower from north to south, passing just below the summit, the route described here is more direct. It starts from **Mount Clinton Road**, a few miles north of Crawford Notch. From the parking area, climb on historic **Edmands Path** as it ascends moderately, passing the tree line at 2.8 miles. With its constant angle of ascent and careful stone paving and cribbing, graceful Edmands Path does a great job of taking the effort out of the climb. At 3 miles, bear right on **Eisenhower Loop** and scramble up ledges to the top, at 3.3 miles. From the grassy, wide-open summit dome, only the mass of Mount Washington interrupts the sweep of the panorama; it looms three miles away as the raven flies. Return by the same route.

An interesting and somewhat ambitious **variation** on this trip is to head north on **Crawford Path** after topping out on Eisenhower. From the summit descend Eisenhower Loop, but instead of heading left on Edmands Path, pick up Crawford Path and head north on the main ridge over relatively easy terrain to the foot of **Mount Monroe** (5,372'). Along the way you pass over a bump on the ridge known as Mount Franklin (5,004'). Climbing Monroe is optional, but definitely worth the trouble. Monroe Loop traverses the summit, Crawford Path bypasses it. The two trails rejoin just above **Lakes of the Clouds Hut**. From the hut, descend on the **Ammonoosuc Ravine Trail** to Base Road (the Cog Railway access road). From the top of Mount Eisenhower to Lakes of the Clouds Hut it is 2.4 miles and it's another 3.1 miles to the trailhead on Base Road, via the Ammonoosuc Ravine Trail.

Mount Eisenhower from Bretton Woods

Approach: From Bretton Woods, take Base Road (toward the Cog Railway) as far as Mt. Clinton Road. Turn right and continue for 1.3 miles to the trailhead.

Maps: Mount Washington and the Heart of the Presidential Range (AMC/Museum of Science); White Mountains Hiking; Presidential Range (AMC); and Trail Map and Guide to the White Mountain National Forest (DeLorme)

68 • Mount Washington 6,288′

Rating: Strenuous
Time: 7-8 hours
Distance: 9 miles
Total climb: 3,800′
Location: Near Bretton Woods, just south of the Cog Railway

Summary: The trail leads past a waterfall and up some extremely steep terrain to an alpine hut just above tree line. Mt. Washington's barren summit cone rises another 1,000′ into the arctic-alpine zone.

The **Ammonoosuc Ravine Trail**, together with a section of Crawford Path, is the classic route up Mount Washington from the west. This interesting trail climbs—at times seemingly straight up—to the Lakes of the Clouds Hut at 5,010', just above the tree line. After a gradual but rather rocky beginning, the trail climbs more briskly and reaches the cascades at attractive **Gem Pool** after 2.1 miles. From this point on, the trail is extremely steep in places, but the footing is good and there is usually something to hang on to. You pass several viewpoints, followed by stream crossings on rock slabs, before emerging from the woods just below the hut. At the level of the hut (3.1 miles), you are in a treeless arctic world of rocks and wind. **Lakes of the Clouds Hut** is open to the public; for overnight accommodations, contact the AMC at Pinkham Notch.

Take a moment to evaluate the weather before continuing. Nearby Mount Monroe (5,372') can be a good alternative to Washington if the weather looks like it may not hold or if a shorter hike is preferable. It is only 0.4 mile to the top of Monroe from the hut. To your left, the summit of Mount Washington beckons, 1.4 miles away and 1,260' higher. Head north on **Crawford Path** (and the white-blazed Appalachian Trail) and stay on it to the top. This will take about an hour. At the beginning of the final, rocky climb up the barren summit cone, Davis Path enters from the right, and immediately thereafter the Westside Trail enters from the left. Follow signs for Crawford Path to the top.

The summit is a busy place during summer! The historic Cog Railway reaches the summit from the west, while the popular Auto Road arrives from the east side. A cafeteria, a souvenir shop, a museum, and a meteorological station are housed in the fortress-like building on the top. Be sure to climb up onto the observation deck to get the least obstructed view. When you are ready to descend, use care to pick up the same trail you used on the way up. You don't want to head down the wrong side of this big mountain.

Lakes of the Clouds Hut and Mount Washington summit

Approach: From Bretton Woods on US 302, follow Base Road (the Mount Washington Cog Railway access road) 5.5 miles to the large parking lot on the right.

Maps: Mount Washington and the Heart of the Presidential Range (AMC/Museum of Science); Presidential Range (AMC); White Mountains Hiking; and Mount Washington Close-up Map

Mount Monroe variation: Once you are at Lakes of the Clouds Hut (5,010'), only a little more effort is required to make the summit of Mount Monroe (5,384'). Panoramic views await: Washington's summit seems close enough to touch. Monroe is good to keep in mind if a planned climb of Washington doesn't work out, or if you find you have enough time and energy to do both. Although only a lowly spur on the side of Washington, it is considered a summit in its own right, the fourth highest in New Hampshire. Follow Crawford Path south, soon branching right on Monroe Loop, and reach the top in about 0.3 mile. Return by the same route, or make the full Monroe Loop/Crawford Path loop.

69 • Traverse of the Presidentials

Rating: Long, very strenuous
Time: One to three days
Distance: 22 miles one way
Total climb: 9,000′
Location: The Presidential Range runs from Crawford Notch north to Gorham and includes Mount Washington
Summary: Spectacular traverse on the longest alpine ridge in the east. The single day traverse is a coveted achievement.

At a minimum, this is an 18-mile route. Its core section along the ridge is from Madison Hut over Mount Washington to Mizpah Hut. There are many variations, but most hikers try to climb all eight 4,000'-ers along the ridge: Madison, Adams, Jefferson, Washington, Monroe, Eisenhower, Clinton (Pierce), and Jackson. Additional summits are Mt. Clay, Mt. Franklin, and Mt. Webster. The grand tour—with all eight high peaks—is 22 miles with a little over 9,000' of climbing—and descending! It has been done in as little as six hours, but a normal time is about 12-14 hours. A brief segment-by-segment description follows.

Appalachia to Madison Hut (3.8 miles)

From the trailhead at Appalachia (on US 2, a few miles west of Gorham), follow Valley Way 3.8 miles (3,550' of climbing) to Madison Spring Hut (4,800') in the col between Mt. Madison and Mt. Adams.

Madison Hut to Edmands Col (2.2 miles)

From the hut, climb Mt. Madison (optional, adds one mile and 500' of climbing) and return to the hut. Head south on Crawford Path across the north flank of Mt. Adams to Lowe's Path (at Thunderstorm Junction). From here, climb Adams (adds 300', 30 minutes) or continue directly to Edmands Col.

Edmands Col to Mount Washington (3.8 miles)

Edmands Col is 0.5 miles north of Jefferson's summit. The Gulfside Trail bypasses it to the east, before continuing over Mount Clay and on to Washington. Jefferson Loop traverses the summit, adding 300' of climbing and 15 minutes.

Mount Washington to Lakes of the Clouds Hut

From the summit of Washington (6,288'), descend (south) on Crawford Path (still on the AT, white blazes) over open, exposed terrain reaching "Lakes" Hut (5,010') after 1.5 miles.

Sea of clouds below Mount Eisenhower

Lakes of the Clouds to Mizpah Hut (4.8 miles)

Mount Monroe (5,372') is the next (optional) summit; Crawford Path bypasses it and continues over Franklin to the col north of Eisenhower. Traversing Eisenhower's summit, via Eisenhower Loop, adds 300' and 0.2 miles. Follow Crawford Path to Mt. Pierce, then Webster Cliff Trail on to Mizpah Spring Hut.

Mizpah Hut to Crawford Notch (4.3 miles)

From Mizpah, continue 1.7 miles to Mount Jackson. From here, Webster (3,910') is one option; descending directly (2.6 miles) to Crawford Notch on the Webster-Jackson Trail is the other.

Approach: From the south, start from Crawford Notch, on US 302. When starting from the north, begin at Appalachia, on US 2, south of Gorham. Other variations exist.

Maps: White Mountains Hiking (Map Adventures); Presidential Range (AMC); and Mount Washington and the Heart of the Presidential Range (AMC/Museum of Science)

70 • Mount Jefferson 5,712′

Rating: Moderately strenuous
Time: 4 hours 30 minutes
Distance: 5 miles
Location: North of the Mount Washington Cog Railway
Total climb: 2,700′
Summary: The most direct approach to Mount Jefferson, with the least amount of climbing. Exposed to wind and weather.

Mount Jefferson is the third highest mountain in New Hampshire, in fact it is the third highest in the Northeast. It is Mount Washington's nearest neighbor to the north, the next major summit of the Presidential Range. Its distinctive west ridge—the **Ridge of Caps**—is the classic route. Starting from high, 3,000-foot Jefferson Notch, the **Caps Ridge Trail** quickly brings you above tree line and onto exposed, rocky terrain leading to the summit. Several short but very steep sections (the "caps") and the rough boulder field in the summit area add to the challenge of this route.

After leaving the parking area, you pass the Link (left) at 1.1 miles. From 1.5 to 2.1 miles, the trail is steep and difficult as it negotiates the various caps. At 2.1 miles you reach the junction with the Cornice Trail, a trail that traverses along the western base of the summit cone. Continue upwards, and at 2.5 miles you reach the open summit with stunning views of nearby Mount Adams and Mount Washington. As always, be prepared for wind and cooler temperatures on the summit. Keep a close eye on the weather, as a significant portion of this route is above tree line. The rough nature of the trail on the upper mountain is not conducive to a quick scamper back down to safety! Return by the same route or by the following variation, which adds a mile and gives you a fuller perspective of this high mountain terrain: take **Jefferson Loop** south off the summit to **Gulfside Trail**. Stay right on it, soon reaching the **Cornice Trail**. Follow this (right) for 0.5 mile back to the Caps Ridge Trail, at the trail junction you passed on the way up. Now descend Caps Ridge Trail back to Jefferson Notch.

A much more ambitious **variation** is to continue from Jefferson on Gulfside Trail over to the summit of Mount Washington, a distance of 3.2 miles. Needless to say, this should be attempted only by strong parties and under good weather conditions.

On the Ridge of Caps, Mount Jefferson   Robert Kozlow

Approach: From Bretton Woods follow Base Road 4.5 miles (towards the Cog Railway), and turn left onto Jefferson Notch Road. Follow this 3.3 miles to the trailhead at the height of land.

Maps: Mount Washington and the Heart of the Presidential Range (AMC/Museum of Science); Presidential Range (AMC); White Mountains Hiking; Trail Map and Guide to the White Mountain National Forest (DeLorme); and New Hampshire Atlas & Gazetteer, p. 44

71 • Mount Adams 5,799'

Rating: Strenuous
Time: 8 hours
Distance: 8.6 miles
Total climb: 4,500'
Location: Northern Presidential Range, six miles north of Mount Washington. Adams rises directly above the hamlet of Randolph
Summary: A very direct route up Mount Adams. Views into King Ravine on ascent, superb panorama from the summit.

Mount Adams is the dominant feature of the Northern Presidentials, the high ridge that arcs north from Mount Washington. Although 500' lower than Washington, Adams' ascent is several hundred feet greater than the Tuckerman Ravine Trail on Washington because the trailhead on Route 2 is only about 1,300' above sea level.

Of the classic routes up Mount Adams, **Air Line** is the most direct. It ascends the famous Durand Ridge and its Knife Edge, giving dramatic views down into the cirque of King Ravine. Starting from **Appalachia**, the Air Line initially coincides with Valley Way, but branches off right immediately. Several trail junctions are passed before Air Line very briefly merges with Randolph Path—follow signs carefully. (Randolph Path takes an unusual line; it makes a long, traversing ascent from Dolly Copp Road, just off Route 2, all the way across the northern flank of Mt. Adams, ending at Edmands Col, just below Mt. Jefferson.) Continuing on Air Line, the climbing steepens—there is a very steep section in the middle—as it ascends the more sharply defined ridge. After the Scar Trail enters (left), views appear, and after passing Upper Bruin and Chemin des Dames (the latter is an escape route from King Ravine), you ascend along the narrow section of **Durand Ridge** known as the **Knife Edge**. Note Crag Camp, an RMC cabin, just across King Ravine, perched on the top of the precipitous south wall. After you pass Air Line Cutoff—it heads left to Madison Hut—join with the Gulfside Trail (the AT) for a few minutes before Air Line splits off towards the summit.

Since it is the second highest mountain in the Northeast, and is placed in the middle of the most extensive alpine landscape in the eastern U.S., bear with us as we exclaim that the views from Mount Adams are among the best! The rocky cone of Mount Madison is less than a mile to the northeast, and Mounts Jefferson and

Airline Trail on Mount Adams Richard Bailey

Washington line up to the south. At your feet, mountain slopes plunge into the void of Great Gulf. The Carter and Baldface Ranges lie a little farther to the east. Descend by the same route or, for variety, and greater protection from nasty weather that may have arisen, head down to Madison Hut. To reach Madison Hut—unless it's foggy it's been in plain view—return to Gulfside and continue (right) on it to the hut. From the hut, you then take Valley Way down to Appalachia and Route 2.

Approach: From Gorham drive west on US 2 for 5.5 miles to the Appalachia parking area on the left.

Maps: Randolph Valley and the Northern Peaks of the Mount Washington Range (RMC); Mount Washington and the Heart of the Presidential Range (AMC); Presidential Range (AMC); White Mountains Hiking; and Trail Map and Guide to the White Mountain National Forest

72 • Mount Madison 5,367'

Rating: Strenuous
Time: 7 hours
Distance: 8.2-mile loop
Total climb: 4,100'
Location: Northern end of the Presidentials, near Gorham
Summary: Ascend directly to the summit, drop down to Madison Hut, then return on Valley Way.

The massive north slope of the Northern Presidentials has an impressive array of trails; every ridge and ravine seems to have a path. Some, like Lowe's Path, Randolph Path, and Air Line are legendary. In our time, **Valley Way** is the most-traveled route to the upper slopes; it provides the fastest and easiest access to Madison Spring Hut and Gulfside Trail. Most hikers climbing Mount Madison from the north use Valley Way up or down, if not both ways. The hike presented here is a variation on Valley Way.

Starting from **Appalachia**, pick up well-marked Valley Way. It climbs at a generally pleasant rate, crossing numerous minor trails, and gradually working its way closer to Snyder Brook. At 2.4 miles (about an hour and a half), branch left on **Watson Path**. After crossing the brook, the trail climbs steeply over rocky, rough terrain; cairns mark the upper section. The view improves steadily as you ascend. At the summit, 3.9 miles from the road, sweeping views including Adams, Washington, the Carter Range, and the North Country are yours. From the top, descend on the white-blazed **Osgood Trail** (the AT) in a westerly direction. (Descending to the east will take you into Great Gulf, a different world.) About 20-30 minutes (0.5 mile) of easy rock scrambling brings you down to the pleasures of **Madison Spring Hut**, right at tree line, and about 550' below the summit. Madison Hut has the alpine feeling: it is high up, yet snuggled in the col between two rocky, nearby summits. A 6-mile link of the AT, the Gulfside Trail, leads high across Adams and Jefferson to Mount Washington's summit. The hut is open during the summer hiking season and has overnight accommodations for 50 people. Contact the AMC for reservations.

Madison Hut (4,800') lies in the saddle between Madison and Adams, and for those that are up for it, the 1,000'-climb of Mount Adams (5,799') takes about 40 minutes via the Gulfside and Air Line trails. At any rate, when you are ready to head down, the most direct route back to Appalachia is Valley Way, a distance of 3.8

Mt. Madison & Madison Hut from Mt. Adams

miles. From the hut, the trail descends moderately and steadily, its upper section running quite close to a rushing brook. About a mile and a half from the hut you pass the junction with Watson Path. Continue down, retracing your steps to Route 2 and Appalachia.

Approach: The trailhead is at the large roadside parking area known as Appalachia, 5.5 miles west of Gorham on US 2.

Maps: Randolph Valley and the Northern Peaks of the Mount Washington Range (RMC); and Mount Washington and the Heart of the Presidential Range (AMC)

73 • Mount Jefferson's east side

Rating: Steep, strenuous
Time: 10 hours, or as overnight
Distance: 14.5-mile loop
Location: A few miles north of Pinkham Notch
Total climb: 4,460′
Summary: Gradual ascent of Great Gulf culminates with an exciting, difficult finish. One of the most demanding trails in New Hampshire.

Of the two main approaches to Mount Jefferson (5,712′), the eastern approach, via the **Six Husbands Trail**, is decidedly more difficult. Traditionally considered to be one of the six most difficult hikes in the White Mountains, it is considerably more demanding than the Tuckerman Ravine Trail on Washington, for example. It's a hike of contrasts. An easy walk up into Great Gulf, the largest glacial cirque in New England, is followed by the extremely steep ascent of Jefferson's east flank.

From the parking area just off NH 16, cross the river on a suspension bridge and pick up the **Great Gulf Trail**. Continue on this over generally quite pleasant ground 4.5 miles to the junction of the Wamsutta and Six Husband Trails. This is a good area to set up camp if you are planning to spread the hike over two days. From here, head right on Six Husbands Trail which soon becomes super steep as it toils up past huge boulders in dense forest: the trail resorts to ladders in two places. Without these ladders, a hiking route would probably not be possible. The gradient eventually eases and you come out onto the open upper slopes of Mt. Jefferson. After crossing the Gulfside Trail, you reach the summit after seven miles and about five hours from the road. There are actually three little summit cones on Jefferson, and they form a kind of sheltered pocket, offering protection from the breeze. Jefferson is a popular summit, and on a fine summer day, you may find yourself joining 50 to 100 others for lunch among the rocks.

For variety and a less demanding return route, consider descending the somewhat easier, but steep and rough **Sphinx Trail**, as follows. From the top, walk south (toward Mount Washington) for 0.3 mile on **Jefferson Loop** to **Gulfside Trail**, and continue on it 0.6 mile to **Sphinx Col**, where the Sphinx Trail descends to the left. At times you walk directly in a rocky streambed, or pass near little waterfalls. The sound of running water is within earshot most of the time. Be careful on the wet

Approaching Mount Jefferson from Mount Washington   Robert Kozlow

rocks, and allow yourself plenty of time for this difficult trail. After climbing down 1,400 feet (and 1.1 miles) head left on Great Gulf Trail. It is 5.6 miles back to the trailhead and highway; you will pass the junction with the Six Husbands Trail after about a mile.

Mount Adams variation: Once on top of Jefferson, a number of more ambitious routes are possible. For example, traversing north across Mounts Adams and Madison and then returning on the Osgood Trail (AT) to Great Gulf makes for a good long day in the most alpine landscape New Hampshire has to offer (14 miles total).

Approach: From the AMC facility at Pinkham Notch, drive about three miles north on NH 16 to the Great Gulf parking area on the left. From Dolly Copp Road, it is 1.5 miles north to the trailhead.

Maps: Mount Washington and the Heart of the Presidential Range (AMC/Museum of Science); Presidential Range (AMC); White Mountains Hiking; and New Hampshire Atlas & Gazetteer, p. 44 and 48.

74 • Mount Washington and Tuckerman Ravine

Rating: Strenuous
Time: 8-9 hours
Distance: 8.2 miles
Location: In Pinkham Notch, on NH Route 16, north of Jackson and south of Gorham
Total climb: 4,250'
Summary: The classic route up New Hampshire's legendary mountain. Together with its satellite peaks, it is the most important hiking mountain in the eastern United States.

From **Pinkham Notch** (2,012'), the east wall of Mount Washington (6,288') is so steep and so high that it is impossible to see the entire mountain, especially the upper portion. The great ramparts of Boott Spur and Lion Head dominate the view, and Tuckerman Ravine, the mountain's most famous feature, is only partly visible. You simply feel very small at the base of a very large mountain. Few mountains in the Northeast have such a powerful presence.

From the AMC's **Pinkham Notch Visitor Center**, the wide, pleasant **Tuckerman Ravine Trail** parallels the Cutler River, passing **Crystal Cascade** after about 15 minutes and Boott Spur Trail (on the left) soon after. Maintaining its width (it is actually a rough tractor road) the trail is much rockier once it starts to climb. Huntington Ravine Trail departs right at 1.3 miles and Raymond Path at 2.1 miles. After about two hours and 2.4 miles, the lean-tos and caretaker's cabin at **Hermit Lake** come into view. The Lion Head Trail departs right just below Hermit Lake.

Here, at the base of the ravine, the impressive flank of Boott Spur (with skiers' Hillman Highway) looms overhead. Above, on the right, are the flanks of Lion Head, Tuckerman Ravine's north wall. Although you are now over halfway to the top in terms of distance, the remaining climb to the top usually takes at least as long as the lower part. After a brief wooded section, the trail is in the open and climbs steeply at times, reaching the innermost recesses of the ravine about 30 minutes from Hermit Lake. In a sense, this is the best part of the trip. Yes, panoramic views of "forest and crag" await at the summit, but it is here, working your way up the headwall of this high alpine basin—a perfect example of a glacial cirque—that many hikers get their first taste of a true alpine envi-

Tuckerman Ravine Trail in the spring Robert Kozlow

ronment. The trail now climbs the extremely steep Headwall of Tuckerman Ravine. In the late spring, thousands of skiers congregate here to test themselves on the 50-degree slopes. The hiking trail ascends the notorious **Headwall**, the best known ski route in Tuckerman Ravine. Clamber out of the ravine. The grade eases dramatically, and the path soon crosses the end of the Alpine Garden Trail.

This is a good point to take a status check. What does the weather look like? How is your group holding up? It is still 0.8 mile and 1,150 feet to the summit—about an hour of climbing on difficult ground. This means two hours of walking before you return to this point on your descent.

To continue, stay on the Tuckerman Ravine Trail reaching **Tuckerman Junction** after a few minutes. Bear right at this intersection and follow Tuckerman Ravine Trail up the final steep slopes—the summit cone—over and across large boulders. This portion of the trail can be quite difficult when wet or icy.

The summit itself may come as a shock; buildings, crowds, cars and motorcycles, the Cog Railway, and the large main building with its cafeteria, museum exhibits, souvenirs, etc. Climb up on the observation platform for a less cluttered view. Descend by the same route, carefully noting trail signs.

There are many variations possible for your descent. If the weather has held and you have the energy for a little extra walking, the following is highly recommended. Take Tuckerman Ravine Trail to Tuckerman Junction, continue straight on Lawn Cutoff over to Davis Path (left), left again on **Boott Spur Trail** out along the top of Tuckerman Ravine. From Boott Spur, there are great views "straight down" to the Hermit Lake area. Continue down to Pinkham Notch on the Boott Spur Trail.

Approach: From North Conway, drive north on NH 16 through Jackson to Pinkham Notch and the AMC's well-marked visitor parking area on the left (west) side of the road.

Maps: Mount Washington and the Heart of the Presidential Range (AMC/Museum of Science); Mount Washington Close-Up Map (Wilderness Map Company); Presidential Range (AMC); White Mountains Hiking (Map Adventures); Trail Map and Guide to the White Mountain National Forest (DeLorme); and New Hampshire Atlas & Gazetteer, p. 44

Huntington Ravine: Tuckerman Ravine and Huntington Ravine are the two dominant features of the east side of Mount Washington. Huntington Ravine is the more precipitous of the two cirques; its headwall and side walls are almost vertical. The "hiking" trail that ascends the headwall—the **Huntington Ravine Trail**— is the most difficult trail in the East, in fact nothing comes close to it for exposure and sustained steepness. More of a rock climb than a hiking trail, it ascends 1,400' in 0.8 mile. It compares to some of the slide climbs in the Adirondacks. To do the route, follow **Tuckerman Ravine Trail** 1.3 miles and branch right on Huntington Ravine Trail. Follow this another 1.3 miles to the floor of the ravine. From here yellow paint blazes lead up the headwall. Do this climb only under dry conditions and with a competent leader. At the top of the headwall, the terrain levels off abruptly, and a variety of options make for a more moderate hike on to the summit. On your descent use either the Lion Head or Tuckerman Ravine Trails.

Winter hiking on Mount Washington

Accessible as it is, and with the Pinkham Notch Visitor Center open year round, Mount Washington probably sees hikers and climbers every day of the year. Huntington Ravine is the primary venue for ice climbers, and the Lion Head Trail—along the right edge of Tuckerman Ravine—is the recommended approach for winter hikers. This designated winter hiking route is a variation on the normal Lion Head Trail and has been routed in such a way to reduce exposure to avalanches. There is also a much easier option, the Mount Washington Auto Road. It is however much longer (7 to 8 miles each way) and completely exposed to the elements for about half its length. None of the summit buildings is open during the winter.

Needless to say, climbing Mount Washington in winter is a serious undertaking—this is when most accidents occur—and hikers should be well-equipped and trained for full winter conditions. Deep snow, ice, high winds, and even avalanches can be part of the experience!

All hikers, climbers, and skiers are advised to avail themselves of the latest weather, trail, and avalanche conditions by checking with the Forest Service Ranger Station south of Gorham or the AMC at Pinkham Notch. See page 294 for telephone numbers.

On the summit of Mount Washington
Robert Kozlow

Beyond the Presidential Range

North of Mount Madison the Presidential Range slides into oblivion in the Androscoggin River Valley. However just to the east, across NH Route 16, the **Carter Range** carries the Appalachian chain northward. The Androscoggin River cuts through the range, and north of the river it is known as the Mahoosuc Range. The Carter Range and its parallel-running companion range to the east, the **Baldface Range**, have their southern beginnings in the hills and low mountains around North Conway. The local landmark, **Kearsarge North** (3,268'), is the dominant mountain here and it is presented as Hike #76. Moving north from North Conway, we have chosen **Carter Dome** (Hike #75), the highest summit of the Carter Range, to represent this group. The short ridge consisting of the five Wildcat summits, is included as part of the Carter Range. Two of the Wildcat summits are official 4,000'-ers, **Wildcat A** and Wildcat D. It is easy to combine a climb of Wildcat A (4,422'), the higher of the two, with the loop hike over Carter Dome. The Imp Trail provides and exciting loop hike possibility and is a good way to climb North and Middle Carter. **Shelburne Moriah** (3,735'), is the northern sentinel of the Carter Range, and its close up views of the Androscoggin River Valley and the Presidential Range are famous.

Just to the west of NH/ME 113 in **Evans Notch**, in the Baldface Range, the often over looked **Baldface Circuit** (Hike #77) is one of the gems of the White Mountains. It features two summits just under 4000 feet, over a mile of open ridge walking, and challenging climbing on crisp, granite slabs.

The rugged and remote **Mahoosuc Range** is traversed by the Appalachian Trail (Mahoosuc Trail). There are a number of open summits on this densely wooded—and heavily logged—range. Perhaps the mountain offering the most exciting views is the curiously named **Goose Eye Mountain**. Although Goose Eye is in the middle of the range, a logging road originating in Berlin, Success Pond Road (together with various side trails), provides convenient access to it and all of the Mahoosuc summits. Hike #78 is the loop over **Mount Carlo** and Goose Eye. The Mahoosuc Range flows into Maine, and more hikes (Mahoosuc Notch, Old Speck) are discussed in the Maine chapter.

Unknown Pond

Leaving the main mountain chain and heading off in a northwesterly direction, one soon comes across the double summits of **Mount Percy** (Hike #79). Near the town of Groveton, reached from Nash Stream Road, North Percy's (3,418') bare granite dome is a surprising sight in these north woods. It is quite striking as far south as Lancaster. Slightly higher **Sugarloaf Mountain** (3,701') is the other popular hike accessed from Nash Stream Road.

South of the town of Stark, a woods road and a trail lead to **Unknown Pond**. From here it is straightforward to climb **Mount Cabot** (4,170') and its satellite peak, the Horn. For a considerably more ambitious trip, continue south from Cabot on the Kilkenny Ridge Trail to **Waumbek** (4,006') and **Starr King** (3,915'). However most hikers will elect to climb this summit pair from the trailhead (in Jefferson) on US 2.

Perhaps the most remote of New Hampshire's main hiking venues is **Dixville Notch**. There are a number of short, interesting hikes here, and Balsams Wilderness Resort has a good hiking map.

75 • Carter Dome 4,832'

Rating: Strenuous
Time: 7 hours
Distance: 10.2 miles (loop)
Total climb: 3,400'
Location: Just across Pinkham Notch from Mt. Washington

Summary: A loop over the dominant mountain of the Carter Range, with a very steep descent to Carter Notch Hut, in the deep notch between Wildcat Mountain and Carter Dome.

Just across NH 16, the Carter Range parallels the Northern Presidentials. Including the Wildcat summits, there are ten significant high points, including five 4000'-ers, along this rugged ridge. The **Appalachian Trail** crosses the highway at the AMC's Pinkham Notch Visitor Center and runs the entire length of the range. Carter Dome is the major peak of range, but its northern satellite, Mount Hight (4,675'), has the view. For a good loop trip across both summits, start out on **Nineteen Mile Brook Trail** from NH 16. After ascending along a rushing stream, branch left onto **Carter Dome Trail** at 1.9 miles, reaching **Zeta Pass** (3,900') on the main ridge at 3.8 miles. The segment to Zeta Pass is noticeably less traveled, as the majority of the hiker traffic runs to Carter Notch and back.

From Zeta Pass head 1.2 miles south (right) on the **Carter-Moriah Trail** to the top of Carter Dome, traversing **Mount Hight** along the way (Hight's summit can be bypassed). The slight detour to Hight is well worth the effort because the summit of Carter Dome consists of a small clearing ringed by trees that obscure the view. Beyond Carter Dome, descend steeply to the two ponds that nestle in **Carter Notch**. Once in the notch, a short stroll (side trail left) takes you to historic **Carter Notch Hut**. The original stone portion of the hut dates from 1914. There is bunk space here for about 40, and AMC staff is on hand year round.

Leaving the hut, hike back past the ponds on Nineteen Mile Brook Trail, and make the short, steep climb to the notch proper. Now begins the 3.6-mile descent back to Route 16. The trail drops steeply at first, then eases lower down. After 1.7 miles you pass the Carter Dome Trail branching right. From here it is 1.9 miles back to the trailhead.

Wildcat variation: from the Notch, you can easily climb **Wildcat A**, at 4,422' the highest of the five Wildcat summits. Head south on

The caretaker at Carter Notch Hut

the AT for 0.7 miles about 1,000 feet of climbing.

Approach: From North Conway, drive north on NH 16 past Pinkham Notch. The trailhead is on the right, 3.5 miles north of the AMC facility at Pinkham Notch.

Maps: White Mountains Hiking; Carter Range-Evans Notch (AMC); and New Hampshire Atlas & Gazetteer, p. 45

76 • Kearsarge North 3,268′

Rating: Moderate
Time: 4 hours 30 minutes
Distance: 6.2 miles
Total climb: 2,600′
Location: North Conway on Hurricane Mountain Road
Summary: A good alternative to Mount Washington if the weather doesn't pan out. Great view of Mount Washington.

The southern outpost of the Baldface Range, Kearsarge North is an area landmark. It is very prominent from Mounts Chocorua and Carrigain, for example. Although only a little over half the height of nearby Mount Washington (as far as the immediate North Conway area is concerned) it is the big kid on the block. And since you start walking at an elevation of only 600', it is a good solid climb to the top. From the open summit, only 15 air miles from Mount Washington, dramatic views of the Presidential Range, the Moats (across the valley), and the lakes of western Maine greet you. Clamber up the old fire tower for the full effect of the view of Mount Washington and Tuckerman Ravine.

Starting out as an old road, the **Kearsarge North Trail** gets rockier and steeper after about a half mile. As it climbs through woods and across intermittent ledge it provides good views of the Saco Valley. Once on the main ridge, the trail swings to the east, making the final push to the top from the north. Descend by the same route.

Approach: From Intervale, a little north of North Conway, leave NH 16/302 and drive east on Hurricane Mountain Road 1.5 miles to the trailhead on the left.

Maps: White Mountains Hiking; Trail Map & Guide to the White Mountain National Forest; Carter Range-Evans Notch (AMC); and New Hampshire Atlas & Gazetteer, p. 45

Mount Kearsarge from Black Cap

77 • Traverse of the Baldfaces

Rating: Strenuous
Time: 7 hours
Distance: 9.8-mile loop
Location: North of Fryeburg, Maine, and about ten miles east of Mount Washington as the crow flies
Total climb: 3,540′
Summary: A challenging circuit hike with some exciting rock scrambling on huge, exfoliating, granite slabs. Several miles of open or semi-open ridge walking.

Although the magnificent loop over North and South Baldface (3,591' and 3,569', respectively) is known to most experienced White Mountain hikers, it is perhaps the least-appreciated of the really outstanding New Hampshire hikes. Think of it as a slightly less-spectacular version of the Franconia Ridge Traverse. Its relative neglect seems to be a case of "if it's not 4,000', forget it." We try to correct that here! From the parking area, cross the highway—the **Baldface Circle Trail** is about 200' up the road—and make the easy stroll into **Circle Junction** at 0.7 mile. As most hikers will probably prefer to ascend rather than descend the difficult slabs on South Baldface, take the left fork at the junction. You soon pass the Slippery Brook Trail (on the left) and after a gradually steepening climb, reach the **Baldface Shelter** at 2.7 miles. The next section—friction climbing on exfoliated slabs—will give you a taste of rock climbing. Ascend these moderately steep, granite slabs, in a step-like fashion, with cracks in the smooth rock, detached blocks, and the occasional bush providing handholds. Soon the grade eases, views open up and, after crossing a minor summit, you reach the top of **South Baldface** (3,569'), 1.2 miles from the shelter.

Your reward is superb views in all directions, although nearby Carter Range blocks the Northern Presidentials. Except for a brief woods section near the summit of South Baldface, the mile-long traverse to **North Baldface** (3,591') is out in the open, with little protection from the elements. After North Baldface (4.9 miles) more open walking leads past the Bicknell Ridge Trail (5.8 miles) to a four-way intersection at 6.1 miles. Here Eagle Link descends left to Wild River Valley, the Meader Ridge Trail continues north, and our route, the Baldface Circle Trail, descends to the right, returning you to Circle Junction. After dropping off the ridge, the trail enters the woods and gradually adopts a mellower rate of descent. From Circle Junction, it is 0.7 mile back to the road.

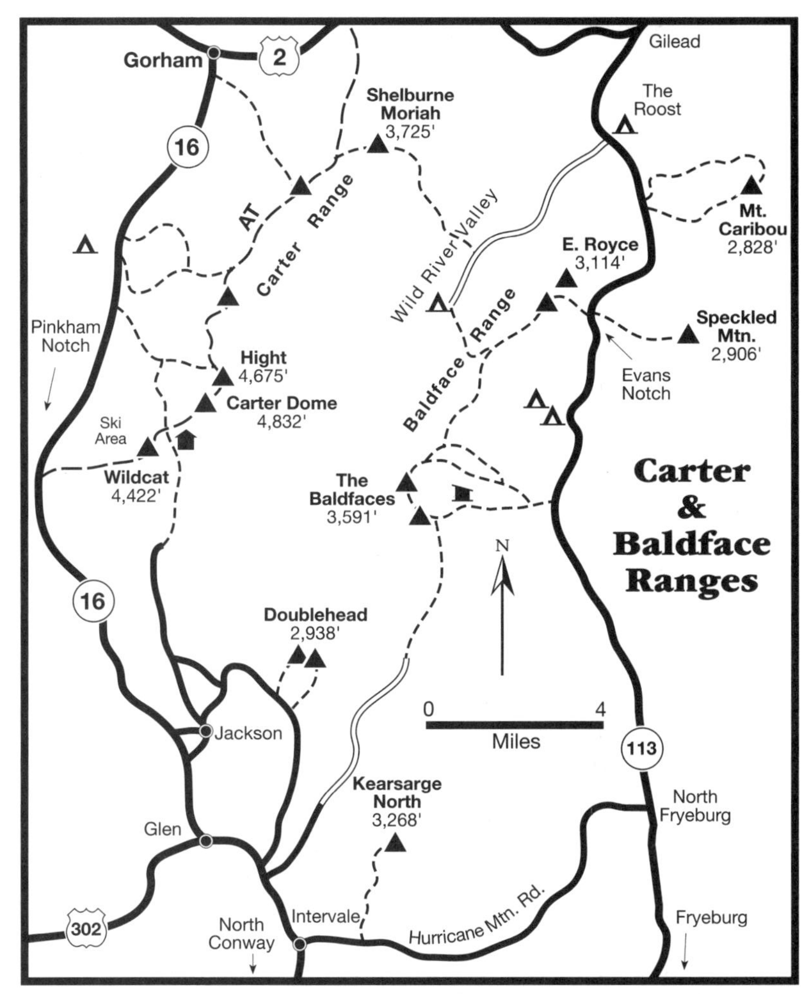

Approach: From Fryeburg (on US 302, just west of Conway), drive north on NH/ME Route 113 for 17.5 miles to the small trailhead parking lot on the right, beyond the AMC's Cold River Camp.

Maps: Trail Map & Guide to the White Mountain National Forest (DeLorme); Carter Range-Evans Notch (AMC); and New Hampshire Atlas & Gazetteer, p. 45

78 • Mount Carlo and Goose Eye

Rating: Moderately strenuous
Time: 5 hours
Distance: 7.5-mile loop
Total climb: 2,575′
Location: In the Mahoosuc Range northeast of Berlin
Summary: These two open summits make a great introduction to the rugged Mahoosuc Range.

Begin your exploration of the Mahoosucs with this one! The views from Goose Eye and Carlo are superb. From **Success Pond Road**, pick up the **Carlo Col Trail**. The first mile from the road is easy woods road walking. The trail then steepens, ascends a ravine, and reaches **Carlo Col Campsite** at 2.4 miles, in a tiny clearing. A lean-to shelter provides accommodation for about eight people, with four tent platforms providing additional space. From the shelter, climb another 0.3 mile to **Carlo Col** and the **Mahoosuc Trail**, which is also the Appalachian Trail. Head north (left) on the MT/AT for 0.4 mile of moderate climbing to reach the broad, open summit of Carlo (3,565'). North of the summit the trail descends over interesting terrain—with spectacular views of the route northwards—into another col, only to climb again, at times very briskly, reaching the junction with **Goose Eye Trail** 1.4 miles from Carlo's summit.

Head left 0.1 mile to the open summit of impressive Goose Eye Mountain (3,860') for the high point of the trip. This is a fine place to take a well-earned breather. From the summit, continue (west) on Goose Eye Trail, first negotiating a small cliff (a helpful piece of rope is provided) just below the summit. From here, the trail glides down into woods, eventually crossing a brook before following a woods road for its final mile. Completing the loop, it rejoins and coincides with the Carlo Col Trail a hundred yards from the trail-head parking.

Approach: From Berlin, about five miles north of Gorham, drive eight miles up Success Pond Road to the signed trailhead, on the right. To locate Success Pond Road when approaching Berlin from the south, turn right off NH 16 just as you are coming into town, and cross the river. At the light, continue straight, and staying on the main road, bear first right, then left. You are now on Hutchins

Along the Mahoosuc Trail

Street, heading north. Measuring from Route 16, it is 1.9 miles to unsigned Success Pond Road. A large sign announcing OHRV parking signals the turnoff on the right.

Maps: North Country-Mahoosuc Range (AMC) and New Hampshire Atlas & Gazetteer, p. 49

79 • North Percy 3,418′

Rating: Moderate
Time: 3 hours 30 minutes
Distance: 4.4 miles
Location: North of Stark near the town of Groveton
Total climb: 2,140′
Summary: A steep, nicely varied climb to an open, granite dome of a summit. Wide views of the forested North Country.

Percy Peak is has two summits: North Peak and South Peak. North Percy's bare rock dome can be spotted from many locations around the area. It is quite prominent from Groveton and the Lancaster area. From Nash Stream Road the first mile or so of the trail climbs moderately along Slide Brook. Abruptly the trail steepens, before branching right and traversing—still in woods—up along a series of low-angle slabs. A moderate climb leads up to the wooded col area between North Peak and South Peak; at one point the trail runs along an elevated rock rib. From the col the route winds a bit through dense forest before finally breaking out in the open on the exfoliating granite slabs that form the broad summit dome. The hike is viewless, but panoramic views are your reward once you reach the summit. A good portion of New Hampshire's northern forest lies at your feet. Return by the same route.

There is a **direct route** up North Percy pioneered by the Underhills in the 1930s. This variation, although quite steep and requiring caution, is still popular, especially with the locals. To find it, follow the route as described above, and after the initial steep section, just where the trail veers right, find an arrow painted on the rock pointing straight up the mountain. Follow it! Cairns and blazes show the way as you ascend very steeply and directly to the summit. There is plenty of loose rock lying about, so be careful not to dislodge rocks onto any climbers below. Descending from the summit by the normal hiking trail makes an interesting circuit; it is also a little safer than coming straight back down.

Nash Stream Road is an important corridor for snowmobilers, and in winter it is gated about a mile and half south of the trailhead. Winter hikers will thus need to add about three miles to the round trip distance.

North Percy Peak from South Percy Richard Bailey

Approach: From Groveton, drive east on NH 110 for 2.5 miles and turn left on Emerson Road. After crossing the river, bear right, and take the second left onto Nash Stream Road. Continue up the Nash Stream valley 2.7 miles to the trailhead, on the right.

Maps: North Country-Mahoosuc Range (AMC) and New Hampshire Atlas & Gazetteer, p. 50

Maine

Southwestern Maine

Maine is the largest of the New England states, with roughly the same area as the other five combined. The twenty-one hikes selected here represent a huge variety, and with the exception of the far north, all corners of the state are represented. The trips run the gamut from quite easy to strenuous and/or difficult. For Maine, more than for the other states, making the selection of hikes to include in this guide involved making some difficult choices. A large number of mountains of more or less equal size and popularity, in addition to a variety of landscapes, is bound to give rise to differing groups of "favorites." We present our hikes from south to north, starting with Evans Notch, north of Fryeburg, moving north to the Mahoosuc Range and Grafton Notch, across to the Weld Region and the Rangeley-Stratton area, over to the Atlantic Coast, and finally ending at Baxter State Park, home to Mount Katahdin, Maine's highest mountain. The hikes for Maine are grouped as follows: Southwestern, Western Lakes, Coastal, and Baxter State Park.

In this first section, Southwestern Maine, five hikes are presented. We start out near the New Hampshire border, with two hikes in the Evans Notch Area, **East Royce Mountain** and **Caribou Mountain**. After that, we move east into the Oxford Hills to **Pleasant Mountain**, home of Shawnee Peak Ski Area. Pleasant Mountain, although low in elevation, has an open summit with a fire tower. The next hike is **Old Speck Mountain**, located in Grafton Notch, which is a little north of Bethel and the Sunday River Ski Area. The Appalachian Trail crosses Maine Route 26 in Grafton Notch, and there are a number of good day hikes north and south along the Trail from Grafton Notch. **Rumford Whitecap**, a low mountain north of Rumford, offering a long, open ridge with great views, is the final southwestern hike.

In addition to the featured hikes, three additional trips are mentioned: the popular and easy hike on **Streaked Mountain**, the notorious stretch of the Appalachian Trail through **Mahoosuc Notch** (see photo page 237), and **Table Rock**, a favorite perch above Grafton Notch.

Photo previous page: Mount Katahdin from the south   Ed Rolfe aerial photo

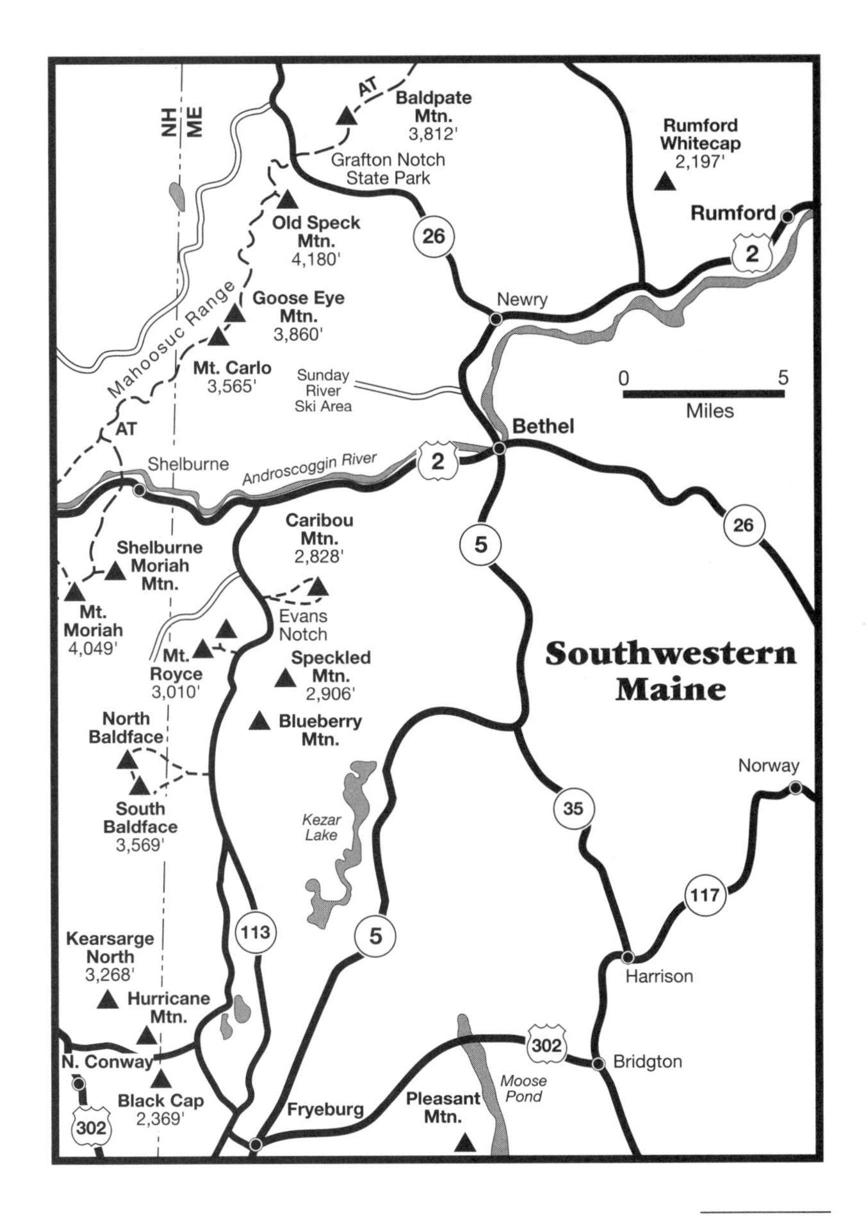
Southwestern Maine
NH
ME
AT
Baldpate Mtn. 3,812'
Rumford Whitecap 2,197'
Grafton Notch State Park
Old Speck Mtn. 4,180'
26
Rumford
2
Goose Eye Mtn. 3,860'
Newry
Mahoosuc Range
Mt. Carlo 3,565'
Sunday River Ski Area
0
5
Miles
AT
Bethel
Shelburne
Androscoggin River
2
Caribou Mtn. 2,828'
26
Shelburne Moriah Mtn.
5
Mt. Moriah 4,049'
Evans Notch
Mt. Royce 3,010'
Speckled Mtn. 2,906'
Blueberry Mtn.
North Baldface
Norway
South Baldface 3,569'
Kezar Lake
35
117
Kearsarge North 3,268'
113
5
Harrison
Hurricane Mtn.
302
N. Conway
Bridgton
Moose Pond
Black Cap 2,369'
Fryeburg
Pleasant Mtn.
302

80 • East Royce 3,116′

Rating: Moderate
Time: 2 hours 30 minutes
Distance: 2.8 miles
Total climb: 1,700′
Location: Evans Notch
Summary: Short hike offering a solid dose of climbing with great views from a rocky summit.

Immediately after leaving the parking lot, the yellow-blazed **East Royce Trail** crosses a wide stream before settling into a long, steep climb. After one mile, the Royce Connector Trail appears on the left. (This leads to West Royce Mountain, which is slightly higher than East Royce.) Staying right to continue to the top of East Royce, about fifteen more minutes of climbing brings you to the open rocks of the summit area. Clamber up to the top to enjoy the full view. The rugged cliffs of nearby West Royce provide a contrast to the mellow landscape of lakes and low hills that stretch away to the east. There is a short spur trail off the summit, leading to ledges offering good views to the north and west. Return to your car the same way you came up.

The Evans Notch area lies along the Maine-New Hampshire border, and Route 113, the narrow road that provides access to the region, weaves back and forth across the border several times. There is excellent hiking on both sides of this valley. The Baldface Circuit (Hike #77)—just over the border in New Hampshire—is discussed in the New Hampshire chapter, while East Royce Mountain and Caribou Mountain (Hike #81) happen to be in Maine and are therefore described in this chapter. The **Caribou-Speckled Mountain Wilderness**, part of the White Mountain National Forest, contains most of the better known hikes on the Maine side of ME 113: Caribou Mountain, Speckled Mountain and Blueberry Mountain. There are four Forest Service campgrounds in the area. Hastings, Cold River and Basin are on, or close to, ME 113, while the Wild River Campground is in the Wild River Valley, a major side valley, northwest of Evans Notch.

Approach: Drive south on ME 113 from Gilead (on US 2 between Gorham and Bethel) for 7.6 miles to trailhead parking on the right.

Maps: Carter Range-Evans Notch (AMC); Evans Notch (AMC Maine); and Maine Atlas and Gazetteer, p. 10

Rainy day on East Royce Mountain

81 • Mount Caribou 2,828'

Rating: Moderate
Time: 5 hours
Distance: 7-mile loop
Location: Evans Notch, north of Cold River Campground
Total climb: 2,000'
Summary: A pleasant loop hike, moderate in length and never really steep, offering excellent views of mountains and lakes.

The loop trip on Mount Caribou is in the **Caribou-Speckled Mountain Wilderness**, and in accordance with Forest Service wilderness area guidelines, a lower level of trail maintenance is in order here. Signs are less frequent, fewer mileages are given, trail blazing is less obtrusive and the trails themselves are narrower. To promote a wilderness camping experience, existing shelters are being torn down or removed.

From the trailhead parking, take the left fork, and follow the yellow-blazed **Caribou Trail**. After about two miles of easy walking and numerous stream crossings, you pass 25-foot high **Kees Falls**. In another mile, you come to the saddle between Gammon Mountain and Mount Caribou. Here, leave the Caribou Trail and turn right on Mud Brook Trail (there is a sign), using it for the final 400' ascent to the broad, open summit of Mount Caribou. As the trail breaks out into the open, a great view of southwestern Maine unfolds. From the top, it is 3.5 miles back to your starting point whether you return the way you came, or by the **Mud Brook Trail**. To complete the loop, follow the Mud Brook Trail (yellow-blazed) south off the summit for a pleasant woods stroll back down to your car. About a half mile below the summit, the trail passes an open ledge with good views.

Approach: Approaching from the north, drive 4.6 miles south on NH/ME 113 from US 2 through Evans Notch to the parking lot on the left. When approaching from the south, the trailhead parking lot is six miles past the entrance to Cold River Campground.

Maps: Carter Range-Evans Notch (AMC); Evans Notch (AMC Maine); and Maine Atlas and Gazetteer, p. 10

Paper birch along the trail

82 • Pleasant Mountain 2,006'

Rating: Moderate
Time: 3 hours and 30 minutes
Distance: 5.7-mile loop, including road segment
Total climb: 1,700'
Location: Moose Pond, between Fryeburg and Bridgton
Summary: A pleasant and varied trail. Great views of southern Maine from the fire tower.

There are at least four routes up Pleasant Mountain. Using two of them, Bald Peak Trail and the Ledges Trail, together with a short road section, an interesting circuit hike is possible. From Mountain Road, ascend **Bald Peak Trail** (1.1 mile), starting out along a stream. At 0.4 mile there's a short spur trail to the left where you can observe an interesting cascade. Continuing up the steep mountainside, stay left where Sue's Way branches off to the right. (This trail connects to the ski area.) A final steep section brings you to the top of the ridge. **Big Bald Peak** at 1,932', the second highest bump on the Pleasant Mountain ridge, is a short distance beyond. From here, the North Ridge Trail (blue blazes) leads to the right along the ridge to Shawnee Peak Ski Area. Heading left on the Bald Peak Trail, you cross over open ledges—a forest fire swept across here many years ago—and through scrubby pines. After you pass through a shallow dip, ascend gradually; you come out on the **Fire Warden's Trail**, an old carriage road, at 2.2 miles. Heading left on this trail, the top (at 2.4 miles) soon comes into view. From the tower there are sweeping views of the Oxford Hills and the local countryside. Mount Washington is clearly visible, 30 miles away.

When you are ready to leave the summit, continue (south) on the **Ledges Trail**. This will take you down to Mountain Road. From the summit, as you walk down along the ridge, views of hills and lakes and stands of pines alternating with cliff top ledges make for a great hiking experience. The total distance down to the road is 1.8 miles. From the trailhead you'll either have your other car (and keys, hopefully), or you can make the half hour stroll along the almost flat road back to your car at the base of the Bald Peak Trail. A popular alternative to the full loop is to hike up and down the Ledges Trail, a total distance of 3.6 miles and about 2 hours and 30 minutes round trip.

Approach: From Bridgton, drive west on US 302 for 4.5 miles and turn left on Mountain Road, after crossing Moose Pond. The parking area for the Bald Peak Trail is 1.8 miles down Mountain Road, past the entrance to Shawnee Peak Ski Area. Those planning to do the full loop may want to place another car 1.5 miles farther on, at the Ledges Trail, to avoid walking the road section.

Maps: Pleasant Mountain (AMC); Maine Atlas & Gazetteer, p. 4

About 20 miles northeast of Bridgton, prominent **Streaked Mountain** (1,770') offers a fun, popular hike to open summit ledges. It is only a half mile to the top, and the views are excellent. After a brief section in woods, the trail transitions onto rock and climbs steeply to the top. The total climb is about 800'. Note: On your descent take care to use the same route! To reach Streaked Mountain from South Paris, drive north five miles from ME 26 (in South Paris) on ME 117, and turn right onto Streaked Mountain Road. The trailhead is then about 0.5 mile in on your left.

Low Impact Hiking

In many areas of our lives we want to make an impact. Not so when hiking or camping! Well-meaning folks can easily do damage by polluting drinking water, stepping or tenting on fragile vegetation, or by destroying trees for firewood.

Low impact means just what it says: disturbing the natural areas we hike in and enjoy as little as possible.

Some tips: Take only pictures, leave only footprints, carry out all your trash, don't camp, bathe, wash dishes, or deposit human waste within 200 feet of a trail, lake, or stream; use a campstove instead of a campfire; use outhouses if available; if not, bury human and pet waste in a hole at least six inches deep. Try to hike without leaving any trace of your visit. If you notice trash or damage from previous parties, you have the opportunity to leave the area better than you found it.

Be especially careful above tree line—a hiker's boot can easily crush a delicate alpine plant. So, when above tree line, be sure to step only on rocks. This applies to dogs as well: owners must keep their dogs on a leash.

83 • Old Speck Mountain 4,180'

Rating: Moderately strenuous
Time: 5 hours
Distance: 7.6 miles
Total climb: 2,700'
Location: Grafton Notch, north of Bethel and Sunday River Ski Area
Summary: A long climb to a wooded summit. The fire tower gets you above the trees.

The climb of Old Speck Mountain—the fourth highest mountain in Maine—is the major hike in the Bethel-Sunday River area. Although large, Old Speck generally does not impress; it is simply the northern of end of the Mahoosuc Range, and the last and highest bump on the ridge. However, when you are in Grafton Notch, the towering northeast flank of the mountain—it is almost 3,000' high— is rather daunting. This is where the route goes.

From the large parking lot at the height of land in Grafton Notch, follow the white-blazed **Appalachian Trail south**, here called the **Old Speck Trail**. Immediately passing the lower end of the Eyebrow Trail (right), the Old Speck Trail begins its climb, and after a series of switchbacks, and passing near some cascades, once again encounters the Eyebrow Trail at 1.1 miles. The AT now works its way up to and along the mountain's north ridge. Finally, at 3.5 miles, you reach the **Mahoosuc Trail**. Now head left 0.3 mile on the Mahoosuc Trail over easy terrain to the flat, forested summit area, where a 28-foot high observation tower lifts you above the trees. The spectacular view includes much of western Maine, Umbagog Lake, and the paper mill town of Berlin.

Approach: From Bethel, drive east on US 2/ME 26 for six miles, where ME 26 branches left 12.5 miles to Grafton Notch.

Maps: Carter-Mahoosuc Range (AMC Maine); MATC, Map #7; and Maine Atlas and Gazetteer, p. 18

Grafton Notch is the centerpiece of **Grafton Notch State Park**, home to a number of interesting features; high cliffs, waterfalls, and gorges. Across the notch from Old Speck is **Table Rock**, a popular, short hike with great views. To climb it, follow the **Appalachian Trail north** from Grafton Notch. Following signs, you immediately cross the highway, and at 0.1 mile, follow the **Table Rock Trail** when it branches right off the AT. Initially it climbs gently but soon (at 0.3 mile) ascends steeply, negotiates a

Waterfall in Grafton Notch Laurie Caswell

series of switchbacks, and leads into a very steep gully, working its way up through imposing rocks, passing the "slab caves." The trail then passes a viewpoint at the base of Table Rock. A short scramble brings you to the spur trail that leads to the rock platform of Table Rock. There are views down into Grafton Notch and across to Old Speck. To complete the loop, continue on the almost level traverse across the mountainside, returning to the AT after 0.5 mile. Head left and descend to Grafton Notch in a little less than a mile.

The Appalachian Trail in Maine

Coming off a traverse of the rugged Mahoosuc Range, the Appalachian Trail enters Maine from New Hampshire just south of Grafton Notch, which is near the town of Bethel. Angling northeast, the Trail ends 281 miles later on the lofty summit of Katahdin's Baxter Peak, Maine's highest point. For over a hundred miles after passing Grafton Notch, the AT takes a grueling route through the most mountainous part of the state, summiting seven 4,000' peaks and passing near three others. After a more moderate section, the Trail's final hundred miles leads the hiker through the largest area of unbroken forest in the eastern U.S., an area with no towns or public road crossings. On this wilderness-like stretch, hikers need a level of self-sufficiency greater than usual. A few miles before the end of the Trail, hikers reconnect with civilization before taking on the finale, a steep, 4,000-foot ascent of Mount Katahdin.

Two of the better known portions of the AT in Maine are the **Mahoosuc Notch** and the 100-Mile Wilderness. Mahoosuc Notch is considered the most difficult mile of the entire Appalachian Trail! While not difficult in the technical climbing sense, it is awkward going with endless ups and downs. Think of it as an obstacle course. You climb over, around, and under huge boulders, making very slow progress for an entire mile. The larger your pack, the greater your struggle! Mahoosuc Notch is a few miles south of Grafton Notch and Old Speck Mountain, and just east of the Maine-New Hampshire border. Day hikers can access it from Success Pond Road: the 2.2-mile Notch Trail climbs gradually to meet the AT at the southern entrance of the deep and shady defile that is Mahoosuc Notch.

At the northern extent of the Trail in Maine, the section of the Appalachian Trail between Monson (southeast of Moosehead Lake) and Abol Bridge (just south of Baxter State Park), is referred to as the **100-Mile Wilderness**. Hikers typically use 7-10 days to complete it. It is the longest stretch on the Trail (99.4 miles) without a public road crossing and thus without a convenient resupply point. Several interesting summits, such as White Cap and the Barren-Chairback Range, are crossed in this remote area. It is a region of hundreds of lakes and streams.

Hiking through Mahoosuc Notch

The Maine Appalachian Trail Club publication, *Appalachian Trail Guide to Maine*, is the best resource for the Appalachian Trail in Maine. The Appalachian Trail and its side trails are described in a handy booklet, and detailed maps and trail profile diagrams are provided on separate map sheets.

84 • Rumford Whitecap 2,197′

Rating: Easy
Time: 3 hours
Distance: 4 miles
Total climb: 1,200′
Location: Northwest of Rumford
Summary: Low mountain featuring about a mile of open ridge. Great views of the northern Presidentials.

Although somewhat out of the way and informally marked, Rumford Whitecap offers an outstanding ridge walk for very little effort. Park along the road and ascend a logging road over steep and at times rough ground. There may not be a sign to mark the trailhead. After 0.5 mile the trail branches sharply left onto another logging road. Shortly thereafter the trail departs to the right and the climb resumes. From here on it is fairly well marked with blazes and tape ribbons. After a little less than 0.5 mile of climbing through woods, you reach the first open ledges of Whitecap's relatively bare ridge crest. The next mile—about half the hike—is increasingly out in the open. On a clear day many mountains and lakes can be seen, and there is a great expansive feeling. The route is marked with cairns and paint blazes and occasionally with ribbons of various colors. It is an undulating climb, passing in and out of brief woods sections and is not always easy to follow. In many places, the spruces have grown in on the trail, making it hard to pick it up again when you are coming off a ledge section. Eventually, at the end of this long ridge, you find yourself on the summit. On your return you will need to pay closer attention, as it is quite easy to stray off the not-so-beaten path. Of the various marking methods employed, ribbons seem to be the most reliable.

Approach: From US 2, 0.5 mile west of Rumford Point (west of Rumford), drive north on ME 5 three miles and turn right, crossing the Ellis River. Now head north (left) on East Side Road for 1.6 miles and turn right on Farmer's Hill Road. Continue 0.8 mile to the informally marked trail (right side of the road) which starts out as a very steep logging road.

Maps: Maine Atlas & Gazetteer, p. 18 and USGS Andover

Cairn on Rumford Whitecap

Western Lakes Region

The **Rangeley Lakes** area is one of Maine's premier recreation spots. Primarily noted for its hunting, fishing, and snowmobiling, the area is also wonderful for canoeing, skiing, and hiking. Large numbers of moose and deer are a special attraction. The Appalachian Trail passes east of the town of Rangeley as it traverses **Saddleback Mountain** (Hike #87) and its two 4,000-foot summits. It can be climbed via the Appalachian Trail or by way of the ski runs. North of Oquossoc, a tiny village a few miles west of Rangeley, popular **West Kennebago Mountain** (Hike #86) stands in splendid isolation. Just south of Oquossuc village, lies little **Bald Mountain**, a very popular short hike.

Closely associated with Rangeley Lakes, and about 20 miles to the northeast by car, is the **Stratton Area**. This compact area is home to eight of Maine's allotment of fourteen 4,000' peaks, including the **Bigelow Range**, North and South Crocker, Spaulding, Redington, and **Sugarloaf Mountain** (Hike #89). The north side of Sugarloaf is home to a major ski area, and the Appalachian Trail passes near but does not cross the summit. The mountain is climbed by a short spur trail off the AT, or by ski runs on the north side. **Mount Abraham** (Hike #88) is a few miles to the south of Sugarloaf, just west of Kingfield. One of Maine's larger lakes, Flagstaff Lake, parallels the Bigelow Range (Hike #90) to the north. In addition to the skiing at Sugarloaf—perhaps Maine's premier ski area—there is plenty of good mountain biking, kayaking, and cross country skiing.

About 35 miles southeast of Rangeley Lakes, the **Weld Region** provides hiking at a less intense level. The mountains are lower and the lakes smaller. It is home to the popular hikes on Mount Blue, Bald Mountain, and favorite **Tumbledown Pond** (Hike #85). There are good camping facilities near the quaint village of Weld along Webb Lake.

A variety of maps is needed for these areas. The Maine Appalachian Trail Club's series of seven maps is the best resource for hikes along the AT, and the AMC's Rangeley-Stratton map does an excellent job, as well. Included on the AMC map is a map panel for the Weld Region.

85 • Tumbledown Mountain 3,068'

Rating: Moderate
Time: 4 hours 30 minutes (loop)
Distance: 3 miles or 5.6-mile loop
Total climb: 2,200' (loop version)
Location: Weld Region
Summary: Popular hike to a pond nestled among rocks. Great swimming and blueberries.

Tumbledown Mountain, as the name may suggest, is a jumbled mass of ridges and knobs. Little Jackson Mountain at 3,434' is actually the highest point of this rugged little mountain. A network of trails leads to open ridges and to the gem of the area, beautiful **Tumbledown Pond**, known as Crater Pond by the locals. From the road, pick up the well-worn **Brook Trail** and make the 1.5-mile climb to Tumbledown Pond. The last half-mile or so is steep. The pond is a popular spot for swimming and relaxing on warm summer days. For many, the trek up to the pond and back down again is probably going to be enough of a hike on a hot summer day. However, the loop version makes for an interesting and worthwhile outing

To continue on the loop, pick up **Tumbledown Ridge Trail** from the pond and follow it west as it threads through blueberry bushes and ascends open ledges to the top of **East Peak** (about 3,000'). Next, drop down into the col separating East and West Peaks, 0.6 mile from the pond, where the Loop Trail descends to the left. From the col, and before descending, take the 0.1-mile spur trail to the top of **Tumbledown West Peak**, the highest point of the hike. Return to the col and make the steep descent (some spots are extremely steep) on the **Loop Trail** back to Byron Notch Road. Upon reaching the road, head left 1.4 miles—it's an easy stroll—back to your starting point at the base of the Brook Trail.

Approach: From US 2 in Dixfield, take ME 142 north to Weld, and head left on Phillips Road (still ME 142) to Weld Corner. From this intersection, continue west (left) on Byron Notch Road 4.4 miles to roadside parking at the trailhead area.

Maps: Weld Region (AMC Maine); Maine Atlas & Gazetteer, p. 19

86 • West Kennebago Mountain

Rating: Moderate
Time: 3 hours 30 minutes
Distance: 4.2 miles
Location: A few miles north of Rangeley Lakes
Total climb: 1,750′
Summary: Hike through interesting woods to a well-preseved cabin before ascending to the summit fire tower.

This is a popular family hike and with good reason. **West Kennebago Mountain** (3,705') is a relatively high and isolated peak with a commanding view of one of Maine's primary recreation areas; mountains and lakes abound. On your climb up the mountain, large spruces with fascinating, exposed roots and lush forest pockets provide pleasant distractions. There is a fair amount of climbing to reach the top, so the old fire ranger cabin (at 1.4 miles) with its view of Kennebago Lake makes a good intermediate goal for younger and other, possibly less motivated hikers.

From the cabin, the trail resumes from the upper right edge of the clearing. Reaching the summit ridge after 15-20 minutes, the route then turns south (left) and passes over easier terrain through a logged area (views) before arriving at the fire tower. If the Maine Forest Service ranger is present, ask to climb the tower in order to see the full panoramic view. With clear conditions, you will be able to see north to Mount Katahdin, west to Jay Peak (Vermont) and Mt. Mégantic (Québec), and to Mt. Washington in New Hampshire. Closer at hand, away to the east, the bare ridge of Saddleback is in plain view. Descend by the same route.

Approach: From the junction of ME 4 and 16 in Oquossoc (7 miles west of Rangeley), drive west on ME 16 for 4.9 miles, then head north (right) on Morton Cutoff Road for 3.2 miles to a junction. Turn right (Lincoln Pond Road) and drive 5.3 miles to the trailhead on the left.

Maps: Maine Geographic: Hiking, vol. 2 (DeLorme) and Maine Atlas and Gazetteer, p. 28

Popular **Bald Mountain** (2,443'), just south of Oquossoc, is less of a drive and an easier hike than West Kennebago. From Oquossoc head west on ME 4 to Haines Landing (1 mile), then south on Bald Mtn. Road 0.8 mile to the trailhead. The 1,000-foot climb leads to an open, ledgy summit.

The Northeast Forest

One hundred years ago the forests of New England were far less extensive than they are today. In those days, New Hampshire and Vermont were only about 20% forested. Today the siutation is reversed. This return of the forests has brought with it the comeback of many of the native wild animals. Deer, bear, wild turkey, moose, and coyotes, which today we tend to take for granted, had been eliminated in many areas. Wild turkeys were re-introduced in Massachusetts in the 1970s, there is an abundance of deer throughout the region, in northern areas the moose population is growing rapidly, and recently there have been several sightings of mountain lions.

This amazing comeback is due mainly to a shift in farming away from the Northeast to the Midwest, and to the decline of wood products relative to petroleum products, but conservation forces have also played a large role. For example, public outcry following devastating logging practices in the Crawford Notch area of New Hampshire eventually led to the creation of the U. S. Forest Service and subsequently the White Mountain National Forest.

Most would agree that the return of the forests is a good thing. The northeastern United States is held up as proof that a large, highly industialized population—70 million people live within a day's drive of New England and the Adirondacks—is not completely incompatible with an ecosystem that seems to be strongly on the rebound. The recent natural history of the Northeast gives hope to the claim that developed and natural environments can exist in close proximity—in fact intertwined—with each other. But with most of the prime land under intense development pressure, and with Maine being logged very aggressively—over half the state is owned by logging companies—the continuation of this recovery is not a given. The Northern Forest Project is an effort dedicated to protecting watersheds, recreation, and wildlife habitats over a 26,000,000 acre extent of forested land stretching from the Adirondacks, across Vermont and New Hamphire, and including more than half of Maine.

87 • Saddleback Mountain 4,116'

Rating: Strenuous
Time: 9 hours
Distance: 13.4 miles
Total climb: 3,670'
Location: A few miles east of Rangeley Lake
Summary: Saddleback Mountain is one of the finest above-tree line ridge walks in the East.

The **Appalachian Trail** traverses Saddleback Mountain's three miles of high, mostly open ridge. The mountain has two summits over 4,000'. **The Horn** (4,041') is 1.6 miles north of the main summit. The trip described here includes both. From ME 4 follow the AT (north) over easy terrain, reaching **Piazza Rock Lean-to** at 1.4 miles. Just beyond the lean-to, a spur trail leads left to an unusual feature known as Piazza Rock. A large mass which juts out from the mountainside, Piazza Rock is a strange and impressive sight. Continuing on the AT, another side trail (left) takes you to an area of jumbled rock slabs and caves. The main trail now ascends steeply, passing three small ponds in succession. Just past the last one, Eddy Pond (at 3.2 miles), the trail coincides very briefly with a road, before departing abruptly right. From here a little less than a mile of steep climbing remains before you finally break out of the forest and onto the open ridge.

Five minutes before the summit, the feeder trail (sign) from the ski area comes in from the left, and at 5.1 miles, you reach the actual summit. The ridge is spectacular with sweeping views, as the scrubby tree growth does not interfere. The route is marked with paint blazes and cairns. The view north to the Bigelow-Sugarloaf region is especially intriguing. The trail works its way across lichen-covered slabs and blocks of granite, the Rangeley Lakes spread out to the west, with Saddleback Lake in the foreground. From the summit, continue on the ridge for few minutes to the top of a drop-off, where you gaze across the 500' dip separating the main summit from the Horn. Skirting around the cliffy section to the left, descend onto the connecting ridge. The climb up the Horn (at 6.7 miles) involves a section in dense woods and is steep (ladder) and rough in a few places. Once on top, the views are again fantastic, with Sugarloaf and its companion mountains somewhat closer. Return by the same route.

Saddleback summit from The Horn

Note: Normal precautions with regard to above-tree-line travel should be observed. Saddleback's exposed upper mountain puts you at the mercy of wind and weather, so keep an "eye on the sky" as you progress along the ridge.

Approach: From Rangeley, drive ten miles east on ME 4 to the Appalachian Trail crossing. The hiker parking area is on the right (south) side of the road. Approaching from the south, the trailhead is 32 miles north of Farmington.

Maps: Rangeley-Stratton (AMC Maine); Maine Appalachian Trail Club, Map #6; and Maine Atlas & Gazetteer, p. 19 and 29

Hiking the ski runs: It is shorter and for day hikers probably more popular to climb Saddleback Mountain from the base of the **Saddleback Ski Area**. From Rangeley, head east on ME 4 for a mile and turn left on Dallas Hill Road. Then follow signs to the ski area base lodge, about eight miles from town. From here, follow the marked route up the ski runs to the top of first one chairlift and then another. The ridge is a few minutes above the second chairlift, and the summit itself is a few minutes farther on, to the north (left). Average climbing time is about an hour and a half.

88 • Mount Abraham 4,049'

Rating: Strenuous; a long climb
Time: 6 hours
Distance: 8 miles
Total climb: 3,000'
Location: West of Kingfield and south of Sugarloaf
Summary: A steep climb to a high, open ridge, with an isolated mountain feel and great views.

From the car the **Fire Warden's Trail** heads straight into the woods. Starting out very gradually, the yellow-blazed trail soon crosses a large brook and climbs steeply for a short way before beginning a long, gently ascending traverse that continues all the way to the old fire warden's cabin at two miles. You will cross a logging road after about 45 minutes, and the trail occasionally dips into a ravine to cross a brook. This entire section of the trail is poorly drained and can be quite soggy.

From the cabin, a listing log structure in a small clearing, the trail immediately commences a very steep climb, offering no significant letup until just before the first open slopes of the upper mountain. After traversing the top of a very steep talus slope, the route—now marked with small cairns—swings left and passes in and out of several brief patches of stunted forest before cresting the final loose rocks of the summit. Here the truncated remains of the old fire tower and a primitive stone shelter greet you. There are views of mountains near and far, with the Kingfield area in the middle distance. Signs of tree harvesting—logging roads and clear cuts—are plentiful. In fact, a logging road appears to come very close to surmounting the connecting ridge between Abraham and Spaulding Mountain, reaching an elevation of almost 4,000'.

Out in the open on this barren summit, the wind and weather will have a say in how long you linger. Return by the same route, exercising care to stay on the somewhat vaguely marked upper section of trail. Note that there is another trail off the summit; the 1.7-mile connector trail to the Appalachian Trail.

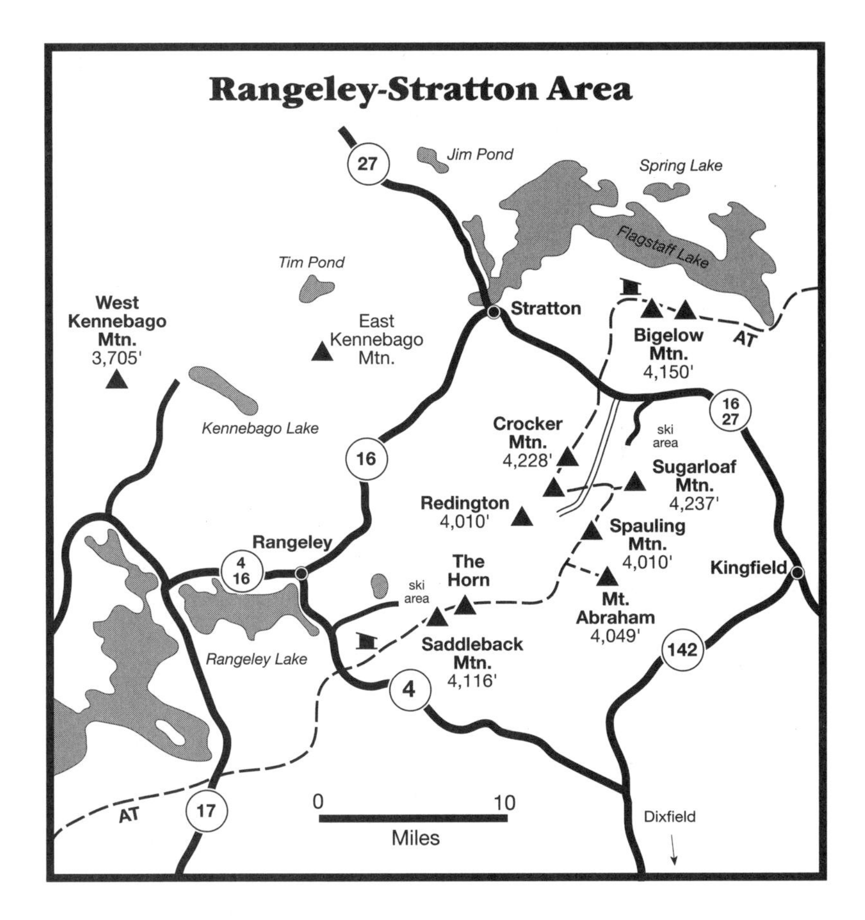

Approach: From Kingfield head north on ME 27 for about 0.5 mile and turn left on West Kingfield Street. Three miles from here West Kingfield St. turns to gravel. At 3.5 miles proceed straight through an intersection, and finally at 3.7 miles, bear right on to a logging road. Continue on this, and at a total of six miles from Route 27, bear left, cross Rapid Stream, and continue another 0.5 mile to the poorly marked trailhead at a "T"-intersection.

Maps: Rangeley-Stratton (AMC); Maine Atlas & Gazetteer, p. 29

89 • Sugarloaf Mountain 4,237'

Rating: Moderate, but very steep
Time: 4 hours 30 minutes
Distance: 5 miles
Location: Six miles east of Stratton and 18 miles north of Kingfield
Total climb: 2,250'
Summary: Maine's third highest peak with panoramic views from Mount Katahdin south to the White Mountains.

The route described here ascends the western and southern slopes of Sugarloaf Mountain, climbing out of the deep valley separating it from Crocker Mountain. Maine's best-known ski area, **Sugarloaf/USA**, spreads across the mountain's broad northern slope. It is possible, and quite popular, to climb Sugarloaf by the ski runs. An easy variation on this is to take the ski lift up and walk down. These various options can be explored by driving up the access road to the base of the ski area. A less civilized and, from a hiking perspective, certainly more interesting alternative is to use the Appalachian Trail and a short side trail to gain the summit.

After driving up the **Caribou Valley Road**, park and pick up the **Appalachian Trail south**. It is on your left as you drive up. Start out by descending through a white birch forest, soon reaching the rushing Carrabassett River. As of fall 1999, the bridge was still out, and getting across with dry feet is not at all easy! In fact with average flow levels, even wading will demand a certain amount of care. (There may be easier crossing points upstream.) Once on the other side, the trail bears right and climbs moderately but soon turns and gives its full attention to the mountain, climbing very steeply—at times it's hand-over-hand up the rocks. Through all this, gnarled white birches provide the occasional hand hold as well as an interesting distraction. Eventually you break out of the dense woods and the grade slackens. Skirting the (north) rim of the little cirque tucked between Sugarloaf and Spaulding, you can begin to reap the rewards of your labors. There is a great view into the headwaters of the Caribou Valley that includes little Caribou Pond. From high above, the Carrabassett River is only a mellow swath through the forest. The Crockers, with their two prominent cirques, fill the view across the valley. The trail now climbs at a more moderate rate to a spur trail (left).

From the spur trail junction—you are now 1.9 miles from the car and at an elevation of 3,600'— the summit of Sugarloaf is 0.6 mile

Appalachian Trail crossing of the Carrabassett River

and 600 vertical feet farther. The **Sugarloaf Side Trail** (blue blazes) climbs (left) moderately steeply to the summit where signs of Schussdown Man are everywhere. Despite this, the views from the open summit are among the best in the Maine. If the weather is clear, you will be able to pick out a good number of the prominent peaks and other landmarks.

Descend by the route you came up. A fun **variation** on this hike is to descend by the ski runs. However, once at the base of the ski area, you are miles from your starting point, the assumption being that you have made the necessary transportation arrangements.

Approach: From the base of the Sugarloaf ski area access road continue west on ME 27 one mile to Caribou Valley Road. Turn left (the road is unmarked) and head south for 4.5 miles to the AT crossing. There are no signs, so look for the white AT blazes and the small parking space on the right.

Maps: Rangeley-Stratton (AMC Maine) and Maine Atlas and Gazetteer, p. 29

90 • Bigelow Range Traverse

Rating: Strenuous, a long day
Time: 8-9 hours or overnight
Distance: 12-mile loop
Total climb: 3,960'
Location: Just to the north of Sugarloaf Ski Area and near the village of Stratton
Summary: An exciting ridge walk with a traverse of four distinct summits at or above the tree line.

The traverse of the four high points of the Bigelow Range is one of the great ridge walks of the East, and it can be conveniently done as a loop hike. If we first ascend the aptly named North and South Horns, the route then takes us east along the main ridge to the highest point, Bigelow's **West Peak** (4,150') and culminates on its eastern companion, known as **Avery Peak** (4,088').

From the parking area, cross the outlet of **Stratton Pond** and continue along the road branching off to the right at 0.2 mile. (Stratton Pond is a good place for a swim.) The **Fire Warden's Trail** climbs over moderate terrain, reaching the junction with the Horns Pond Trail at 1.6 miles. Our route now heads left on the more gradual Horns Pond route, while the Fire Warden's Trail climbs directly, and at times extremely steeply, to the col between Avery and West Peaks. (You will descend this way on your return.) The **Horns Pond Trail** climbs moderately, eventually passing an open bog area on the right where there is a good view of South Horn. At 4.1 miles you reach the ridge and the **Appalachian Trail** (Bigelow Range Trail). Head right and in a few minutes the lean-tos of Horn Pond come into view. **Horns Pond** is just beyond and to the left; you can't miss it.

From the pond, our route (the AT north), climbs steeply up South Horn. Just below the top, a 0.2-mile spur trail leads left to **North Horn** (3,810') with views along the summit ridge. Return to the AT and finish the climb up slightly higher **South Horn** (3,831'). Here the views are even better. At this point you have hiked 5.3 miles, and it is 2.1 miles along the ridge to West Peak. Either summit makes a good stopping point for lunch. The trail dips into forest before again climbing above the trees to the top of West Peak, which is the highest point of the ridge. After enjoying the views and a well-earned rest, drop down into the col between Avery and West Peak.

West Peak from Avery, Bigelow Range

Here is the **Avery Memorial Lean-to** (and caretaker cabin) and the junction with the Fire Warden's Trail. At this point some may opt to begin their descent on the Fire Warden's Trail, but the full version of the hike requires a short scramble up Avery Peak, 0.4 mile and a 300' climb. The views from Avery are considered to be the best of the entire ridge. When you are ready to head down, return to the col and begin your descent. The Fire Warden's Trail turns out to be very steep indeed, the first 1.5 miles drops about 1,500'. Eventually the plunging descent slackens and an easy stroll brings you back to Stratton Pond and your car.

Approach: From Kingfield drive north on ME 16/27 towards Sugarloaf and Stratton. From the base of the Sugarloaf Ski Area access road, continue northwest on ME 16/27 for 3.2 miles to Stratton Brook Road, on your right. Follow this rather bumpy dirt road past the AT trailhead (at 1.4 miles) to our trailhead and a small parking area at 1.6 miles.

Maps: Rangeley-Stratton (AMC Maine); MATC, Map #5; and Maine Atlas & Gazetteer, p. 29

Coastal Maine and Acadia National Park

The coastal town of **Camden**, about two hours south of Mount Desert Island, supports a network of hiking trails. Mount Battie (see below), directly above town, is the best known hiking destination. While not the area's highest point, it provides a fun climb to good ocean and harbor views. Other popular hikes are Maiden Cliff and Mount Megunticook.

Monhegan Island, a proud fist of land at the outer edge of Maine's offshore islands, offers breezy strolls along its grassy headlands. The mile and a half long island is reached by an hour ferry ride from Port Clyde, which is south of Rockland.

Mount Desert Island is home to **Acadia National Park**, our only Atlantic Coast national park. Reached by a bridge from the mainland, Mount Desert is about an hour south of Bangor and three hours from Portland. Roughly circular in shape, the island measures about 13 by 16 miles. It is perhaps appropriate that this rugged, glacially scoured landscape is home to the only fjord on America's eastern seaboard: Somes Sound almost splits Mount Desert Island in two, creating distinct eastern and western halves. The eastern lobe receives the majority of the attention: **Bar Harbor**, Northeast Harbor, Cadillac Mountain, Jordan Pond, Thunder Hole and most of the mountains are here. Although the mountains are low—the highest, Cadillac, is only 1,530'—the trailheads are at, or near sea level, so there's plenty of climbing to be done. The summits are usually bare, and much of the hiking is on open granite ledges, and the wonderful ocean views are never hidden for long. Much of Maine, and this area in particular, is famous for blueberries. For those not inclined to toil upwards, there are several popular walks that lead along the wild shoreline where spruce forests end abruptly on granite bluffs.

The Park's well-developed hiking trail network and unique system of gravel carriage roads makes an almost unlimited variety of hikes possible; anything from one or two summits, to the long traverse from Somes Sound over **Cadillac Mountain** to Bar Harbor. The carefully engineered carriage roads and masterful stone bridges are the legacy of a bygone era. Most of what is now Acadia

91 • Mount Battie 800′

Rating: Easy
Time: 1 hour
Distance: 1 mile
Total climb: 570′
Location: Camden, on the coast
Summary: A short hike to spectacular coastal views.

Mount Battie rises steeply from town. It is a subsidiary summit of Mount Megunticook, at 1,385', the highest of the Camden Hills. This compact coastal range lies just east of US 1 and runs north from Camden. Most of it is contained in **Camden Hills State Park**. A network of hiking trails makes it possible, for example, to continue from Mount Battie on to Megunticook Mountain and beyond to Maiden Cliff above Megunticook Lake. The AMC's Camden Hills map panel (included with the Maine Mountain Guide) does a nice job of displaying this area.

From Megunticook Street, the half-mile **Mount Battie Trail** climbs at a moderate grade through woods to ledges just below the top. Then a final scramble up easy slabs brings you to the summit, where a low stone tower enhances the view considerably. The town of Camden is directly below—its harbor usually full of boats—with beautiful Penobscot Bay unfolding in the distance. Return by the way you came up.

Approach: From US 1 in Camden, drive out Mountain Street (ME 52) to the fourth right. Take this, then head left on Megunticook Street to limited roadside parking at its upper end.

Maps: Camden Hills (AMC Maine); Maine Atlas & Gazetteer p. 14

Park was donated by the Rockefeller family, and during the 1930s, John D. Rockefeller took a keen interest in developing roads suitable for horse-drawn carriages. These gently graded, lightly graveled carriage roads are closed to cars and are thus a great resource for hiking, biking, and cross country skiing.

Twenty-five miles southwest of the hustle and bustle of Mount Desert Island, but still a part of Acadia National Park, **Isle au Haut** is a favorite of those seeking a coastal hiking experience with a measure of solitude. Isle au Haut is reached by ferry from Stonington, on Deer Isle.

92 • Cadillac Mountain 1,530′

Rating: Moderate
Time: 3 hours
Distance: 4 miles
Location: Mount Desert Island, Acadia National Park
Total climb: 1,450′
Summary: A good hike to terrific views of Mount Desert Island. Go early or late to avoid the tour buses at the top.

Cadillac is the Mount Washington of Mount Desert Island and Acadia National Park. It is the island's highest point; there is a road to the top, and it's immensely popular. At the risk of contributing to the summer crowds, we include it here. The mountain is too important to omit from our selection. Of the several routes and their variations, we have chosen the popular and very scenic **North Ridge Trail**. From the road, pick up the signed trail and start climbing. The trail alternates between cool woods (spruce, birch) and open granite ledges. After only a few minutes the summit comes into view and Eagle Lake is visible off to the right. Soon you will catch glimpses of the ocean on your left, and after passing close to the summit road (at 0.5 mile), the trail leads up stone steps in a beautiful birch wood. You are now about halfway. After grazing the road two more times, the trail climbs up across extensive open sections to finally merge with the road at 2 miles. There are plenty of blueberries in season and the views out across Frenchman's Bay are terrific. Bear left and walk on stone paving the remaining 300 or so yards to the top. The summit is a flatish, broad dome, so if you walk out on the ledges to the south and east, you'll be able to fully enjoy the stupendous, sweeping views. The Cranberry Islands are straight south, Bar Harbor is behind you to the north, and the bulk of Mount Desert Island rolls away to the west and south. Return by the same route.

A **variation** on the above is to do a traverse of Cadillac and its slightly lower neighbor to the east, **Dorr Mountain** (1,270'). From the Nature Center at the Sieur de Mont Spring, follow the **Dorr Mountain Trail** as it ascends steeply, at times on stone steps, to the open summit of Dorr with its great views of the ocean. Slightly higher Cadillac Mountain looms nearby. From the top of Dorr drop down about 300' into the interesting ravine-like trough between Dorr and Cadillac, then clamber up the final steep ledges of Cadillac on the **Dorr Mountain Notch Trail**. The distances are as

Mount Desert Island with Cadillac Mountain in the center Acadia National Park

follows: to the top of Dorr, 1.5 miles; to summit of Cadillac, 2.4 miles. From the summit of Cadillac descend on the **North Ridge Trail** as described above (2 miles). You will need to arrange to be dropped off and picked up at the trailheads.

Approach: From Bar Harbor, take ME 233 west to Park Loop Road. Turn left, then bear left again onto the one-way section of Park Loop Road, heading east towards Sand Beach. (Ignore the sign for Cadillac Mountain, as this is for the road to the top.) Park along the road 0.6 mile farther on.

Maps: Acadia National Park (Park Service); Mount Desert Island and Acadia National Park (DeLorme); Map of Acadia National Park/Mount Desert Island (AMC); Maine Atlas & Gazetteer, p. 16

93 • Penobscot Mountain 1,194′

Rating: Short distance, but very steep in places
Time: 2 hours and 30 minutes
Distance: 3.2 miles (or 5 miles)
Total climb: 1,000′
Location: West of Jordan Pond in Acadia National Park
Summary: Short hike to great views. Steep sections have ladders and railings bolted to the rock.

From the **Jordan Pond House** parking area, pick up the 0.1-mile connector trial to **Penobscot Mountain Trail**. The trail heads west from the carriage road, crosses a stream, and meets another carriage road at 0.4 mile. Just to the right of this junction the **Jordan Cliffs Trail** departs right and runs north, traversing the east flank of Penobscot Mountain. After little less than a mile, a difficult section is negotiated using iron rungs and handrails. (Note: This section is extremely difficult for dogs, and they will need to be carried.) The trail then turns sharply left and ascends steeply to the ridge crest giving exciting views of Jordan Pond and nearby mountains like the Bubbles and Pemetic. The most direct return route is to take Penobscot Mountain Trail south off the summit. This trail, together with the connector trail, takes you back to Jordan Pond. For a popular extension of this hike, read on.

The summit of **Sargent Mountain** (1,373') is only one mile distant. To visit it, take the **Sargent Pond Trail** north off the top of Penobscot, reaching Sargent Pond after 0.2 mile. From here it is 0.8 mile on the **Sargent Mountain South Ridge Trail** to the summit of Sargent. To return, retrace your steps to the summit of Penobscot. From the top, it's 1.5 miles back to the Jordan Pond House, as for the shorter variation, described above.

Situated at the south end of Jordan Pond with its view of the two rocky peaks known as the Bubbles, Jordan Pond House is one of the primary attractions of Acadia Park. Not just a feast for the eyes; its teas and pastries (popovers!) are probably more famous.

Approach: From Bar Harbor, drive to Jordan Pond House at the south end of Jordan Pond. Use the Park Loop Road, or take Route 3 to Seal Harbor and the Park Loop Road from there.

Maps: Acadia National Park (Park Service); Mount Desert Island and Acadia National Park (DeLorme); Map of Acadia National Park/Mount Desert Island (AMC); Maine Atlas & Gazetteer, p. 16

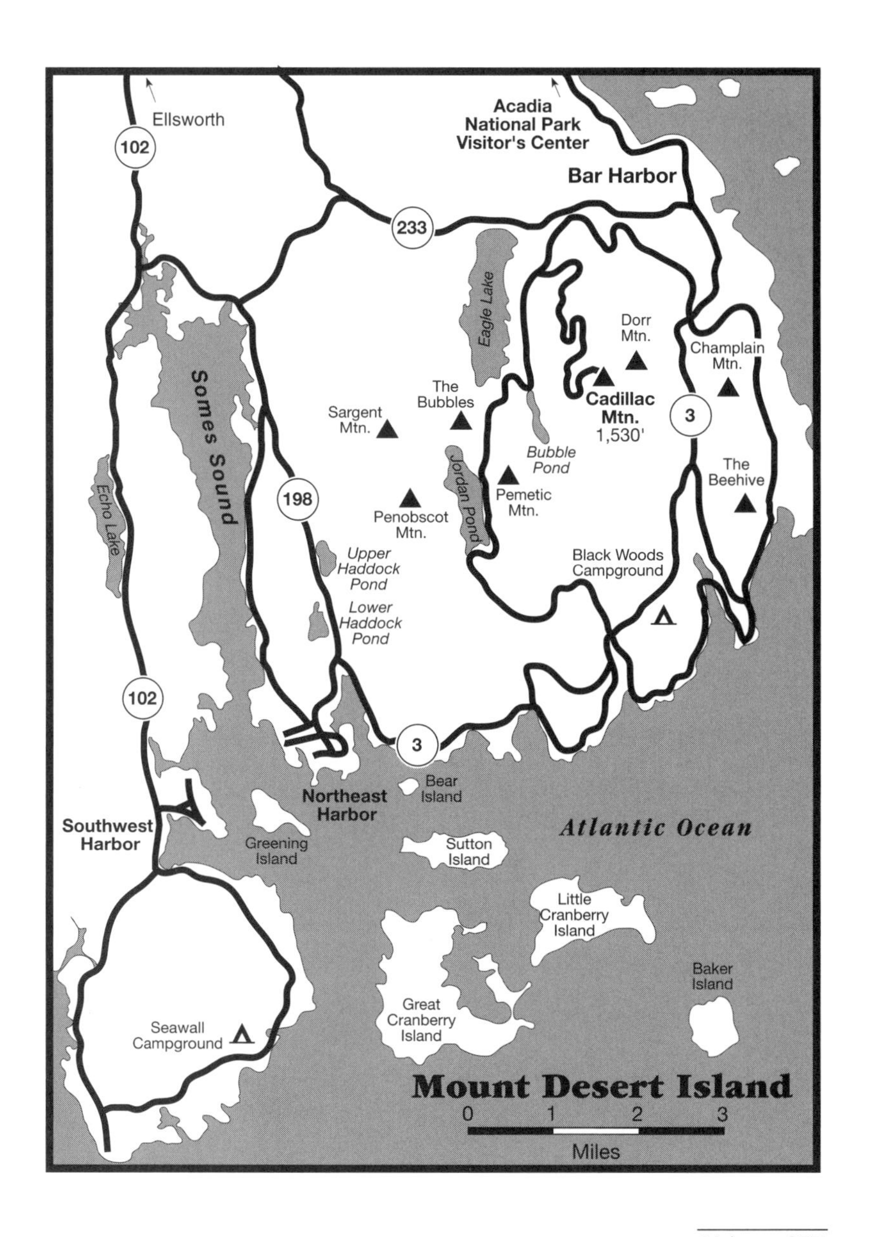
Ellsworth
102
Acadia
National Park
Visitor's Center
Bar Harbor
233
Eagle Lake
Dorr
Mtn.
Champlain
Mtn.
Somes Sound
The
Bubbles
Sargent
Mtn.
Cadillac
Mtn.
1,530'
3
Bubble
Pond
Jordan Pond
The
Beehive
Echo Lake
198
Pemetic
Mtn.
Penobscot
Mtn.
Upper
Haddock
Pond
Black Woods
Campground
Lower
Haddock
Pond
102
3
Bear
Island
Northeast
Harbor
Southwest
Harbor
Atlantic Ocean
Greening
Island
Sutton
Island
Little
Cranberry
Island
Baker
Island
Great
Cranberry
Island
Seawall
Campground
Mount Desert Island
0
1
2
3
Miles

94 • The Beehive 520′

Rating: Short, but extremely steep
Time: 1 hour and 30 minutes
Distance: 1.2-mile loop
Location: Acadia National Park
Total climb: 500′
Summary: Iron rungs aid you on the tricky parts of this climb. Not for the faint-of-heart.

Along the eastern edge of Mount Desert Island, directly south of Bar Harbor, runs a low mountain ridge. **Champlain Mountain** (1,058') is its highest point and an interesting area for hikers; there are four routes to the top. In particular, the **Precipice Trail**, which ascends the cliff on Champlain's east face, is an exciting experience. Resorting to iron rungs and ladders to provide a "hiker's" route up the almost sheer rock face, it is not a place for acrophobes! Unfortunately—for hikers—peregrine falcons find these cliffs to be a good place to make their nests. To protect the young birds, the National Park Service keeps the Precipice Trail closed much of the time. Those wanting to climb this route should contact the Park Service first.

All is not lost. A similar experience can be had on the Beehive, a lower summit about a mile south of Champlain. From the **Sand Beach** parking area, pick up the **Bowl Trail** and climb moderately 0.2 mile through woods to a trail junction. Here bear right and make the steep, breathtaking rock climb—iron rungs are placed at critical spots—to the summit. As for the Precipice Trail above, this is not a place for those uncomfortable with drop-offs. From the top, there are views of Frenchman's Bay, Champlain Mountain, and the rest of the rugged landscape of Mount Desert Island.

For an easy descent route off the Beehive, take the continuation of the trail down the northwest side of the mountain. After a steep descent (only 0.2 mile) you reach the intersection with the **Gorham Mountain Trail** and the **Bowl Trail**. Keeping to the left, walk 0.5 mile over easy terrain to return to your car.

Approach: From Bar Harbor, drive south on Park Loop Road to Sand Beach and a large parking lot on the left. The trail starts across the road, just north of the entrance to Sand Beach.

Maps: Acadia National Park (Park Service); Mount Desert Island and Acadia National Park (DeLorme); Map of Acadia National Park/Mount Desert Island (AMC); Maine Atlas & Gazetteer, p. 16

Summit of Champlain Mountain

Ocean Path, a gentle shore path from Sand Beach to **Otter Cliffs**, is a great way to experience Maine's rugged coastline without leaving the comfort of an easy path. Park at Sand Beach. The more or less level path runs right (south) from the parking lot. Walk as far as you like; it is 1.8 miles all the way to Otter Cliffs. About half way you pass **Thunder Hole** where waves crashing into an indentation on the shore cliffs make an explosive sound.

Note on maps for Maine: DeLorme's Maine Atlas and Gazetteer does a good job of getting you to the trailhead, and it is referred to throughout the text. Once at the trailhead, various AMC maps (Rangeley-Stratton, for example) and the Maine Appalachian Trail Club's excellent "Appalachian Trail Guide to Maine" give more detailed information. The latter booklet includes seven topo/trail profile maps which treat the AT in great detail. Baxter State Park and Acadia National Park each have a number of good maps: the AMC's "Map of Acadia National Park/Mount Desert Island", DeLorme's "Mount Desert Island and Acadia National Park" and "Baxter State Park and Katahdin," and Wilderness Map Company's "Katahdin-Baxter State Park" are all excellent. DeLorme's "Maine Geographic" series on hiking is useful for the less visited areas.

Baxter State Park

"A sanctuary for wild birds and beasts" that shall remain "forever in its natural wild state." Taken from the charter of Baxter State Park, the above statement conveys the core philosophy of Maine's unique 201,000-acre wilderness park. Located in the north central part of the state, about 250 miles north of Portland, this large expanse of forest and mountains is enjoyed by thousands of hikers, campers, climbers, and fishermen every year. It is the home of **Mount Katahdin,** Maine's highest and best-known mountain and the northern terminus of the 2,100-mile **Appalachian Trail.**

The existence of the park is the result of a lifelong crusade by one man, Percival Baxter. As a young legislator and later as governor, Baxter worked hard but unsuccessfully for the creation of a wild preserve for the people of Maine. Commercial interests, primarily logging, continually stymied his efforts. After retiring from public life Baxter was able, with his own funds, to realize his dream. By 1944, after purchasing the land in piece by piece fashion, he had acquired 114,000 acres. This he deeded to the State of Maine with explicit preservationist covenants and instructions. After his initial gift he continued to add parcels, bringing the park up to its present size.

Today, while the Park is a paradise for outdoor enthusiasts, the number of visitors is strictly limited. It is in the charter of the park to give wilderness preservation first priority and the needs and wants of hikers and other recreationists second priority. Thus the number of cars at each parking area is carefully monitored. This means that when the Roaring Brook parking area is full, you will have wait for another day to climb Katahdin by the Chimney Pond route! Arriving at the entrance gate early is the best strategy, as reservations are not taken for day use. Camping reservations can be made by contacting the **Baxter Park Authority** in Millinocket (207-723-5140). There are two roads which provide access to the campgrounds and trailheads. These are narrow, gravel affairs that require—and this is intentional—a slow rate of travel. The Park is open from May 15 to October 15, with day use allowed after mid-October, dependent on weather conditions. For example if Katahdin receives a couple inches of snow, say in late October, the Knife Edge on Katahdin will be closed for hiking. Lower elevation hikes (e.g. South Turner), however, may still be open. Note that the access roads are not plowed. Despite its remoteness and inconvenient access, Katahdin receives a good number of visitors in winter as well. Special application must be made to the Park Authority for winter hiking and climbing.

Bull moose Robert Kozlow

Some might say the **Moosehead Lake** area has the opposing philosophy to Baxter State Park. This is logging and hunting country, and that most unrestrained of animals, modern man, runs wild here. Moosehead Lake is huge, and on its eastern shore Mount Kineo juts up unexpectedly, providing a unique vantage point.

White Cap, a 3,644' summit with outstanding views, is located on a remote section of the Appalachian Trail. The lengthy road access is via the historic Katahdin Iron Works, a former iron smelting site, where the old blast furnace is still visible. Gulf Hagas, a narrow canyon carved out of the slate bedrock, is nearby. A four-mile loop hike provides a tour of Maine's "little Grand Canyon."

95 • Mount Kineo 1,806′

Rating: Easy
Time: 2 hours
Distance: 2 miles
Location: Western shore of Moosehead Lake
Total climb: 880′
Summary: A short hike to a cliff top vantage point over one of Maine's largest lakes. Cross the lake to get to the trailhead.

A different hike, indeed. For all intents and purposes, this is a journey to an island, as road access to the Kineo Peninsula is closed to the public. From Rockwood, strike out across the lake. Land your boat on the south shore of the peninsula and head left on the shoreline path. (The dock in Kineo Cove is not open to the public.) The trail used to climb Kineo is the **Indian Trail**. It branches right from the shore path and ascends along the edge of the cliff face, offering increasingly dramatic views as you gain elevation. As you walk along the lake, the junction for the Indian Trail occurs where the shoreline juts out to the left. The old fire tower on the summit may be unsafe, so exercise caution if you feel the need to climb it. There are various side trails off the top which lead to good vantage points.

Mount Kineo is thrust out into Moosehead Lake, resulting in unique views. Return by the same route, careful not to follow either of the side trails that depart first left and then right off the Indian Trail.

Approach: From Greenville drive northwest 20 miles on ME Routes 6/15 to Rockwood. Here you can rent a boat (or launch your own) to make the approximately one mile crossing to Mount Kineo on the opposite shore.

Maps: Maine Geographic: Hiking, Volume 3 (DeLorme) and Maine Atlas & Gazetteer, p. 42

Looking across Moosehead Lake to Mount Kineo Maine Office of Tourism

Big Moose Mountain (3,196'), formerly Squaw Mountain, lies at the southern end of Moosehead Lake and is the highest mountain in these parts. The views from its summit are exceptional, with Moosehead Lake practically at your feet, Katahdin to the north, the Bigelow Range to the southwest, and dozens of other mountains and lakes scattered about. A half-mile trail links the top of Squaw Mountain Ski Area with the mountain's actual summit. To reach the **Fire Warden's Trail**, the usual hiking route to the summit, drive (5.2 miles) north on ME 15 from Greenville. Turn left (west) on the Scott Paper Company Road, and continue for 1.2 miles where the trail heads off to the right as a wide logging road. It is a little over 3 miles and 2,000' of climbing to the top, with the round trip taking about 4 hours. The fire warden's cabin (abandoned) is reached at 2.5 miles. From the cabin onward, the trail is steep. Use care when climbing up the unmaintained fire tower.

96 • White Cap Mountain 3,644′

Rating: Moderate
Time: 3-4 hours
Distance: 4.2 miles (or 6 miles)
Location: Near Katahdin Iron Works, west of Millinocket
Total climb: 900′
Summary: Superb mountain and lake views. Mount Katahdin is the next big peak to the north. Possible side trip to Gulf Hagas.

White Cap Mountain is well inside the so-called **100-Mile Wilderness**. It is a prominent peak and the last significant mountain before Katahdin, about 75 hiking miles to the north. A series of gravel roads makes White Cap accessible to the day hiker. A day usage fee is charged near the site of the old **Katahdin Iron Works**, as these are private roads. The gate attendant will be able to answer questions and provide up-to-date road information. An important geological feature, **Gulf Hagas**, is nearby. Carved out of the slate bedrock, this four-mile long gorge has a trail running along both sides of the river, and a visit is highly recommended.

If you succeed in following the somewhat complicated approach instructions, you will find yourself at the trailhead of the blue-blazed **White Brook Trail**. Initially it leads across a logged-over area and passes the ruins of the warden's cabin at 0.5 mile, before reaching the **Appalachian Trail** at one mile. Turn right on the AT, and make the remaining 1.1-mile climb (steep at the end) to the summit where your panoramic reward awaits. By air, Mount Katahdin is only 30 miles to the northeast and Moosehead Lake is about 16 miles to the west. However it is the grandeur of Maine's vast North Country—forest and lakes stretching away to the north—that is captivating. After enjoying a (hopefully) warm and sunny time on the summit, retrace your steps to your car, taking care not to miss the junction for the White Brook Trail.

Gulf Hagas is a deep, narrow canyon cut in to the slate bedrock by the Pleasant River. Dubbed Maine's "Little Grand Canyon," its total length is about four miles. If you walk along the edge, you will see rapids, slot-like canyons with vertical sides, and waterfalls. There is a trail along one side of the Gulf and a rough road on the other, so it's possible to do a loop hike. The loop distance is nine miles and takes 4-5 hours. Use the same parking area as for White Cap Mountain, above.

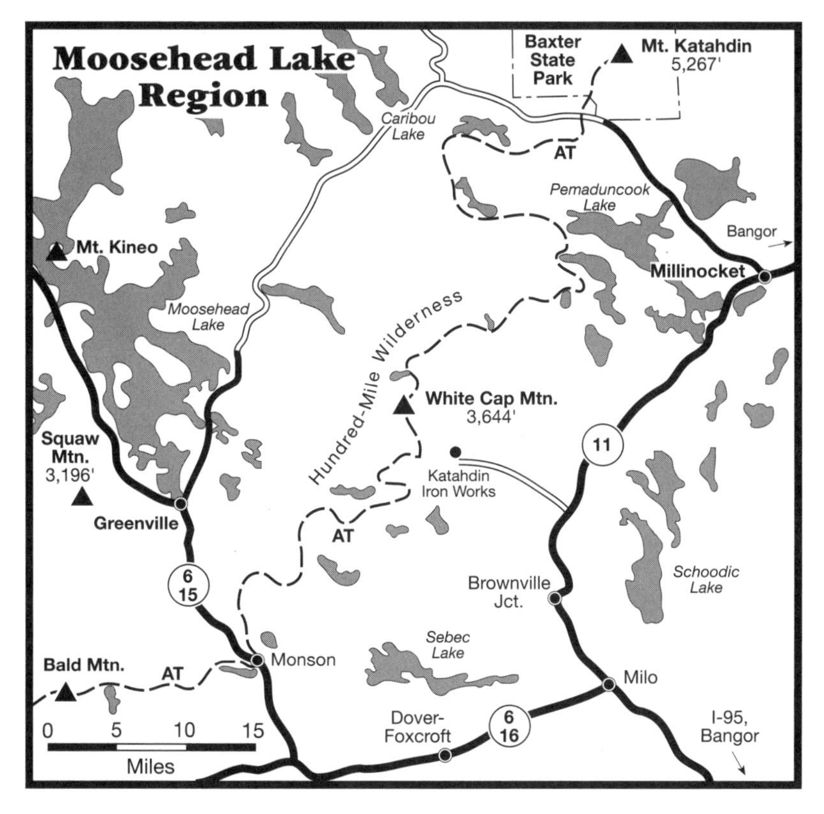

Approach: From Brownville Junction on ME 11, drive north 5.5 miles to K I Road where there is a sign for Katahdin Iron Works. Follow this gravel road 6.8 miles (left) to the Iron Works, a state historical site. After paying the small fee, pass through the gate and immediately turn right, crossing the river. Continue for three miles, bear right, and just after crossing a rather dubious bridge (at 5.8 miles), you will come to an intersection. Continue straight here, and after four more miles park along the road, safely out of the way of trucks. The trail coincides with a rough logging road for a mile, and this may or may not be negotiable for vehicles.

Maps: Free map provided at Katahdin Iron Works Site; MATC, Map #2; and Maine Atlas & Gazetteer, p. 42.

97 • North Brother 4,143′

Rating: Moderately strenuous
Time: 6 hours
Distance: 7.6 miles
Total climb: 3,000′
Location: In Baxter Park, 4.5 miles northwest of Mt. Katahdin
Summary: Long climb to an open, rocky summit. Sweeping views of Baxter Park and northern Maine.

North Brother is the third highest mountain in Baxter Park, and it ranks seventh in Maine. It is a little over four miles northwest of Katahdin, and the views from its open summit are unique and impressive. North Brother and its companion, South Brother, form the northwest flank of the barrier that encloses the high, swampy no-man's-land known as the **Klondike**. You look across the Klondike as you gaze over to Baxter Peak. With a vertical ascent of 3,000', North Brother offers a solid climb. Strong hikers will be able to make the round trip in five hours or less, but on the average hikers should plan on at least six hours.

From the Perimeter Road at **Slide Dam**, the blue-blazed **Marston Trail** starts out paralleling Slide Brook. After crossing some slide rubble, the trail climbs through woods and after a num-

Fir waves on The Owl, seen from Hamlin Peak

Summit of North Brother — Richard Bailey

ber of stream crossings, reaches the junction with the **Mount Coe Trail** at 1.2 miles. A few minutes beyond, cross Roaring Brook, and at 1.9 miles you reach the floor of a steep-sided ravine and pass a small pond on the right. For the next half mile, the trail climbs quite steeply, finally gaining the ridge at about 3,200'. The trail now works its way up to the col area between North and South Brother. From here, at the upper junction with the Mt. Coe Trail, **South Brother** (3,942') is 0.8 mile to the right. Heading left, it is 0.7 miles to the summit of North Brother. After a brief section of easy going, the climbing begins again in earnest. A few minutes below the summit, the trail breaks out in the open. Enjoy the great views before retracing your route back down.

Approach: From Baxter Park's main entrance at Togue Pond, drive 13.5 miles up the Perimeter Road past Katahdin Stream Campground to Slide Dam Picnic Area and the trailhead.

Maps: Baxter State Park and Katahdin (DeLorme); Baxter State Park (AMC Maine); Katahdin (Wilderness Map Company); and Maine Atlas and Gazetteer, p. 50

98 • The Owl 3,736′

Rating: Strenuous, exposed
Time: 5 hours
Distance: 6.6 miles
Total climb: 2,670′
Location: Baxter State Park, just west of Mount Katahdin
Summary: A rigorous hike with outstanding views from its summit.

The Owl is the prominent, domed summit about two miles west of Baxter Peak (Katahdin's highest point) as the crow flies. The route up the Owl coincides with the **Hunt Trail** (Appalachian Trail) for the first 1.1 miles, before branching off to the left and climbing the left side of the valley formed by Katahdin Stream. The final portion of the route ascends the steep southwest shoulder. Although the route up the Owl partially overlaps with one of the most popular hikes in the Park, the Owl is visited by only a fraction of the Katahdin-bound hikers.

From **Katahdin Stream Campground**, follow the white-blazed Hunt Trail as it parallels Katahdin Stream, climbing gradually. At 1.1 miles, the blue-blazed **Owl Trail** branches left and continues climbing through woods. At about 2.7 miles, things become quite steep indeed, and a bit farther on, at 3.1 miles, the trail comes out onto an old slide. After passing a huge boulder teetering on the edge of a cliff, you soon reach the uppermost part of the mountain and can see the summit a short distance away. Note that some of the final climbing is over exposed terrain.

From the top, panoramic views of lakes and mountains include Baxter Peak, the Northwest Plateau, North and South Brother, Mount O-J-I, and the Klondike. You will also notice a curious feature of the forest: bands of lighter color (dead trees, actually), in a kind of wave pattern. The phenomenon is known as "fir waves" (see photo page 266) and its origin is unknown. It occurs fairly commonly on high mountain slopes in New England. Descend by the same route.

Approach: From Millinocket, drive 18 miles west to the park entrance at Togue Pond. After registering, follow the Perimeter Road (the "tote road") 7.7 miles to Katahdin Stream Campground.

Maps: Baxter State Park and Katahdin (DeLorme); Baxter State Park (AMC Maine); Katahdin (Wilderness Map Company); and Maine Atlas and Gazetteer, p. 50-51

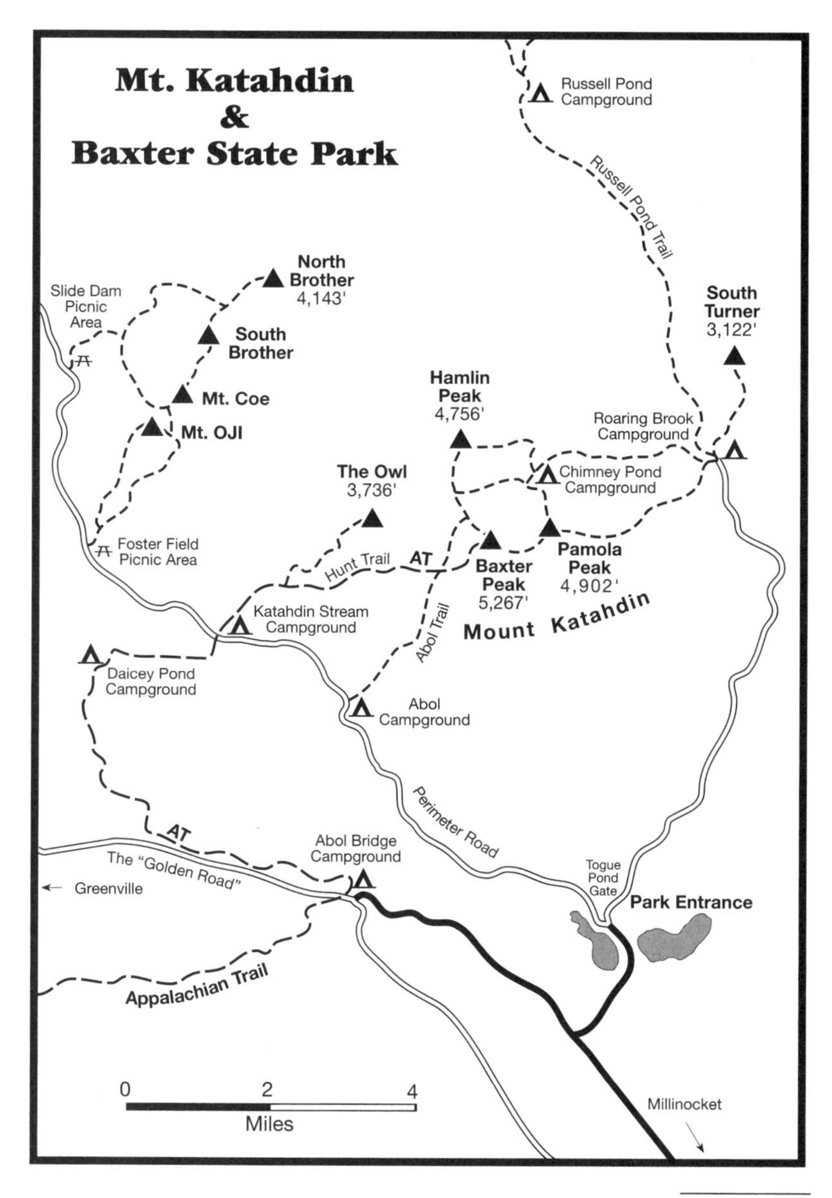
Mt. Katahdin
&
Baxter State Park
Russell Pond
Campground
Russell Pond Trail
North
Brother
4,143'
Slide Dam
Picnic
Area
South
Brother
South
Turner
3,122'
Mt. Coe
Hamlin
Peak
4,756'
Mt. OJI
Roaring Brook
Campground
The Owl
3,736'
Chimney Pond
Campground
Foster Field
Picnic Area
Hunt Trail
AT
Baxter
Peak
5,267'
Pamola
Peak
4,902'
Katahdin Stream
Campground
Abol Trail
Mount Katahdin
Daicey Pond
Campground
Abol
Campground
Perimeter Road
AT
Abol Bridge
Campground
The "Golden Road"
Greenville
Togue
Pond
Gate
Park Entrance
Appalachian Trail
0
2
4
Miles
Millinocket

99 • Mt. Katahdin via the Knife Edge

Rating: Very strenuous
Time: 8-10 hours
Distance: 11.2 miles
Total climb: about 4,000′
Location: Near Millinocket in northern central Maine, in Baxter State Park

Summary: Katahdin is the most alpine mountain in the East, and the traverse of the precipitous Knife Edge is one of the most famous hikes in the country.

As the highest mountain in Maine and the northern terminus of the Appalachian Trail, Mount Katahdin is a mecca for hikers. Despite its remoteness (4 hours north of Portland) and a very protective park management policy, about 20,000 people climb it every year. The southwestern slopes are relatively moderate (this is the side the AT ascends), but the north side is another matter entirely. This complex of glacially scoured basins and granite walls surpasses New Hampshire's Mt. Washington in alpine character.

The loop hike detailed here is one of several standard variations, and it can be done in either direction. It is usually done as a day hike from **Roaring Brook Campground**, but if space is available, consider spending the night at Chimney Pond.

From Roaring Brook Campground follow **Chimney Pond Trail** 3.3 miles up to **Chimney Pond** and its cluster of lean-tos, a bunkhouse, and ranger station. After signing out at the ranger station, head left on the **Dudley Trail** which almost immediately has you grappling with enormous granite boulders (fun stuff!) as you begin the climb of this extremely steep mountain wall. Mercifully, most of the lower portion of the route is tucked into trees (gnarly birches), and there is negligible awareness of the drop-off. Higher up, the route is out in the open and not as steep, although there is a brief section with SUV-sized boulders requiring careful attention. After a very tough 1.1 miles from Chimney Pond you reach the sharp, rocky summit of **Pamola Peak** (4,902').

From here, make the short rock climb descent into a notch (called the Chimney) and scramble up the other side, reaching the top of Chimney Peak and the beginning of the **Knife Edge**. Keep your eyes on the route—in places the ridge is only three feet wide—ignoring the drop-off on either side as the ridge descends gently to its low point before climbing steeply on easier rocks to **South Peak** at 5,240'. A few minutes of rock hopping over more level terrain brings you to Katahdin's main summit, **Baxter Peak** (5,267'), where you can relax and enjoy the views. You may find yourself in the company of AT through-hikers basking in the glory of their achievement and attempting to grasp that it's finally over!

Descending from the summit, take the **Saddle Trail** west down moderate slopes for a mile where it bears right off the ridge and plunges down to Chimney Pond. The steepness, together with very

Hikers along the Knife Edge

loose rock for the first fifteen minutes or so, demands extreme caution. After re-entering the woods (beautiful mountain birches), the gradient moderates and the descent is on stable rock. Back at the pond area, sign out at the ranger station and follow the Chimney Pond Trail back to the parking lot.

Aerial view of the Knife Edge and Pamola Peak, Dudley Trail on left Ed Rolfe

Note:

1) Take at least two quarts of water per person. There is no water for 3-5 hours.
2) Assess the weather very carefully before venturing out onto the Knife Edge.
3) Take warm clothing, including mittens or gloves. Gloves are helpful on the rough rock surfaces.

Approach: From Portland, drive north four hours on I-95 to Millinocket (Medway, exit 56). Continue west 18 miles to Togue Pond, Baxter Park's South Entrance. From here it is 8 miles to Roaring Brook Campground. Since park authorities limit the number of cars at the trailheads, you should plan to arrive at the gate early in the morning. Call the park office at (207) 723-5140 for more information. The day fee is $8.

Maps: Baxter State Park and Katahdin (DeLorme); Baxter State Park (AMC); Maine Atlas and Gazetteer, p. 50-51; and Katahdin (Wilderness Map Company)

Approaching the summit of South Turner — Richard Bailey

South Turner Mountain (3,122')

Only four air miles from Baxter Peak, popular South Turner Mountain is one of the better places to contemplate Mount Katahdin's alpine splendors. It is also a good consolation prize if your trip on Katahdin does not pan out. The four-mile round trip, with a vertical gain of 1,700', will take about three hours. From the ranger station at **Roaring Brook Campground**, start out on the path to Russell Pond, but continue straight at 0.2 mile onto the **Sandy Stream Pond Trail**, reaching the pond at 0.4 mile. Contour (right) around the pond, and at 0.7 mile the **Turner Mountain Trail** branches off to the right. After passing some boulders, you begin the steep climb up South Turner. At 1.8 miles the trail comes out into the open, with blazes and cairns leading the way. After enjoying the view, return to Roaring Brook Campground by the same route.

100 • Mount Katahdin 5,267' via the Appalachian Trail

Rating: Strenuous, a lot of climbing
Time: 8-10 hours
Distance: 10.4 miles
Total climb: 4,200'
Location: Baxter State Park
Summary: The final section of the Appalachian Trail and a beautiful, demanding hike in its own right.

The **Hunt Trail** is the Appalachian Trail's final leg, the culmination of the 2,100-mile footpath originating in northern Georgia. Typically a "through-hiker" will start from Stone Mountain, Georgia in April, and by sometime in September or October, after 5-6 months of walking, will arrive at **Katahdin Stream Campground** here in Baxter State Park, at the base of Hunt Trail.

From the campground, the white-blazed AT runs along Katahdin Stream and at 1.1 miles reaches the junction with the Owl Trail (left). Soon after passing a side trail (left) to Katahdin Stream Falls, the trail climbs more steeply, through spruce woods, reaching a kind of cave shelter formed by two big boulders at 2.7 miles. Above here the trail soon breaks out into the open and winding among huge boulders, with cairns showing the route, gains a crest—and easier ground—in about a mile. This barren, rocky landscape is called the **Tableland**. After about a half mile you reach the four-way intersection at **Thoreau Springs** (a rather unreliable water source). You are now 4.2 miles into the climb. From this intersection, the Abol Slide Trail departs right, shortly to descend steeply—at times extremely so—to Abol Campground, 2.8 miles distant. To the left, Baxter Peak Cutoff heads left in 0.9 mile to the Saddle. The Cutoff provides an important bypass of the summit for hikers headed on to Chimney Pond, should bad weather or other factors force this.

Continuing on the AT from Thoreau Springs, the ascent is easy to moderate among scattered boulders, with the summit continuously in view. It is one mile and 600' to the top. If the weather seems unstable, evaluate whether you should turn back, as this is not a pleasant place to be caught in a storm.

Upon reaching the summit, a markedly different landscape appears. The east side of the mountain falls away so steeply that you can't see much of it. Chimney Pond is nestled in woods far

Summit of Baxter Peak and the end of the Appalachian Trail

below. The cliffs of the main cirque are partly visible to your left and to your right. A short distance to your right, the slightly lower South Peak marks the beginning of the Knife Edge, the narrow connecting ridge to Pamola Peak. If the weather is good, you are almost certain to find yourself sharing the summit with hikers doing one of the east side routes. It's a popular mountain! When you are ready to descend, follow the Hunt Trail/Appalachian Trail back down to Katahdin Stream Campground.

Approach: From the main gate of Baxter State Park, at Togue Pond (18 miles west of Millinocket), drive 7.7 miles to Katahdin Stream Campground and the trailhead. The town of Millinocket is about 4 hours north of Portland via I-95.

Maps: Baxter State Park and Katahdin (DeLorme); Katahdin (Wilderness Map Company); Baxter State Park (AMC Maine); and Maine Atlas and Gazetteer, p. 50-51

Four Thousand-Footers

New Hampshire

	feet	meters
1. Washington	6288	1917
2. Adams	5774	1760
3. Jefferson	5712	1741
4. Monroe	5384	1641
5. Madison	5367	1636
6. Lafayette	5260	1603
7. Lincoln	5089	1551
8. South Twin	4902	1494
9. Carter Dome	4832	1473
10. Moosilauke	4802	1464
11. Eisenhower	4780	1457
12. North Twin	4761	1451
13. Carrigain	4700	1433
14. Bond	4698	1432
15. Middle Carter	4610	1405
16. West Bond	4540	1384
17. Garfield	4500	1372
18. Liberty	4459	1359
19. South Carter	4430	1350
20. Wildcat	4422	1348
21. Hancock	4420	1347
22. South Kinsman	4358	1328
23. Field	4340	1323
24. Osceola	4340	1323
25. Flume	4328	1319
26. South Hancock	4319	1316
27. Pierce (Clinton)	4310	1314
28. North Kinsman	4293	1309
29. Willey	4285	1306
30. Bondcliff	4265	1300
31. Zealand	4260	1298
32. North Tripyramid	4180	1274

33. Cabot	4170	1271
34. East Osceola	4156	1267
35. Middle Tripyramid	4140	1262
36. Cannon	4100	1250
37. Hale	4054	1236
38. Jackson	4052	1235
39. Tom	4051	1235
40. Wildcat D	4050	1234
41. Moriah	4049	1234
42. Passaconaway	4043	1232
43. Owl's Head	4025	1227
44. Galehead	4024	1227
45. Whiteface	4020	1225
46. Waumbek	4006	1221
47. Isolation	4004	1220
48. Tecumseh	4003	1220

Maine

1. Katahdin, Baxter Peak	5268	1606
2. Katahdin, Hamlin Peak	4756	1450
3. Sugarloaf	4250	1295
4. Old Speck	4170	1271
5. Crocker	4228	1289
6. Bigelow, West Peak	4145	1263
7. North Brother	4151	1265
8. Saddleback	4120	1256
9. Bigelow, Avery Peak	4090	1247
10. Abraham	4050	1234
11. Saddleback, the Horn	4041	1232
12. South Crocker	4050	1234
13. Redington	4010	1222
14. Spaulding	4010	1222

Vermont

1. Mansfield	4393	1339
2. Killington	4235	1291
3. Camel's Hump	4083	1244
4. Ellen	4083	1244
5. Abraham	4006	1221

New York

Adirondacks

1. Marcy	5344	1629
2. Algonquin Peak	5114	1559
3. Haystack	4960	1512
4. Skylight	4926	1501
5. Whiteface	4867	1483
6. Dix	4857	1481
7. Iroquois Peak	4850	1479
8. Gray Peak	4840	1475
9. Basin	4827	1471
10. Gothics	4726	1440
11. Colden	4714	1437
12. Giant	4627	1410
13. Nipple Top	4620	1408
14. Santanoni Peak	4607	1404
15. Redfield	4606	1404
16. Wright Peak	4580	1396
17. Saddleback	4515	1377
18. Panther Peak	4442	1354
19. Table Top	4427	1350
20. Rocky Peak Ridge	4420	1348
21. Macomb	4405	1342
22. Armstrong	4400	1341
23. Hough Peak	4400	1341
24. Seward	4361	1330
25. Marshall	4360	1329
26. Allen	4340	1323
27. Big Slide	4240	1293

28. Esther	4240	1293
29. Upper Wolf Jaw	4185	1276
30. Lower Wolf Jaw	4175	1272
31. Street	4166	1270
32. Phelps	4161	1269
33. Donaldson	4140	1262
34. Seymour	4120	1256
35. Sawteeth	4100	1250
36. Cascade	4098	1249
37. South Dix	4060	1238
38. Porter	4059	1238
39. Colvin	4057	1237
40. Emmons	4040	1232
41. Dial	4020	1226
42. East Dix	4012	1223
43. Blake	3960	1207
44. Cliff	3960	1207
45. Nye	3895	1188
46. Couchsachraga	3820	1165

Catskills

1. Slide	4180	1274
2. Hunter	4040	1232

Glossary

alpine - steep mountainous terrain with narrow ridges and pointed summits. Characterized by a transition from temperate forests to the treeless, arctic zone.

arctic vegetation - plants found above tree line. A wide variety of plants thrive in the harsh arctic environment: mosses, lichens, and many different kinds of wild flowers.

blaze - paint (usually) marking on rock or tree to indicate the route. Usually rectangular.

bushwhack - to travel through woods without the benefit of a trail

cairn - pile of rocks used to indicate a route; often a succession of cairns marks a route across featureless terrain

cirque - a hollow scooped out of a mountainside by glacial erosion. Tuckerman Ravine is a cirque.

clove - a steep-sided mountain pass, a notch or a gap. Used in the Catskills, comes from the Dutch "kloft", similar to English "cleft"

col - a high pass, or a shallow dip on a mountain ridge

dike – layer of rock either more, or less, resistant to erosion than the rock on either side. Often appears as a trough or a ridge, or is of a different color.

exposed - unprotected from wind and weather. In the context of rock climbing, it describes a spot with a drop-off.

Forty-sixer – hiker who has climbed all 46 of the Adirondack High Peaks over 4,000' in elevation.

frostbite - the freezing of skin, usually on the face, but in more serious cases, of the hands and feet.

gap - a spot of lower elevation in a mountain ridge, a pass, or a notch. Vermont usage.

glacial erratic - a boulder transported by a glacier from its original location. Eractics can weigh hundreds, even thousands of tons.

headwall - steep upper end of a valley or cirque.

herd path – informal, unmaintained path created by hiker traffic. Adirondack usage only.

hypothermia - lowering of the core body temperature. Marked by disorientation, uncontrolled shivering, and incoherent speech.

krummholz - stunted, ground-hugging trees (spruce or fir) that live at tree line.

lean-to – three-sided log shelter. Popular along the Appalachian Trail and in the Adirondacks.

peakbagging – avid pursuit of all the summits over a fixed height in a particular region, for example the 4,000' mountains in NH.

puncheons – walkway of logs and planks to carry a trail across a wet area

ravine - steep-sided gully or narrow valley on a mountainside.

scree – loose rock, see talus

talus - a loose accumulation of rocks and boulders on a slope, usually at the base of a cliff.

tarn - a small mountain pond, usually at a high elevation

timberline – same as tree line

trailhead - starting point of a hike, where the trail meets the road.

tree line - zone on a mountain at which trees are less than 8 feet tall or become non-existent. Determined mainly by latitude and elevation. Usually a brief, well-defined transition.

tundra - open areas in an arctic environment. In summer, usually grassy with bushes, gentle to moderate terrain.

waterbar - rocks or logs placed at an angle across the trail to deflect surface water, thus reducing erosion damage.

whiteout - dense fog, especially in the context of a treeless and snow-covered landscape. Creates an environment with few reference points, making travel difficult.

wind chill - the perception of body termperature as affected by wind. The temperature is effectively lowered by the wind; for example, on exposed skin, at 32 degrees, a 20-mph wind feels the same as zero degrees.

Notes

Notes

Notes

Notes

Notes

Index

ADK Range Trail 82
AMC Hiker Shuttle 185
Abol Slide Trail 274
Abraham, Mount (ME) 246
Abraham, Mount (VT) 122
Acadia National Park 252
Adams, Mount............190,202,207
Adirondacks, The.............40,76-78
Adirondack Mountain Club ...50,53
Adirondack Mountain Reserve ...82
Adirondack Museum..................45
Adirondack Park........................40
Adirondack Trail Improvement
Society (ATIS) 50
Adirondak Loj 53,57
Algo, Mount 106
Algonquin Peak 58
Air Line Trail 202
Ammonoosuc Ravine Trail 194,196
Ampersand Mountain 52
Appalachia 198,202,204
Appalachian Gap......................123
Appalachian Mountain Club 187
Appalachian Trail
104-105,107,112,190,214,260
Arctic-alpine zone 190
Arnold, Lake 66
Ascutney, Mount 120
Ascutney State Park 120
Ausable Lake (Lower) 82
Avalanche Lake......................64,98
Avalanche Pass 64,66
Avalon Trail 186
Avery Peak 250

Bald Mountain (ME) 242
Bald Peak (NY) 85
Bald Peak Trail (ME)................232
Baldface,
North and South 212,218
Baldface Shelter.......................218
Bar Harbor................................252
Bascom Lodge 112
Bash Bish Falls 104
Basin Mountain (NY) 72
Battell Trail..............................122
Battie, Mount...........................253
Baxter Park Authority 260
Baxter Peak 270-275
Baxter State Park 260
Bear Mountain (CT) 107
Bear Mountain (NY)...................24
Beaver Brook Trail 170
Becker Hollow Trail 36
Beehive, The 258
Bicentennial Trail 110
Big Moose Mountain.................263
Big Slide Mountain 74
Bigelow Mountain 250
Bigelow Range Traverse...........250
Black Dome...............................38
Black Mountain 46
Blackhead Mountain..................38
Blackhead Range Trail 38
Blue Mountain 44
Blue Mountain Lake 45
Blueberry Ledge Trail..............166
Bond, Mount 182
Bondcliff 182
Boott Spur 210
Boquet Lean-to 86
Bowl Trail 258
Breakneck Ridge 26
Brook Trail 241
Brothers, The............................74
Brownsville Trail 120
Brownsville Rock.....................120
Bubbles, The 256
Bucklin Trail...........................116
Burke Mountain 142
Burnt Rock Mountain..............116
Burroughs Range 35
Burrows Trail 127
Bushnell Falls Lean-to 78

CCC Road (Mt. Mansfield) 136
Cabot, Mount 213
Cadillac Mountain 254
Camden Hills State Park...........253
Camel's Hump...........................126
Cannon Cliff..............................177
Cannon Mountain.....................172
Caps Ridge Trail........................200
Cardigan Lodge........................151
Cardigan, Mount 150
Caribou Mountain.....................230
Caribou-Speckled Mountain
Wilderness 228
Caribou Valley...........................248
Carlo, Mount......................212,220
Carlo Shelter.............................220
Carrigain, Mount......................188
Carrigain Notch Trail 188
Carter Dome 212,214
Carter Moriah Trail 214
Carter Notch 214
Carter Notch Hut......................214
Carter Range 212
Cascade Mountain 68
Catamount Mountain................100
Catamount Ski Trail 132
Cathedral Forest Trail 151
Champlain Mountain.............258-9
Champney Falls Trail................164
Chapel Pond................................84
Chimney Pond...........................270
Chin, The 136,138
Chocorua, Mount 164
Circle Junction 218
Clark Trail 150
Clay, Mount..............................198
Colden, Lake 66
Colden, Mount 66
Connery Pond Trail.....................96
Cornice Trail.............................200
Crane Mountain..........................48
Crane Mountain Pond................49
Crawford Notch ...185,190,192,199
Crawford Notch Hostel.............185
Crawford Path............194,196,198
Crocker Mountain.....................248
Crystal Cascade 208
Cube, Mount 152

Dept. of Environmental
Conservation (NYSDEC) 50
Dartmouth Outing Club 170
Dartmouth Skiway....................152
Deer Leap Rock 116
Devil's Path............................36-37
Desolation Trail 188
Dicey's Mill Trail.......................166
Dickey Mountain 158
Dix Mountain..............................86
Dixville Notch...........................213
Dorr Mountain..........................254
Dudley Trail..............................270
Dunderberg Mountain................24
Durand Ridge 202

East Dix 89
East River Trail 83
East Royce Mountain 228
Echo Lake (NH) 177
Echo Lake (NY)...........................28
Edmands Col............................198
Edmands Path...........................194
Eisenhower Loop......................194
Eisenhower, Mount...................194
Elk Lake......................................88
Ellen, Mount 123
Escarpment Trail...................30,38
Esther Mountain 94
Evans Notch 212
Everett, Mount 108

Falcon Spring 148
Falling Waters Trail..................174
Ferncroft...................................166
Fire Warden's Trail
(Mt. Abraham, ME) 246
Fire Warden's Trail
(Bigelow, ME)..........................250
Fire Warden's Trail (Pleasant
Mountain, ME).........................232

Firescrew 150
Forehead, The 138
Forest City Trail........................126
Forty-Sixer............................71,77
Franconia Notch.........174,177,178
Franconia Ridge Traverse 174

Galehead Hut 179,181
Garden, The 72,74,78
Garfield, Mount 178,180
Garfield Ridge Trail.................180
Gem Pool..................................196
George, Lake..............................46
Giant Mountain 84
Giant's Nubble 84
Giant's Washbowl.......................84
Glen Ellen Lodge 123
Goodnow Mountain 43
Goose Eye Mountain..........212,220
Gothics.......................................82
Gothics Col 72
Gothics Trail 82
Grafton Notch...........................235
Grand Junction........................151
Great Gulf 206
Great Range..........................72,82
Green Mountain Club 128-9
Greenleaf Hut 176
Greenleaf Trail.........................175
Greylock, Mount 112
Gulf Hagas 264
Gulfside Trail.............198,200,206
Guyot Campsite 182
Guyot, Mount...................178,182

Hamlin Peak 266
Harriman State Park 24
Haystack, Little 78
Haystack, Mount 78
Headwall 209
Heart Lake 57
Hermit Lake.............................208
Hermit Lake Shelters 208
High Peaks 41,50-89,97
High Peaks Information Center 57
Hight, Mount 214
Hitch-Up Matilda 65
Holt Trail 151
Hopkins Mountain.....................70
Hopper Trail 112
Horn, North and South
(Bigelow Mountain) 250
Horn, The (Saddleback, ME).....244
Horn Pond................................250
Hough Peak 89
Hudson Highlands...........22,24-27
Hudson River........................22-23
Hundred-Mile Wilderness 236,264
Hunger, Mount 130
Hunt Trail 268,274
Hunter Mountain.......................36
Hunter's Pass 86
Huntington Ravine...........208,210
Hurricane Mountain..................90

Indian Falls 60
Indian Trail..............................262
Iroquois Peak 59
Isle au Haut 252

Jackrabbit Trail 99
Jackson, Mount 192
Jefferson Loop 200,206
Jefferson, Mount 190,198,200,206
Jefferson Notch Road 201
Jo, Mount 56
Johns Brook Lodge (JBL)
.............................53,72,75,99
Jordan Pond.............................256

Kaaterskill Falls....................31-32
Kancamagus Highway.............183
Katahdin Iron Works 264
Katahdin, Mount 260,270-275
Katahdin Stream C.G.........268,274
Kearsarge, Mount 153
Kearsarge North 212,216
Keene Valley.....................80,82,84
Kees Falls 230
Killington Peak 116

Kineo, Mount 262
King Ravine 202
Kinsman Notch 170
Kinsman Ridge Trail 172
Klondike, The 266
Knife Edge (ME) 270-272
Knife Edge (NH) 202

Lafayette, Mount 175,178
Lafayette Place Campground....172
Lafayette Place 172,174,178
Lake Road (Adirondacks) 82,99
Lakes of the Clouds Hut 194
196,198
Lambert Ridge Trail 152
Lincoln Gap 122
Lincoln, Mount 175
Lincoln Woods 183
Lion Head Trail....211
Little Haystack 174
Livermore Road
(Waterville Valley) 160
Lonesome Lake 172,176
Lonesome Lake Hut....172
Long Path (Catskills) 38
Long Trail (Mount Jo) 56
Long Trail (Vermont)
....118,122,126,128,136

Macomb Mountain....88
MacIntyre Range 58
Mad River Glen Ski Area 123
Madison Hut 198,204
Madison, Mount....190,204
Mahoosuc Notch 236
Mahoosuc Range 212,220,234,236
Mahoosuc Trail 220
Maiden Cliff 253
Maine Appalachian Trail Club
(MATC)....229
Major, Mount 154
Major Welch Trail 24
Mansfield, Mount....136,138
Maple Ridge....139
Marcy Dam 60,64
Marcy, Mount....50,51,60-63
Marston Trail....266
Middle Sugarloaf (NH)....184
Millinocket....260
Mizpah Spring Hut 192,199
Monadnock, Mount....148
Money Brook Trail....112
Monhegan Island....253
Montclair Glen Lodge....126
Monroe, Mount 194,197,198
Monroe Skyline Traverse....123
Moosehead Lake 261
Moosilauke, Mount 170
Mossy Cascade Trail 70
Mount Clinton Road 194
Mount Desert Island....252
Mt. Washington Auto Road......209
Mt. Washington Cog Railway ...196
Mud Brook Trail 230

Nash Stream Road....222
Nineteen Mile Brook Trail....214
Noonmark Mountain 80
North Brother....266
North Lake 30
North Point....31
North Ridge Trail (ME) 254
North Slide Trail (NH)....160
Nose, The....140

Ocean Path....259
Old Bridle Path 176
Old Speck Mountain 234
Orebed Trail....72
Osceola, Mount....160
Osgood Trail 204
Otter Cliffs 259
Overlook Mountain....28
Owl, The 268
Oxford Hills 226

Pack Monadnock....146
Pamola Peak....270
Passaconaway, Mount....166
Peakbagging....12,71

Pemigewasset Wilderness.........178
180,182
Penacook, Camp 164
Penobscot Mountain 256
Percy, Mount 213,222
Phelps Mountain.........................60
Phelps Trail 72,74,78
Piazza Rock Lean-to 244
Pine Cobble...............................113
Pine Hill Trail 110
Pinkham Notch.........................208
Pinkham Notch
Visitor Center 208,211
Pinnacle Trail 134
Piper Trail................................164
Pisgah, Mount 142
Pitchoff Mountain.......................68
Placid, Lake 50
Pleasant Mountain....................232
Poke-O-Moonshine Mountain 92
Porter Mountain 69
Potash, Mount...........................162
Precipice Trail 258
Presidential Range 190,198
Profanity Trail 137
Pulpit Rock 142
Pyramid Mountain.....................82

Race Brook Trail.......................108
Rainbow Falls 82
Randolph Mountain Club 190
Rangeley Lake 240
Ravine Lodge............................170
Ridge of Caps...........................200
Roaring Brook Trail 84
Roaring Brook Campground 270
Rocky Peak Ridge Trail 85
Rollins State Park.....................153
Rollins Trail.............................166
Round Pond 86
Rumford Whitecap....................238

Sabbaday Falls 163
Saddle Trail.............................271
Saddleback Mountain (ME) 244
Saddleback Mountain (NY) 72
Saddleback Ski Area (ME) 245
Sand Beach 258
Sandwich Range 164,166
Sargent Mountain.....................256
Sawyer River Road 188
Shawangunks 22
Shelburne Moriah.....................212
Shorey Short Cut 72
Short Trail 56
Signal Ridge Trail.....................188
Six Husbands Trail 206
Skyline Ridge Trail 135
Slant Rock Lean-to 73
Sleepy Hollow 30
Slide Dam.................................266
Slide Mountain 34
Slide Mountain Brook Trail 74
Smarts Mountain......................152
Smugglers Notch......................137
Snake Mountain.......................124
Snowy Mountain........................42
South Brother 267
South Dix...................................89
South Meadow 99
South Slide 160
South Trail...............................142
South Turner Mountain...........273
South Twin Mountain........178,181
Sphinx Trail 206
Squam Lake 154
Squaw Mountain.......................263
Starr King, Mount 213
State Range Trail.......................78
Sterling Pond...........................116
Stimson Trail 80
Stony Clove 36
Stowe Mountain Resort 136
Stowe Pinnacle 134
Storm King Mountain.................27
Stratton Mountain....................118
Stratton Pond (ME)...................250
Stratton Pond (VT)...................118
Streaked Mountain 233
Success Pond Road 220

Sugarbush Ski Resort...............123
Sugarloaf Mountain (ME).........248
Sugarloaf Mountain (NH).........213
Sugarloaf Side Trail..................249
Sugarloaf/USA Ski Resort.........248
Summit Road............................110
Sunday River Ski Resort 234
Sunset Ridge 138,141

Table Rock 235
Tableland, The 274
Taft Lodge 136
Tear of the Clouds, Lake 63
Tecumseh, Mount 160
Thomas Cole Mountain...............38
Thoreau Springs.......................274
Thunder Hole............................259
Togue Pond 272,275
Tongue Mountain Range............47
Trap Dike 66
Tree line.......................63,141,190
Tripyramid, Mount 160
Tuckerman Ravine....................208
Tumbledown Mountain.............241
Tumbledown Pond 241
Twinway 178

Underhill State Park.................138
Undermountain Trail................107
United States Forest Service
(USFS)..............................156,243

Valley Way................................204
Van Hoevenberg Trail............58,60

Wachusett Mountain.................110
Washington, Mount
..............145,190,196-199,208-211
Washington, Mount (winter) 211
Waterbury Trail 130
Waterville Valley 160
Waumbek, Mount.....................213
Watson Path 204
Webster Cliff 192
Webster, Mount 192
Welch Mountain 158
Weld 240
West Bond 182
West Kennebago Mountain.......242
West Peak (Bigelow) 250
West Rattlesnake 154
West Ridge Trail 150
West River Trail..........................83
Wheeler Mountain 142
White Brook Trail 264
White Cross Trail......................148
White Dot Trail 148
White Mountain National
Forest (WMNF) 156
White Cap Mtn. (ME).........261,264
Whiteface, Mount (NH)...........166
Whiteface Mountain (NY) 94
Whiteface Mountain
Memorial Highway 94,99
Whiteface Landing......................96
Wild River Valley......................228
Wildcat Mountain 214
Wilderness Trail.......................182
Willard, Mount.........................186
Willoughby, Lake 142
Wilmington Trail 94
Wilmot Trail.............................153
Wind Gap 126
Winnipesaukee, Lake...............154
Winslow State Park..................153
Wittenberg-Cornell-Slide Trail ...35
Wonalancet Out Door Club 166
Wright Peak 58

Zeacliff 179,182
Zealand Falls Hut..............179,182
Zealand, Mount........................178
Zealand Road 179,182
Zeta Pass 214

Useful telephone numbers & websites

New York, Catskills and Hudson Highlands

New York-New Jersey Trail Conference 212-685-9699
www.nynjtc.org
NY State Dept. of Environmental Conservation......914-256-3000

New York, Adirondacks

Adirondack Mountain Club 518-668-4447
www.adk.org
NY State Dept. of Environmental Conservation (NYSDEC)
www.dec.state.ny.us 518-897-1200

Vermont

Vermont Dept. of Forests, Parks and Recreation 802-244-8711
Green Mountain Club 802-244-7307
www.greenmountain.org
Green Mountain National Forest 802-747-6700

New Hampshire

Appalachian Mountain Club (Pinkham Notch) 603-244-2725
www.outdoors.org
AMC Hut Reservations...603-466-2727
Franconia Notch State Park...................................603-823-5563
U.S. Forest Service (Gorham)................................603-466-2713
U.S. Forest Service (Conway) 603-447-5448

Maine

Acadia National Park...207-288-3338
www.acadianationalpark.com
www.acadia.net
Baxter State Park Authority...................................207-723-5140
U.S. Forest Service (Evans Notch) 207-824-2134
Grafton Notch State Park.......................................207-824-2912

Appalachian Trail Conference 304-535-6331
www.atconf.org

About the author

Jared Gange has hiked and cross country skied in New England and the Adirondacks for 15 years. He has hiked and climbed in the Cascades, the Rockies, the Alps, Norway, Pakistan and Nepal. He has previously written two hiking guides, one for New Hampshire and one for Vermont, and produced numerous recreation maps for areas in New England.

The author on Camel's Hump — Marty Beede

About Huntington Graphics

Located in Burlington, Vermont, Huntington Graphics publishes and distributes recreation guides and maps for New England. Titles include Hiker's Guide to the Mountains of Vermont, Hiker's Guide to the Mountains of New Hampshire, the Vermont Recreation Handbook, and An Ice Climber's Guide to Northern New England.

Other titles from Huntington Graphics

Hiker's Guide to the Mountains of New Hampshire
by Jared Gange

Hiker's Guide to the Mountains of Vermont
by Jared Gange

Secrets of the Notch: A Climbing Guide to Cannon Cliff and Franconia Notch
by Jon Sykes

An Ice Climber's Guide to Northern New England
by Rick Wilcox

Vermont Recreation Handbook
by Diane Carter, Kate Carter and Jared Gange

Recreation Map & Guide to Stowe and the Mount Mansfield Region of Vermont

Climb Mount Washington
A pictorial map and guide

Huntington Graphics
P.O. Box 373
Burlington, Vermont 05402
www.letsclimb.com